LOSING HEART

*The Moral and Spiritual Miseducation
of America's Children*

LOSING HEART

The Moral and Spiritual Miseducation
of America's Children

H. Svi Shapiro

Lawrence Erlbaum Associates
Taylor & Francis Group

New York   London

Cover design by Tomai Maridou

Library of Congress Cataloging-in-Publication Data

Shapiro, H. Svi.
Losing Heart : the moral and spiritual miseducation of America's
children / H. Svi Shapiro.
          p. cm.
Includes bibliographical references and indexes.
    ISBN 0–8050–5721–4 (cloth : alk. paper)—ISBN 0–8058–5722–2
(paper : alk. paper)
    1. Education—Social aspects—United States.   2. Educa-
tion—Moral and ethical aspects—United States.   3. Educational
change—United States.   I. Title

LC191.4.S53 2006
370.11'4–dc22   2005050716

Books published by Lawrence Erlbaum Associates are printed on
acid-free paper, and their bindings are chosen for strength and durability.

Printed in the United States of America
10 9 8 7 6 5 4 3

To all those who teach for Tikkun Olam

Not everything that can be counted, counts. And not everything that counts can be counted.

—Albert Einstein

The real voyage of discovery consists not in seeking new landscapes, but in having new eyes.

—Marcel Proust

God is hiding in the world. Our task is to let the divine emerge from our deeds.
—Abraham Joshua Heschel

The material needs of my neighbor are my spiritual needs.

—Rabbi Israel Salanter

We are given fire to see against the dark,
to think, to read, to study how we are to live,
to bank in ourselves against defeat and despair
that cool and muddy our resolves, that makes us forget
what we saw we must do. We are given passion
to rise like the sun in our minds with the new day
and burn the debris of habit and greed and fear.

—Marge Piercy

Contents

Foreword

David E. Purpel

Both the phenomena of compulsory public education, and the professionalization of education are relatively recent events in American history. Because the federal constitution does not deal with education, issues of public policy of education had traditionally been a matter of state and local concern and systematic efforts at mandating public education at the state level did not begin until well into the 19th century. Indeed, it was the 20th century before all the states had adopted some form of compulsory public education. Moreover, the movement for a profession of education involving professional training and scholarly research did not take on momentum until the late 19th and early 20th centuries.

The impulses for publicly supported schooling are many and there are differences of opinion on what were (and continue to be) the dominant motivations for creating the extraordinarily complex and costly web of institutions focused on public schools that have come to have such a powerful presence in our society. For many, the original purposes focused on the pressing issues of an emerging and fledgling American society—the need to foster loyalty to the new federal nation and solidarity among the states; the concern for nurturing support for the democratic ethos; and the determination to create a uniquely American culture. Then as now, certain themes dominated the discourse of public educational policies, for example, the need to support commerce and industry; the responsibility to teach literacy and to develop personal character, the impulse to nurture the arts and sciences, the demand to prepare the young for gainful employment; and the concern for socializing and acculturating a population of varying ethnicities, religions, races, cultures, and classes.

This attention to formal public education was, of course, part of the much larger and profound project of Enlightenment and modernism, which was nothing less than the redemption of mankind through reason, law, art, technology, and science with the benevolent involvement of the state as its engine, a consciousness that was at the heart of the American Revolution. Permeating this perspective is an optimistic attitude of human nature in general and a deep faith in the capacity of people to learn and apply the tools of Enlightenment. Thus, a necessary element in this project was to develop a coherent theory of education as well as to discover the conditions under which people can to learn the ways to create a meaningful, just, and prosperous society. Indeed, by the late 19th and early 20th century, a lively and energetic systematic and public dialogue on all aspects of public education had emerged, encompassing such matters as curriculum, pedagogy, and school administration, public financing, learning and teaching theories. This dialogue was to be rigorous, creative, and critical subject to the highest standards of philosophy and science. In this way the country could overcome centuries of superstition, dogma, and inertia that had characterized much of early American schooling.

This movement, as we all know, was to blossom into a vast and complex profession replete with myriads of training programs, elaborate research and development endeavors, any number of professional journals, conferences, networks, and the establishment of professional standards and ethics to provide infrastructure for an incredible array of educational institutions involving millions of people and billions of dollars. This relatively new field of education has produced any number of distinguished scholars, theorists, critics, and practitioners and with it a confidence in its capacity to provide the nation with the expertise needed to create a dynamic and effective system of public schools. Although it has had its successes it has had to often operate in a context of significant financial constraints and skeptical, if not hostile, public scrutiny.

Much was expected from the interaction of these movements—thoughtful and compelling educational visions supported by careful and rigorous research would provide the nation with the necessary foundation for forging educational policies that would resonate with its highest ideals and most pressing needs. A dedicated and expert profession, in partnership with a well informed public committed to the common good, would be able to implement practices and procedures that could contribute to the realization of the American dreams and hopes of liberty and justice for all.

Like many dreams, however, fragments of this one have been realized, but mostly, it has turned about to be largely fantasy and not a little nightmarish. It is true that there is a great deal of support for public education and that vast numbers of students have attended the schools and have learned a great deal from them. It is also true that the profession has become increasingly knowledgeable and sophisticated and has passed a lot of that knowledge and sophistication on to the public. Furthermore, the issues of educational policy have risen to the very top of the political agenda at every level of government (local, state, national; executive, legislative, judicial) as well as becoming among the very highest priorities for families. What makes this dream not so pleasant has to do, however, with some disturbing questions involving what actually have students learned or not learned and what has been the impact of all this energy and attention on the well-being of the community and its quest for a better world.

Professor Shapiro has examined these issues (and a lot of other related ones) in considerable depth and with great acuity in this book and what he reports is not a pretty picture at all. Indeed it is a very disturbing one that details ill advised educational policies reflecting disheartening social, political, and cultural trends that call into serious question the basic moral character of our society and our schools. Shapiro's trenchant analysis requires us to confront the realities of how we as a nation and as a profession have addressed our commitments to work for a more just and loving community. What I, and many others, see is a society much more bent on making a lot of bucks rather than easing the needless pain and suffering of our fellow human beings, a culture obsessed with self-gratification and personal advancement; one that increasingly privileges the individual at the expense of the larger community. We are the richest and most powerful nation in the world and a people who ritually and routinely asks God to bless us and whoever pledges allegiance to a country that stands for liberty and justice. The ways in which this commitment has been so widely and cynically undermined are carefully and fully documented in this book and constitute nothing less than a desecration of our most cherished traditions and a betrayal of the legions of people who have worked so hard to make real our moral commitments.

Our government speaks passionately about peace, freedom, and democracy but goes about dispassionately conducting war, increasing inequality, and reducing civil liberties. Many of our most powerful leaders affirm the importance of a spiritual grounding but the dominant spiritual voice reflects a zealous, narrow-minded, intolerant, and mean-spirited religious sensibility. The semi-official implicit avowal of a "Christian" oriented agenda hardly corresponds to the Christianity of the Sermon on the Mount or to Christian traditions of humility, compassion, peace, and tolerance. How "faith based" policies can justify military and political aggression, abide widespread hunger and poverty, and piously adopt a posture of arrogance and defiance is far beyond my stretching capacity.

The dream of a culture that would be capable of settling social disputes and controversies through good faith dialogue under girded by a reliance on rational analysis and a system of common values has been threatened by an atmosphere of hostility, cynicism, and paranoia. Our ancestors foresaw this possibility and believed that an education grounded in the development of critical and creative thinking as well as the nurturance of a democratic ethos would be its antidote. Instead, our basic perspectives on the public schools have shifted dramatically and have gone through radical changes in an astonishing short amount of time as our educational policies reflect ideas that would have been unthinkable a decade ago. Who would have thought that the federal government would become the major player in determining the specifics of public school operations in a society where the tradition of local control of schools was once considered sacred? Who would have been pessimistic enough to predict that our curriculum would be largely determined by principles of uniformity and standardization, for example, by a vast and cruel system of high stakes testing? Surely, no one could have guessed that issues of reading pedagogy and the teaching of biology would be become matters of bitter partisan debate. No educator with only the modest amount of optimism would believe that the teaching of art, music, and physical education would be sharply curtailed or that recess would be seen as a threat to our political and economic survival. We live in a time when such concepts as citizenship education, student governance, interdisciplinary studies, experiential education, and learning by discovery have become, at best, the stuff of nostalgia or, at worst, been consigned to the rubbish heap.

There are some haunting and pressing questions involved in this situation for the profession to ponder. What is our responsibility for this debacle, for the dismantling of so much that the profession has fought for, for our failure to gain the public's confidence, and for the surrender to an oversimplified and primitive educational discourse? I am convinced that only a few have actively colluded in the attempt to disable authoritative professional institutions and undermine the quest for an education dedicated to the enrichment of democracy but what of the rest of us? Were (are) we asleep? Afraid? Indifferent? Impotent? Beyond the matter of how we have responded in the past, however, is the even more critical question of how we are to respond in the present and future. Indeed, the difficulties I have broadly sketched have been significantly exacerbated by a growing sense of pessimism to the point of despair both in the profession and in the larger culture. There surely is good reason for pessimism as the forces of reaction, greed, and zealotry seems formidable and well-entrenched, whereas many of those who are committed to more progressive and liberatory policies seem to be in disarray and demoralized. Yet, we cannot and must not succumb to these impulses as they are toxic ones that will only speed up and deepen the current regime of arrogance, greed, and aggression.

What Svi Shapiro has done for us in this book is to provide us with a powerful and eloquent response to the question of how we might to respond to the clear and present danger of an educational process that takes us down the path of mindless vulgarity and ruthless competition. His analysis is unsparing in its depiction of the breadth and depth of the challenges we face and yet his response to the question of what can be done avoids the equally ineffectual approaches of either suggesting a future of utter gloom and doom or predicting that all will soon be sunshine and delight.

This book meets the scholarly standards of rigor and precision and at the same time is readily accessible to a larger audience, surely a vital part of any strategy of changing the cultural tide that must include energetic political and professional activism. However, Professor Shapiro rightfully acknowledges that the ultimate resources for acquiring the hope and energy required for the task of regaining the momentum of the quest for a better world are of a spiritual and personal nature. He demonstrates through his own personal narrative how one can integrate political commitment and academic rigor with moral and spiritual affirmation without recourse to sentimentality or cant. Let us not cede the moral and spiritual ground to those who would divide the world into the worthy and the unworthy, but instead heed Shapiro's call for an education that could nourish our impulse to create a community of peace, justice, love, and joy.

Preface

It is a strange thing indeed that at this time of extraordinary human challenge our vision of education should seem so little related to the questions and concerns that beset us as a society and as a community. There is hand wringing over "grade inflation"; anguishing over the results of newly published test scores; alarm that students seem not to know historical dates and events; anxiety that classes are not rigorous enough, or that students are not choosing the hard courses; concern over employers' complaints that graduates are not sufficiently able to follow instructions in the work place; and much talk over the need for students to be technology literate. But, disturbingly, where is the concern over the absence of a critical and questioning attitude among young people towards the violent, and often dehumanizing, world they are inheriting? Where is the concern that our graduates lack a passionate commitment to eradicating poverty, or making our world more just? Where are the public questions about whether education is helping our young people to resist the materialism and greediness of the consumer culture? Where is the apprehension that young people are not finding in their education some understanding of what it might mean to live an ethical and purposeful life? Where are the public voices that wish to hold schools accountable, not for failing to ensure requisite levels of test scores in math or reading, but because education has lost all connection to nurturing democratic beliefs, values, and behavior among young people? Or that our students find in school little that awakens their passions and interest in healing and repairing our torn world. What voices are raised in outrage that few young people find in their education the moral and spiritual inspiration that might enliven their wish to care for, and nourish, life on this planet and ensure its survival? And who can be heard raising concern that among the dreariness and instrumentalism of school life today there is very little that might fill young people with appreciation for the awe, wonder, beauty, and preciousness of life?

This book is about two crises in our society. The first concerns the effects of the effort to reform education that have been going on for almost two decades now, but has reached its extreme manifestation in the piece of federal legislation called No Child Left Behind. These efforts to reform American education have had a disastrous influence on the quality of education for our children. Driven by an unprecedented focus on performance standards and "high stakes" testing, schools have become more and more like factories where the only things that really count are the demonstrably measurable outputs of student learning. Classrooms spend more and more time on preparing for tests, schools are compelled to measure their success in the most limited of human terms, and teachers are warned off spending time on anything that might detract from the minutely prescribed curriculum goals of the state. Not surprisingly, the education of our children has become an increasingly stress-filled experience where the joy or meaningfulness of learning recedes from everyone's concern. It is not surprising that the teachers, especially the new and creatively minded ones, leave the profession in droves as the opportunities for truly thoughtful and imaginative learning disappear. Parents, too, increasingly protest at the pressures and unfairness of the emphasis on standardized testing, which makes school an oppressive environment for so many children. And students are increasingly bored, alienated, and frustrated by the deadening consequences of this new regime of education. The dreariness and competitiveness of schools offers little to young people that stirs their imagination, provokes a critical thoughtfulness, encourages their creative vision, or speaks to their hearts and souls about human possibility and commitment.

What is most surprising about our present moment is just how few people there are in the public or professional world that appear to have the insight or courage to articulate any real alternative to the present concerns of education. Among political and civic leaders there is certainly criticism of the shortcomings and inequities of current educational policies, but little that amounts to a coherent attempt to refocus the purpose and point of our children's education. It is as if the doors of human imagination have closed in regard to what we might envisage are the goals of education, aside from usual attention to job training, the "needs" of the economy, "mastering" basic skills, raising test scores, and getting more students to attend college. Aside from some eloquent voices within the academy, and the marginalized, and often threatened, efforts of some determinedly resistant teachers and school administrators, we hear little, for example, about the need to connect education to the cultivation of a democratic citizenship, or the search for lives of purpose and meaning in these ethically and spiritually challenged times.

Parallel to the crisis of education, this book also explores a second much broader crisis that afflicts our society. We live in a time of unmatched material wealth, but one that is being emptied of the meanings that can offer us spiritually rich and sustaining lives. Who can deny that the most influential and insidious values that shape all our lives—most especially those of the young—are the ones that emanate from the world of the consumer marketplace? There are few aspects of our lives that are not in some way shaped by the ethic of buying and selling; the worth of everything seems be a matter of the price tag it has attached. We are in danger of creating a world where every aspect of our lives is turned into a commodity. The consumer world is one of show, glitz, image, and celebrity. It is one of short-lived pleasures and passing fads. It is one in which social inclusion is a matter of what you possess or can buy, rather than your capacity to participate in civic life. The credit card is the passport to social and cultural membership. This market mentality teaches us to see things like politics and education, not as intrinsically valuable experiences, but as merely instruments to get what we want. It is an inherently individualistic world in which human beings jostle and compete to maximize their advantage in what is often a ruthless struggle for survival and success. The last two decades, particularly, have seen the lifting of social and political constraints on the market as a "religion" of untrammeled capitalism has reasserted itself. It can be of little surprise that we now find ourselves facing an unprecedented crisis of cheating and corruption in our public institutions as the ethic of winning and success at any price has taken hold at every level, from the classroom to the boardroom. Nor is it surprising that it is a culture that has produced extraordinary levels of material wealth for some, while so many others are deprived of even the basic requirements of a decent life. The selfish, materialistic world of our consumer culture leaves little room for lives predicated on responsibility and obligation to others. Nor does it provide us with an ethic of care toward the earth, which is viewed as merely an unlimited storehouse of inanimate resources that fuels the world economy. The crisis of our culture reaches every level of our existence as social, moral, and spiritual creatures, posing to us profound challenges as to the meaning of being human, the way we live with one another, and the very purpose of life itself. The integration of the world into a single economic system, the immense power of technology to reshape the earth and human life, the unprecedented influence of the media to influence human consciousness and beliefs, and the awful capacity to inflict violence on a mass scale underline the questions and challenges that now face human beings as we enter this new millennium.

   In writing this book, my central concern is the disconnection between education and the world we and our children must face. The education we now insist on offering our children has been emptied of its capacity to provide young people with what they need most—the ability to cope with, and address, the moral, cultural, and spiritual challenges of the world they inhabit. What we provide to them now in no way helps them develop the things that they will need most in their lives—the capability to discern meaning and purpose in their lives; the ability to question and challenge the dehumanizing dimensions of our culture; and the sense of wonder and appreciation at the richness and beauty of life. The crisis of the culture is not hard to detect and is felt, if not always understood, throughout the society, and experienced in the daily lives of all of us. The crisis of education is the product of blindness, denial, and conformity to the imperatives of interests and forces who have convinced us that education should speak to the most pragmatic and shallow of human aspirations. And its consequences are the killing of that quest for meaning and purpose without which a worthwhile or satisfying life are impossible.

This is a book about educational vision written at a time when our dominant vision for education has lost all connection to the moral and spiritual wellsprings of a meaningful human existence. Without a compelling educational vision we can only continue to submit our schools, and our children's lives, to the most crass and vulgar influences of the larger culture. In the introduction to a book on visions of Jewish education, Seymour Fox wrote, "Lacking a directive guide to the future, the system becomes repetitive and uninspired, prey to past habit, incapable of justifying itself to new generations of our youth in the worlds they will inhabit." Fox noted that an educational vision is not meant to be a detailed blueprint for what we need to do in all facets of schoolwork. But it does offer a guiding purpose and a comprehensive understanding of the nature and goal of our efforts as educators, parents and interested citizens. He continued: "A sense of purpose is active, not passive; it is a call to engagement and thus energizing of latent capacities. A school or community with reflective purpose is liberated from slavery to the mindless momentum of the past, as well as the fads and fashions of the present, free to pursue the lead of deliberate and self-renewing ideals."[1]

What I offer here is a radically different vision for what our schools should be about. But it is not written as wishful fantasy. It is, instead, an attempt to provide a guiding purpose for the education we offer young people rooted in the "practical possibilities of the present." What I have tried to offer in this book is not just a badly needed sense of meaning for education, but a suggestion of some of the practical directions and implication that flow from following this path. In this sense, my goal is to sound both a call to action based in the prophetic tradition of alerting a culture to the dangers it faces, and a road map that illuminates some of the directions and strategies we may follow to find our way out of the present social, moral, and spiritual morass.

I have, in this book, talked interchangeably about education and public education. This may be somewhat confusing. In truth, I am most focused on trends and issues in the public side of education, which is where most of our young people spend their formative years. But I also believe that much of what I have to say is relevant and applicable to private and parochial schooling in the United States. Still, I do not want to detract from some of the really significant and radically different aspects of some of these schools. I will leave it to the readers to find the relevance to their own situations. It is also true that much of what I say is more palpably applicable to the middle and high school experience than to the younger years. Sadly, however, the playful and curiosity-centered moratorium that early and elementary education once provided is now being abandoned in favor of the test-dominated, performance-judged character that is found in the later grades.

More than anything, my effort to describe a different vision for our schools is meant to energize, and stimulate, action that can lead to a different kind of culture and society. To define education in the narrow and utilitarian way we do now is to trivialize not just education but our sense of human possibility. To see education as an end in itself is a kind of idolatry, or a fetish, robbed of its wonderful potential to transform the way we live together. A transformative vision is always impelled by a deep set of convictions about the real meaning and purpose of human life. In my case, these convictions have been stirred and nourished by a many influences not least however has been my identity as a Jew. It is this part of my experience that has so impressed on me the importance of human liberation, the concern for social justice, the preciousness of each single life, and the value of community to human fulfillment. It sowed the seeds of my passion for *Tikkun Olam*—the imperative to heal and repair the world. We need, I believe, to find, and "tap into," those wellsprings that feed all of our deepest impulses for a better world for ourselves and our children. It is in this spirit that I have allowed my "Jewish self" to speak—and cry out—for a life more purposeful and ennobling than the one we presently offer to our children.

—Svi Shapiro
Raleigh, NC

NOTES

1. From Fox, S., Scheffler, I., & Marom, C. (2003). *Visions of Jewish education*, p. 8. Cambridge, UK: Cambridge University Press.

Acknowledgements

The ideas in this book were developed in the years I have spent teaching courses in the social and philosophical foundations of education, and in the discussions and concerns raised in those classes. They are also the product of the countless conversations I have had with students including those in high schools, undergraduates, and graduate students. Among the latter have been numerous individuals who teach or administer schools. My doctoral students at the University of North Carolina at Greensboro have played a special role in both listening to my ideas as well as challenging me to justify or be more cogent in my arguments. My association with *Tikkun* magazine has also been an important vehicle that has allowed me to present my beliefs and ideas to a wider non-specialized audience, and to more freely articulate my educational concerns to the wider challenges of our moral, cultural, and spiritual lives. In this regard I want to note the profound influence that the editor of that magazine, Rabbi Michael Lerner has had on my thinking, and on my willingness to frame the educational crisis confronting us in ways that speak to our ethical commitments and on the struggle for lives of meaning. No one has had a greater impact on my life as a teacher and scholar than my long time colleague David Purpel who taught me what it means to view the work of teaching through the prism of prophetic commitment. My hope is that this book continues and extends the form of moral critique and affirmation that his writing so powerfully embodies. I want to express my appreciation to Naomi Silverman, editor at Lawrence Erlbaum who has been so supportive of my work. Much of the writing of this book took place during a research leave from the University of North Carolina at Greensboro. I am certainly very appreciative of that opportunity. Finally there is the debt to my wife Sherry whose love and camaraderie are constant. In the lighter times she shares my laughter, and in darker moments helps me rediscover the day.

1
▼▼▼▼▼

Education or Schooling?

Rabbi Shnur Zalman, the Rav of Northern White Russia (died 1813), was put in jail in Petersburg, because the *mitnagdim* had denounced his principles and his way of living to the government. He was awaiting trial when the chief of the gendarmes entered his cell. The majestic and quiet face of the *rav*, who was so deep in meditation that he did not at first notice his visitor, suggested to the chief, a thoughtful person, what manner of man he had before him. He began to converse with his prisoner and brought up a number of questions which had occurred to him in reading the Scriptures. Finally he asked: "how are we to understand that God, the all-knowing, said to Adam: 'Where art thou?'"

"Do you believe," answered the *rav*, "that the Scriptures are eternal and that every era, every generation and every man is included in them?"

"I believe this," said the other.

"Well then," said the *zaddik*, "in every era, God calls to every man: 'Where are you in your world? So many years and days of those allotted to you have passed, and how far have you gotten in your world?' God says something like this: 'You have lived forty-six years. How far along are you?'"

When the chief of the gendarmes heard his age mentioned, he pulled himself together, laid his hand on the rav's shoulder, and cried: "Bravo!" But his heart trembled.

The rabbi's answer means, in effect: "You yourself are Adam, you are the man whom God asks: 'Where art thou?'" It would thus seem that the answer gives no explanation of the passage as such. In fact, however, it illuminates both the situation of the biblical Adam and that of every man in every time and in every place. For as soon as the chief hears and understands that the biblical

1

question is addressed to him, he is bound to realize what it means when God asks: "Where art thou?," whether the question be addressed to Adam or to some other man. In so asking, God does not expect to learn something he does not know; what he wants is to produce an effect in man which can only be produced by just such a question, provided that it reaches man's heart—that man allows it to reach his heart.

Adam hides himself to avoid rendering accounts, to escape responsibility for his way of living. Every man hides for this purpose, for every man is Adam and finds himself in Adam's situation. To escape responsibility for his life, he turns existence into a system of hideouts. And in thus hiding again and again "from the face of God," he enmeshes himself more and more deeply in perversity. A new situation thus arises, which becomes more and more questionable with every day, with every new hideout. This situation can be precisely defined as follows: Man cannot escape the eye of God, but in trying to hide from him, he is hiding from himself. True, in him too there is something that seeks him, but he makes it harder and harder for that "something" to find him. This question is designed to awaken man and destroy his system of hideouts; it is to show man to what pass he has come and to awake in him the great will to get out of it.

Everything now depends on whether man faces the question. Of course, every man's heart, like that of the chief in the story, will tremble when he hears it. But his system of hideouts will help him to overcome this emotion. For the Voice does not come in a thunderstorm which threatens man's very existence; it is a "still small voice," and easy to drown. So long as this is done, man's life will not become a way. Whatever power he may attain and whatever deeds he may do, his life will remain way-less, so long as he does not face the Voice. Adam faces the Voice, perceives his enmeshment, and avows: "I hid myself"; this is the beginning of man's way. The decisive heart-searching is the beginning of a human way. (from Martin Buber, *The Way of Man.* Citadel Press, 1994, p. 9–11)

For the past 25 years I have taught high school students, students who are preparing to be teachers, teachers who have come back to the university to gain advanced degrees, individuals pursuing doctoral degrees so that they can assume positions of leadership in schools, and a whole variety of assorted people who have an interest in education and educational matters. In addition, I have talked to countless numbers of people, both informally and in invited settings, about what I see as the real issues that confront educators in today's world. I don't know how many people this totals: in the hundreds certainly, and quite possibly in the thousands. In addition, over the years I have written a good deal for both academic as well as less specialized audiences about educational matters. Still, as I sit down today to begin this new process of writing about education, schools, and the world our children face, I do so with the feeling that many of us face in our middle years. It is a moment of self-reflection and of soul searching, a time to take stock. What has it all added up to? What difference have my heartfelt efforts made to what is happening to children in our schools? Have all of those classes, discussions, articles, books made a dent on the kind of world and the kind of culture that we as adults are making for a new generation?

Of course, by now, I like to think I have shed some of the hubris that grips one's younger years. Not without difficulty, I have begun to come to terms with the more limited effect that most of us (all of us?) have on things. The more ego-centered dreams that we have in our youth about heroically reshaping the world have had to give way to a more limited, more modest, set of expectations. The struggle of middle age, at least for those who came of age in the 1960s possessed of dreams of radical transformations in both our personal and social lives, is to hold in balance the more limited expectations about what any one of can do during our short sojourn on earth, while believing that whatever we do is not enough. Somehow the internal struggle—what is really a spiritual struggle, I believe—is to accept the finitude of our life and our human energies without succumbing to the sense that in this world of huge and terrible needs our efforts are so puny that it matters little whether or not we try.

So on this grey North Carolina day I set out to recount, to renew, and to reassert those beliefs that have animated my professional life. And I do this with no illusions. An honest balance sheet that weighs up what has been achieved makes for less than happy reading. Put very simply, if my professional energies have been about the struggle to make educators aware of their important responsibilities in regard to bringing about a more socially just, a more compassionate, a more democratic, and a more ethical culture, such concerns are very far from what animates our public concerns around schools today. Today, even those who have only a passing interest in what constitutes the public discussion about education in the United States know that most of our time and energy centers on whether Johnny or Sally have improved their scores on the most recent round of standardized tests. It seems to matter little whether our political leaders are Democrats or Republicans. Each candidate, we can be sure, promises to be the education president or governor. And they will do this by making schools more accountable, more efficient, and more successful by instituting a new layer of standardized tests for our children. This dizzying world of ever more pervasive testing has managed to monopolize most of what we now talk about in regard to education. This public discourse has disastrously narrowed, squeezed, and distorted what might count as meaningful talk when it comes to discussing the educational hopes and dreams for our children. Pick up any newspaper and turn to the education page or column and what you will find is the endless rumination on performance standards, measurable results, and student achievement scores. Here, for example, is a sample from the Raleigh News and Observer that appeared on the very day I wrote this chapter:

> For the first time since North Carolina launched its school accountability program in 1997, with a sole focus on testing, education leaders are talking openly about raising the standards used to measure those test results.

> In all 73 percent of the state's 2,221 schools included in the mandatory accountability program exceeded their goals for expected progress based on

student test scores. The year before, only 35.5 percent of the state's schools showed the same level of performance.

Improvement among the state's elementary schools was even more pronounced: 95 percent of all elementary schools topped their goals for student progress, compared to just 44 percent a year earlier ...

"We're at the point where we should be looking at whether we need to ratchet up the standards," said Howard Lee, chairman of the State Board of Education and previous leader on education issues in the state Senate.

Lee continued:

"We want to keep challenging students, and we want to keep challenging teachers," Lee said. We're going to have to keep the pressure on."[1]

To be honest about this report, one needs to add that part of what was driving the concern to "raise standards" was the fact that so many schools had done well on the yearly round of tests. This meant that the extra cash promised to teachers because of their success in getting students to pass the tests was straining the already seriously stretched state budget. So there was a somewhat cynical side to this concern to make schoolwork more challenging for students. Yet, even beside this, we need to sit up and take note of all that is implied in these words and, of course, the millions of others like it that daily fill our newspapers and media when the subject turns to education. Success in educating our children means success in passing standardized tests. To challenge our children means to make these tests more rigorous. Improvements in our schools means, first and foremost, more kids getting higher test scores. Progress in educating our kids mean that a higher percentage can pass the tests this year than the year before. And in all of this we are asked to watch the bouncing ball of percentages. Just as if we are talking about the production and output of manufactured goods, schools measure their products and compare their results to the efficacy of previous years, and, of course, to the output and productivity of their rivals in other schools, in their own state, or to the results of schools systems elsewhere in the country.

THE EMPTINESS OF LEARNING

Something deeply disturbing is going on here, but perhaps, like the frog that is placed in a pot where the temperature of the water is slowly raised, the deadly nature of what we are about eludes us and, at least for now, may even seem reasonable and quite comfortable. The frog may not know the exact point when the water was no longer pleasantly warm but pointed to his demise. We, too, have lost track of when schools became for our children places of never-ending judgments and invidious comparisons, while all the time claiming to be places where all our children were nurtured and supported. Prepping for the test, taking tests, checking the results, comparing them to the results of others is, quite simply, taking over kids' (and of course, teachers') lives in schools. And we as a nation have learned to watch the process like we have come to watch the ups and downs of the Dow Jones index. As the latter purports to be an indicator for the economic and social health of the nation, so the standardized test results purport to represent the educational health of our children. Neither, I believe, is correct!

There is plenty of evidence about the extraordinary increase in the extent and pervasiveness of testing in our schools. In my daughter's public school system in North Carolina (a state often touted as a leader in educational reform), there has been something like a seven-fold increase in the past 10 years. Indeed, a colleague of mine likes to quip that public education ought to be retitled as public evaluation. But perhaps what really brings home to me the effects of all this on education is reflecting on my own daughter's experience. Sarah was a good, even excellent high school student, hard-working and diligent in terms of her work and assignments. She was part of that group of predominantly middle-class to upper-middle-class students who are the real winners in the high school selection process. One of that group of students who most teachers prefer to teach, and administrators look to, to validate the academic reputation of their school. Her school is generally regarded as one of the better, more successful public high schools in the state in terms of the percentage of seniors going on to college, the prestige of the colleges or universities they attend, and the dollars awarded in scholarships. Nor should my reflections on her education suggest that she was unhappy in this environment. She made good friends, enjoyed the camaraderie of her peers, was recognized and affirmed for her achievements, and was served well in terms of the tickets that needed punching in order for her to be able to choose the four-year college she would subsequently attend. In terms of the many students in her school (typically of lower income and disproportionately Black) who fared much less well at school in terms of their academic success, Sarah's achievements could certainly be viewed as enviable. Yet there is more to this story than simply celebrating an education for what it provided one fortunate individual in the way of recognition and success. Many parents may have felt delighted with such good fortune and be ready to laud the school for what was afforded to at least some children. Unfortunately, I could not ignore what appeared to me to be the vulgar degeneration of the educational experience. I had seen "up close and personal" what education had really become for so many young people in this time of supposedly rigorous academic standards and the demand for measurable accountability of what young people were learning.

The educational experience for Sarah was a study in just how deadening and dispirited learning had become in American schools in the early years of the 21st century. Most classroom instruction had come to resemble that process of "banking education" so pointedly described by the famous Brazilian educator Paolo Freire. Most successful students worked hard to fill their heads with an endless array of information, quotes from books, selections from speeches, literary themes, scientific laws, grammatical rules, mathematical formulas, historical dates, thematic descriptions, paragraphs from the constitution—indeed, anything that they were able to parrot back as required by their teachers and as demanded by the *test du jour*. The sheer volume of the material that Sarah and her friends were constantly required to memorize seemed, however, to be in inverse proportion to the extent that it could be called either meaningful or useful to the students' lives. The blizzard of disconnected bits and pieces of information seemed to have more in common with the game Trivial Pursuit than with the kind of understanding that might help young people begin to give some purpose or value to their world, or help them "map" or make sense of the culture that was confronting them. High standards and rigorous assessment in our schools, it was quite obvious, meant most of all the capacity to remember extraordinary amounts of information and the ability to "regurgitate" it when required on a test or exam. We sometimes laughed at home at the fact that teachers were giving so many tests it seemed to leave little time to actually engage in anything that resembled teaching or learning. The quest for greater academic rigor had, it seemed, become a matter mostly of more material to be covered, more information to be memorized, and more tests to discover whether or not you had remembered, at least for a day or two, what you had been taught. (One wit has suggested that the difference between those who are successful at school and those who are not is that the former forget what they learn after the test rather than before it!).

I want to be clear about my criticisms here. My dissatisfaction is not at all about the value of serious intellectual engagement. Indeed, education, I believe, ought, at the very least, to be about teaching young people to think and learn what it means to become critically minded human beings. This is the great legacy of enlightenment values: the belief that our humanity is deepened and enriched by the development of the capacity to go beyond the accepted dogma or the conventional assumptions of a culture. This, certainly, is a casualty of our current preoccupations in education. Schools are becoming quite simply crude, cramming factories. They are increasingly distant from being places where young people learn to reason, question, and critically interrogate the assertions that are placed before them, or to think deeply about the meaning and implications of the ideas, beliefs, or knowledge they encounter. Such a vision of education is, instead, replaced by one in which higher standards mean, quite simply, the drive to fill up young minds with a huge array of facts and information that resides in our brains for only as long as it is needed for the next test. (For an influential example of where this thinking is taking us, pick up one of those popular tomes by E. D. Hirsch[2] optimistically titled *Cultural Literacy* with its extraordinary, and surely absurd, lists of those things that an "educated" person is supposed to know.)

The current "ratcheting" upward of educational standards has made school an increasingly demanding and competitive place in terms of what it takes to be successful. This really means that success requires increasing amounts of time and effort in playing the "game of schooling." More effort than ever is now required to familiarize, memorize, and regurgitate the bits and pieces of knowledge that ensure the good grades without which college admissions and scholarships will remain a pipe dream. This accounts, too, for the extraordinary increase in both the time spent in school and in the amount of homework demanded. A University of Michigan study[3] showed that students spend 8 more hours in school now than they did 20 years ago. It noted, too, that in this time homework has nearly doubled. In 1981, 6- to 9-year-olds averaged 44 minutes a week of homework. In 1997 it was more than 2 hours. In their book *The End of Homework*, John Buell and Etta Kralovec[4] argued that "both research and historical experience fail to demonstrate the necessity or efficacy of ever longer hours of homework." They also noted that many students, especially, junior and senior high students, are suffering from the "fatigue factor" of putting in 50 or 60 hours a week of class time, which may burn them out before they go to college. Even among young children there is an increasing emphasis on making school a place of increasing productivity where there is reduced time for play, and more time is devoted to raising test scores and results. This is evidenced in the fact that since the 1980s hundreds of elementary schools have eliminated recess. Betsy Taylor[5] noted the "extraordinary cultural pressure to put kids on the fast track by the age of two." Parents, she said, are enrolling young toddlers in a myriad of precurricular activities to ensure they can compete and be successful in school. All of this effort and time may provide decent, or even exceptional, grades and test results. But we need to ask ourselves, what in the world does all the material students are now required to "cover" have to do with our proudest and noblest vision of a citizenry that knows how to reason, question, and think? Is there any connection between all of these increased demands and the development of the capacity to become creative, imaginative, or reflective human beings? Filling the minds of young people in this way may have much more in common with that venerable tradition of stuffing the turkey at Thanksgiving. Each may be the precursor to a celebration, but neither should be confused with the rejuvenation of an active, curious life. Perhaps our confusion over what it means to really know something, as opposed to merely "banking" knowledge, is testimony to just how far we have learned to detach the education we expect for our kids from any vision of learning that speaks to the quintessential human need to make or find meaning, to become reflective and thoughtful beings, or even to solve individual and societal problems in creative and responsible ways. We have made a Faustian bargain for our kids—a schooling that promises higher standards and test scores, instead of an education that enlivens and enriches how our children engage their world.

To walk into too many classrooms today is to see just how much this devil's bargain has deadened the minds of our kids and dispirited their sense of active engagement with the world. It is, I believe, time that we as parents and as citizens recovered our sense that there is something being tragically destroyed in our restrictive obsession with grades, test results, and grade point averages (GPAs). It is education itself that is being eviscerated by this process of intellectual narrowing and by the reduction of learning to those things that can be assessed through the simplistic yes/no answers of standardized bubble sheets. Although the sad results of this might be most evident in high schools, we should not imagine that elementary or middle schools have escaped the effects of the testing regime and its deadly effect on the possibility of joyful, creative, and thoughtful classrooms. Here is some of what a teacher of 8-year-olds recently wrote in a letter to our local newspaper[6] expressing her frustration at the demand for additional pressure on schools to "raise standards":

> Please—the pressure is already more than most of us can tolerate. Teachers, administrators, parents, and yes, children most of all, are drowning in unrealistic expectations put on us by people who have no idea how we are affected. Imagine a world where 8-year-olds take a test every year that lasts longer than an SAT or GRE (three half-days of testing) and determines whether they will be retained or not the following year. Imagine having once passed that test, only to be required to take a similar test the next year and the next and every school year thereafter, each determining pass/fail for the next year. The very same children squirm every year and either get trapped or squeak by, knowing the relief may only be temporary.

I have heard such feelings expressed numerous times in my graduate classes, where experienced and dedicated teachers must daily struggle with what the relentless focus on tests and so-called "high standards" is doing to education and the children they teach. What I hear again and again is how destructive all this is to making classrooms that interest, stimulate, and challenge young minds!

BECOMING MANIPULATIVE, THINKING INSTRUMENTALLY

Of course, when I return to my daughter's experience it must be said that not all was darkness. Certainly there were classrooms that were challenging, that came alive with dialogue and discussion, even occasional incidences when the classroom focus resonated with her own experience and concerns. And, of course, with the deadening hand of the regime of tests and standards is the presence of teachers trying hard to make their subject material matter to kids beyond whether it is worth 10 points on the next quiz. But we need to look here not at the heroic and ingenious exceptions to the general trend, but at the trend itself. Often in my conversations with some of these very good and dedicated teachers, the mountains they were being asked to climb daily to do keep their classrooms places that emphasized the capacity to reason, or to be creative, or to encourage the capacity of students to challenge and question, were becoming just too difficult. I have witnessed these teachers agonizing over the choice of whether to leave teaching, or to accommodate to the assessment factories our schools have become. There is, sadly, evidence that it is often the most thoughtful and creative teachers who are the first to leave among those who have recently entered teaching. A recent report noted that nearly one in six public school teachers did not return to their school systems in the subsequent year.

In actual fact, it is less than accurate to say that students in school do not think. Of course, conscious humans are always engaged in some kind of thought process. The issue is really, thinking about what, and in relationship to what set of meanings or purpose? We knew, for example, that Sarah had become very good at statistical computation. She was able to maintain, in her head, a complex accounting of her current grades in any subject, feeding into them all the various permutations relating to the numerical weight of different assignments, quizzes, exams, and other course requirements. Like all of the students around her, she was able to rapidly discern the best way to distribute her energies with the greatest efficiency, to maximize the numbers and grades in her classes. This was no small feat, and there were others who demonstrated quite extraordinary capabilities in this regard. Indeed, she was simultaneously impressed, and also chagrinned, by the real hustlers in her classes who had developed an amazing capacity to beat the numerical system to ensure their own success. If nothing else, using one's wits in this way might be excellent training for those thinking about becoming Wall Street traders or even Las Vegas casino sharp hands. I often wondered whether this is what people had in mind when they talked about school preparing young people for the real world. It was frequently those who were the best "wheelers and dealers" in this process that received the most generous offers from the most selective universities. What all this focus on playing the numbers surely does produce is a strategically attuned mind set—a highly instrumental or manipulative attitude toward one's own education. Students learn in the competitive, test-driven, and grade-obsessed school environment that what counts has little do with the pleasure of learning, or the intrinsic value of greater understanding. And certainly what is learned does not have much to do with increasing the wisdom we have about the purpose or significance of our lives, or our capacity to help shape a more just, free, or compassionate culture. In contrast to this, students learn to see education as mainly about how one can manipulate the system to get the best results with the least expenditure of effort. And who can really blame kids for that? Isn't that what we as adults are really conveying by giving so much attention to grades, test scores, GPAs, even the dollar amounts attained by schools in scholarships.

It should come as no surprise that the extraordinary increase in testing has been paralleled by evidence of widespread cheating both among school personnel and among students. A simple surf of the Web provides examples of a whole industry that now feeds on the instrumental, results-driven character of present-day schooling. Outfits like *Paperpimp* brazenly offer their services to any student who has learned the cynical message of contemporary education, which is to do whatever it takes to get the right grades or exam results. Increasingly it seems that this is the only thing that now really seems to count in our schools—win, or at least survive the game, by any means possible. A survey by the Josephson Institute of Ethics of nearly 21,000 middle and high school students found that 70% of high school students admitted to cheating at least once on an exam in the previous 12 months; 45% of these students agreed with the statement, "A person has to lie or cheat in order to succeed." Over a third of the students questioned would be willing to cheat if it would help them get into college. In another survey of high school students,[7] 80% of students admitted to cheating to get to the top of their class. More than half said that they didn't view cheating as a big deal.

In the context of this increasingly dog-eat-dog world of public education, the incidence of professional employees cheating has also increased. In the past 2 years, schools in New York, Texas, Florida, Ohio, North Carolina, Rhode Island, Kentucky, and Maryland have investigated reports of improper or illegal attempts by teachers, principals and other administrators to raise test scores. In Texas a deputy superintendent was indicted on 16 counts of criminal tampering after central administrators and principals boosted scores by changing the identification numbers of students whose failing grades they did not want counted. In New York City cheating was so pervasive that it led to the resignation of a school superintendent. With the implementation of the Bush administration's No Child Left Behind legislation, and its even greater emphasis on test results and sanctions against schools that fail to show "adequate yearly progress" in their test scores, we should expect more and more examples of dishonest practices by both teachers and school administrators seeking to save jobs or avoid public embarrassment. Of course, in this age of corporate scandals related to extraordinary ethical abuses of deception and cheating, it is hard to see schools as places that are alone in the tendency to emphasize the importance of winning at any cost. It is the results that count—whether this be in the form of grades and test scores, or profits and stock values—and the smartest and most successful individuals, it seems, are those who have learned how to play the game to their greatest advantage. David Callahan recently made this argument in his book *The Cheating Culture*,[8] in which he noted that the free-wheeling economic climate of the past 20 years has produced a society in which cheating and dishonesty are rampant. The unfettered market is reflected in corporate scandals, doping in sports, plagiarism by journalists and students and corner-cutting in the most mundane matters. The "winning class," argued Callahan, has the money and clout to cheat without consequence, whereas others come to believe that not cheating will cost them their only shot at success in a winner-take-all world. This manipulative, win-at-all-costs mentality is the stuff that now provides our entertainment in so many "reality" TV shows.

DE-MEANING EDUCATION

For students, educational chatter about knowledge and understanding is just "sweet talk" little related to the daily grind of schooling and the preoccupation with winning, getting ahead, or just surviving. Education becomes increasingly a high-stakes game in which success is defined almost entirely by one's ability to test well through whatever means necessary. For educators, the extraordinary extent and pervasiveness of standardized tests in American schools put a choke-hold on all other educational goals and purposes. In this process, as we have seen, education becomes the intellectually thin process of memorization and regurgitation of predigested information. Classroom instruction is more and more given over to "test prep." In this context, schools offer little that can be taken as a source of personal meaning, as a stimulus to critical thought, or as the catalyst for imaginative interpretation of human experience.

The effect of all this on students' interest, curiosity, and participation in their own learning is a devastating one. Study after study reveals that the longer kids stay in school, the drearier it becomes. The interest and excitement that is usually present during the first years of school gives way increasingly to the boredom of high school. Observers of high school have continually remarked on the vapid nature of the educational experience, the shallowness of the way knowledge is engaged, and the alienated and manipulative attitudes of students. In a particularly vivid recent account of life in a suburban high school, the journalist Elinor Burkett described the shamelessly instrumental attitudes of students across the range of academic abilities. Some of what she wrote is worth quoting here:

> The philosophy driving education was capitalism in its purest form. Every-thing was about the reward, and the reward had to be delivered in the cur-rency of teenage life: points and grades. Learning, students had been taught, was an exercise in venture capitalism and ... they expected a decent return. "How many points is this extra-credit question worth?" students badgered teachers who offered special questions at the end of exams. "I haven't decided yet," a substitute once responded. "How can we know whether we want to do it then? replied the students, clearly confounded.

> Amanda Halvorson went one step further in the January issue of the *Laker Times*, the student newspaper, suggesting that schools pay students for good grades. "The majority of students today said they don't try their hardest in classes because they feel there is no point," she wrote: "They also say these things to teachers all of the time: Why do we have to do this?' This is useless, and I will never actually use any of this in life.'"

> In the absence of such monetary compensation, students were clear about the purpose of their education: "Grades are what school is about," they declared. And they received few signals that they were wrong. "Work hard, get good grades," their parents urged, not "Work hard, and expand your horizons."[9]

Not surprisingly, such nakedly instrumental attitudes toward education produced an entirely amoral view of cheating. School was a game with no compelling individual or social purpose beyond getting the best grade you could get with the least effort. As long as you can get away with it, why not do whatever is needed (a sentiment that interestingly parallels that found among executives at Enron and WorldCom). One student described it this way:

> "My belief is that every part of life is a game," he said, without a trace of cyni-cism. "I even see it with my dad and his work. The question is: What can I get away with before it's a problem?"[10]

This student described how he "worked" the teachers, pretending that he was engaged and performing "careful cost-benefit analyses" about what work was likely to pay off in A's. Elinor Burkett found such attitudes to be the norm in a school, she was careful to point out, that was rated among the best in the state and nation as measured in the usual currency of college admissions—SAT results and AP scores. Cheating, she noted, in the school was near universal.

> In a world without much shame, students weren't ashamed of copying friends' work or pulling papers off the Internet. When Joe Goracke asked his Psychology students about the morality of the practice, they were candid and forthright. "How many of you have never cheated? he posed the question to his class that morning. Although Goracke was infamous for his toughness, his students seemed entirely relaxed and open in discussions. In response to Goracke's question one girl out of the group of twenty raised her hand. When her friends glared at her suspiciously, she lowered it halfway. "Well, I've never cheated on a test, just on worksheets," she said timidly. "That doesn't count," the students declared unanimously. "Why not?" Goracke pushed. "That's just homework, it's different, they answered. "What about tests, then?" Inquired Goracke. "I wouldn't plan to cheat on a test, but if the situation arose ... " one boy ventured.[11]

I would be less than fully honest to say that there was not some relief in my daughter Sarah's capacity to cope successfully with this game of schooling. After all, the rewards are clear—admission to a good university, scholarship money that lightens the heavy financial load of a middle-class parent, and the avoidance of the constant clashes and crises faced by parents dealing with children who were in a constant mode of resistance toward the school regime. Within my community I have seen, for example, the pain of parents whose children (more often boys) find the school game meaningless and refuse to knuckle down and do what is required of them. There is a special poignance to the fact that these parents often, themselves, share with their kids the sense of the mindlessness of what schools require, but are caught between empathy for their offspring, and fear for the economic and social consequences of school failure. It is also fully apparent that for many working-class and poorer families the rules of the educational game remain the privileged knowledge of students from predominately White, middle- and upper-middle-class backgrounds. This becomes painfully obvious at every school gathering where honors and academic recognitions are distributed. So to whatever extent Sarah's success eased our burdens, I confess that I possess no great sense of triumphalism in this process. The capacity to play the game makes life more comfortable, that is for sure. But this must not be confused with any deep satisfaction at what is being accomplished in terms of the quality and value of the educational experience. The end, here, can in no way be allowed to obscure or justify the means. After all, success is the capacity or willingness (often because of fear of authority or the need to conform—the reason, I believe, that girls now do better at school than boys, rather than because of any blossoming of feminist assertiveness) to play the school game. This means, in the schooling that so many of our children now face, a readiness to subordinate much of the human capacity for creativity and imagination, a questioning thoughtfulness, and the expectation that what we learn might enrich or add meaning to our lives. All of this is forced, much of the time, to give way to the shallow and often manipulative search for points, scores, and grades. In our fixation on the issue of achieving a better education it is as if we have substituted the currency of success for any real sense of meaning, purpose, or wisdom in what we do. It seems to parallel the way that the fetish of accumulating money or possessions has substituted for the question of how wealth might improve the quality of our lives. Day in and day out we drum this message into the heads of our children. Forget that learning might have something to do with the understanding that might, in turn, help us live fuller and more purposeful lives. Or that knowledge offers us the capacity to strip away the deceit, pretenses, and distortions of our grotesquely deceptive culture and, perhaps, empower us as citizens. Schooling is steadily removed from the quest for wisdom, meaning, or the capacity to think, question, and challenge. In its place we subject young people to an increasingly inane regimen of learning in which higher standards and rigor are confused with more tests, more pages to memorize, and more information that can be parroted back to the teacher. All of this is driven by crude economic pressures that suggest that better test scores mean a more competitive workforce, politicians with simplistic promises for educational reform and improvement, and a public hungry for demonstrable evidence of change and accountability.

And at the end of the day, all talk about education and educational change is reduced not to the quality of the human experience but to the quantifiable measures of so-called learning. In other words, it is all brought down to numbers that can measure results and show relative gains and losses, akin to the profit and gain spreadsheets of business. In this one-dimensional world of educational accounting, what is being lost, as we flatten out the extraordinarily complex world of human growth and understanding and reduce it to the crudity and simplicity of a few digits on a school report or the assessment of a school system's adequacy, are any real references to the joy of learning, or the capacity to engage knowledge as the means to live as more discerning, engaged, and conscientious members of the human community. Einstein was surely right when he quipped that "not all that can be counted, counts, and not all that counts can be counted." This is clearly a message not heard by the legions of politicians, legislators, school administrators, and the corporate and academic industry that has supported our brave new world of educational reform. How can one not be darkly amused by reports in our local newspapers that the latest school accountability measures demonstrate that new levels of excellence have arrived in the schools of North Carolina? My everyday experience encountering the graduates of these schools in the college classroom reveals the real impoverished nature of this education—minimum knowledge of events in the world, lack of the ability to question or challenge ideas, incapacity at voicing contrary ideas in the classroom, incredulity that education should have something to do with democracy and critical examination of our culture, surprise at the application of education to the quest for meaning and purpose in our lives, and astonishment at the idea of education as a vehicle for affirming a position of moral responsibility toward the world in which we live. They are, however, familiar and moderately competent with essay "outlines," predigested readings, and, most importantly, clear delineation of the relative weight of assignments to the overall value of the final grade. I find little to celebrate in the claimed great march forward of "high educational standards." It seems to produce mainly intellectual timidity, the capacity for rote learning, a shallowness of thought, and an absence of imagination. More than this, it has left many students with a detached and cynical attitude to any education that doesn't have tangible connections to a better grade and job opportunity.

RETHINKING EDUCATIONAL REFORM

The present era of educational reform is generally considered to have begun in 1983 with the Reagan administration's report *A Nation at Risk*. This report blamed the country's economic woes on the "rising tide of mediocrity" in the nation's schools. Strangely, when 10 years later the United States began the longest economic boom in the past 50 years, little was said either to congratulate schools on the good economic times, or to modify the theory that connected increased productivity and technological inventiveness to the quality of public education. Here is not the place to make sense of the ideological and political influences that had come together to blame schools for job losses, industrial decline, and a general crisis of confidence about this country's cultural and military superiority. Whatever the cogency of the indictment of schools, the influence of the report in setting in train the next 20 years of educational reform can hardly be doubted. Certainly we are still living through the push for higher standards and increased public accountability in our schools. Interestingly, much of the debate around public education has been framed as a conflict between the liberal influences of the 1960s and 1970s with their concern for the psychological well-being of kids, and the defenders of academic standards—conservatives, who want to "return" schools to their true educational mission of ensuring young people have mastered fundamental skills and acquired "basic" knowledge. The former are blamed for permitting lax academic and moral standards in their zeal to create environments where all kids can feel okay about themselves. The 1960s and liberals (especially among the teaching profession and their allies in university schools of education) are accused of undermining clear standards of achievement and behavior by encouraging relativistic values. Whether in terms of affirming multiple forms of intelligence, the value of process over product, history that emphasizes multiple perspectives, or the incommensurable value of different languages and cultures, these liberals stand accused of pandering to the goal of making everyone "feel good" about who they are and what they know, to the detriment of legitimate standards of what might be considered "true" and "good." Of course, there is a good deal of confusion in the conservative critique. For example, among some, schooling ought, indeed, to strongly reinforce the values of authority, hierarchy, and unquestioning respect for the knowledge one receives in school. Yet for others, educational traditionalists, education ought to provide students with the capacity to thoughtfully analyze ideas and to discern the cogency or illogicality of texts. For the latter the shallowness of understanding required in the new regime of standardized tests ought to be cause for alarm. Certainly, report after report has made the point that educational reforms are producing forms of learning that require little critical engagement with ideas, and little more than the most superficial kinds of knowing or understanding to "pass" one's classes. It is also worth noting that careful study of changes in school practices over the past 50 years dismisses the idea that public schools ever really embraced the kind of openness or permissiveness that right-wing critics accused them of, or moved that far away from teacher-centered learning organized around the traditional subject-based curriculum. And, certainly, schools have never gone that far from giving up their roles as social "gate-keepers"—institutions that are engaged in the process of sorting and sifting students for future success and opportunity. Much of the criticism seems to have depended on a caricature of changes in schools that would support or enable the kinds of reforms that have become familiar in the last 20 years. In many senses there was what David Berliner and his associates[12] called a "manufactured crisis" of falling standards, declining abilities, and sinking levels of knowledge. This is not to say that things in our schools were fine, only that the sense of a major disruption in how schools functioned that represented a departure from significantly better earlier times is a far cry from what was actually the reality of the overwhelming continuity and lack of fundamental change in what was going on in the nation's classrooms.[13]

   In fact, this conflict has always been about much more than what and how we should teach in our schools. It quite obviously touches serious tensions in our culture that have to do with the promise of democracy—something we return to later in this book. In some respects the conflict grows out of the anxieties and fears about what cultural observers and scholars refer to as postmodernity. A consequence of our postmodern world has been the unleashing of immense challenges to the certainties and clear categories that shape our world. What can we truly depend on today as fixed, reliable, and assured? What part of our lives does not feel under siege or fragile? What do we know or believe that can be stated with absolute certainty? How secure is my economic future, my social relationships, or even my physical existence? In a world of increasingly permeable borders, and with easy access to an amazing array of new ideas, beliefs, sensibilities and identities, the solid secure self is now the willing subject of endless "make-overs." With the promise of change and novelty held ever more tantalizingly before us, the familiar and comforting contours of home, relationships, and community no longer seem so dependable or permanent. In this sense, schools have become places where we enact (frequently with only limited awareness) the tensions, anxieties, and fears of our precarious and uncertain times. Debates over educational practices are often our attempts to come to grips with issues that are about much more than how much math kids should learn in the eighth grade, or whether learning to read through phonics is better than "whole reading" instruction. In this sense, as David Purpel has argued, there are really no educational issues, only human, cultural, moral concerns played out in the arena of schools, and in terms of the hopes and desires we have for our children's lives. Sadly, and misguidedly, we often continue to talk about education as if it is a world apart from all of these wider concerns, anxieties, fears, and hopes, not the mirror and repository of them.

After 20 years of living in the shadow of *A Nation At Risk*, it is time, I believe, to begin to rethink what education for our children needs to be about. It is time to begin a new era of educational thinking, one that starts with rethinking the vision of what it means for our children to become educated in a time of profound economic, technological, cultural, and moral change. Such a vision needs to connect education to our hopes for our children's lives in the context of a world in which the present often seems menacing, and the future precarious. Our vision will have to connect education's work to our best hopes for what it means to be human and how we might live with others both within our own nation as well as in the larger world. In this new bold assertion of education's mission, questions of identity, culture, and ethical commitment are integral to our educational concerns, and explicitly stated. In the face of such large and profound considerations, our present obsessions around schools will come to seem downright trivial if not ludicrous! Yet it is often hard to reimagine what could or should be—to think, as the expression goes, "out of the box." What we do and think now is so much a part of our common sense, the taken-for-granted way we make sense of things, that it is really quite difficult to radically reshape the terms of our thinking and to reenvisage how things could be. Sometimes, however, by looking around us we can discover the seeds of alternative thinking in familiar places. Answers to some of our questions may stand right before us. We need only to re-contextualize what we are looking at so as to see how it might provide inspiration and insight in areas that we have never before felt relevant to it. This is the case, I believe, with my daughter's experience of summer camp.

THE LESSONS OF NONSCHOOL EDUCATION

For a number of years now, Sarah has been an avid and enthusiastic participant at Camp Ramah. This Jewish summer camp, held each year for several weeks in Clayton, Georgia, is affiliated with the Conservative movement of American Judaism (conservative not in the usual terms of being right-wing but in its commitment to maintaining the traditional rituals and practices of the Jewish faith while, at the same time, recognizing the need to reinterpret religious practices and values in the context of a changing culture). Like all summer camps, this one provides the usual opportunities for play, adolescent sociability, and release from the usual surveillance of parents and teachers. It is, as such, a world with rules, regulations, and controls, but, at the same time, it offers considerable opportunities for the spontaneity and pleasure of youthful exuberance and the expression of pent-up adolescent energies. Yet it is also, I have come to appreciate, much more than an adolescent playpen. No less than school, it claims to be a place for education. I have reflected often on what it means for this same word to be applied to both these sites but with a significance in each that seems so profoundly different. In the superficial sense both camp and school provide places to read and study, to discuss issues and to develop skills. Yet this seems in no way to capture the profoundly different character of learning in each place. Although my daughter was competent and successful in school, this in no way was comparable to the transformational experience of learning at her camp. One provided the satisfaction of good grades and the modest recognition of scholarly success; the other moves her soul and infuses her life with meaning and purposeful identity. One offers her the promise of instrumental rewards, the other the inspiration of ethical ideals and a life lived with, and toward, community. One crowned hard work with a transcript that celebrated individual distinction and status; the other connected learning to feeding the spirit's passion for finding existential significance in life's short journey. Of course, these are my words, not Sarah's. Yet I am convinced about the profound distinction that exists in regard to what education means within the context of her school, and within her camping experience. And it is the key to what for her, and other adolescents, is the joyful and moving experience of the latter, and the dreary, mechanical, and alienating experience of school learning. The totality of the camp experience—its formal classes, religious rituals, shared music, dance and aesthetic experiences, informal social life, and the important responsibilities and roles of adolescent peers—establishes an environment for education quite different from the one we expect, and have come to accept, for the 180 days of each school year. School offers only the hollow shell of meaningful experience to our children. In its zeal about academic achievement, test scores, grades, point averages, college acceptance, and the rest, it has turned our eyes away from what is most important in the process of human development and maturation. In focusing our attention on winning, getting ahead, being a success, we have offered kids little that speaks to what it means to live a good and purposeful life in the context of social relationship and communal responsibility. In the place of an education that seeks to connect knowledge and understanding to living lives of worth and significance, we have substituted the junk "education" of the grade game and test prep. If there is something important to be learned from my daughter's very different experiences, it is that the real crisis of the education we offer to our children today is not in declining achievement scores or poor test results, but in our inability to offer an environment that helps nourish the quest for meaningful lives. I am convinced that it is in the crisis of meaning, not in the crisis of test scores, that we may begin to seek understanding of what ails our lives and our culture. All of the tremendous energy we currently pour into our educational reforms will do little to help us address—and, even more importantly, to prepare our children to positively engage—this world of violence, intolerance, social injustice, alienation, addictive materialism, egoism, and spiritual emptiness. All of our present attempts to "fix" education are very far removed from anything that speaks to the needs of human life and human community at this moment in time. There is little or nothing in all of our educational reforms that offers young people the capacity to deal with the deepening social and cultural crises that are engulfing us. My lifelong colleague and university collaborator David Purpel, in attempting to bring this point home, liked to pose to his students—mainly teachers and school administrators—two questions. The first was to list what they thought were the top 10 problems that now faced humanity (typical answers included war, prejudice, hatred, poverty, HIV/AIDS, social inequities, materialism, and so on). His second question was to have them consider how, and in what ways, the education we presently offer young people attempts to address these issues. There was usually a stunned silence as they recognized how removed our educational focus and work have become from anything that attempts to help us engage and change the human condition in the contemporary world. Education, for all the sound and noise of our local and national reforms, was increasingly disconnected from attempting to provide the knowledge, the understanding, the practical experience, or the moral and emotional climate that might guide young people in their struggle to build lives of meaning and purposeful commitment in a world that, for better or worse, is their home. It is a sad fact that the cramming factories that are our present schools have all but eclipsed any vision of education that might speak to the mind, heart, and spirit of our children so that they might become critically thoughtful, sensitive, and engaged members of the human community. As parents, as citizens, as teachers both in and out of the classroom, we must find a way to redefine, to reenvisage, and to reconstruct what it now means to educate our children. What is at stake in this quest is far more important than the academic acumen of our children. What concerns us here is nothing less than the conscience, the awareness, and the moral commitment of those who will shape human life in this nascent century.

NOTES

1. Success breeds concern for ABC's. (2003, October 13). *The News and Observer* [Raleigh, NC], p. B1.
2. J. Trefil, J. F. Kett, & E. D. Hirsh, eds. (2002). *The new dictionary of cultural literacy: What every American needs to know*. New York: Houghton Mifflin.
3. John de Graaf, ed. (2003). *Take back your time* (p. 48). San Francisco: Berrett-Koehler.
4. John Buell & Etta Kralovec. (2001). *The end of homework*. Boston: Beacon.
5. Betsy Taylor. (2003). *What kids really want that money can't buy*. New York: Warner Books.
6. Letter. (2003, October 21). *The News and Observer* [Raleigh, NC], p. 12A.

7. *The 29th who's who among American high school students. 1996.* Lake Forest, IL. Educational Communications, Inc.

8. David Callahan. (2004). *The cheating culture.* New York: Harcourt.

9. Elinor Burkett. (2001). *Another planet* (pp. 190, 191). New York: Harper Collins.

10. Ibid. (p. 188).

11. Ibid. (p. 193).

12. David C. Berliner, James Bell, & Bruce J. Biddle. (1996). *The manufactured crisis.* New York: Perseus.

13. Larry Cuban. (1997). *Tinkering towards utopia: A century of public school reform.* Cambridge: Harvard University Press.

2

Crisis of Meaning

The tale is told about a nineteenth-century mystical master. Zusia of Onipol was the poorest of masters for many years. Before he revealed himself as a master, he wandered, Buddhist style, from city to city disguised as a beggar. In one city, he would often seek the assistance of a particular wealthy patron, but to no avail. The patron had little time for the likes of him. Later in Zusia's life, he was revealed as a master and came not only to fame but also to fortune. As it happened, he had reason to pass through the town of this wealthy patron again and was of course invited to sup at the patron's table. Zusia accepted.

However, a very strange scene ensued. Zusia would take the fine food from the patron's plate and instead of putting it in his mouth, he would ever so delicately dump it on his clothes.

The patron was aghast. He tried to restrain himself, but as the master kept dumping food onto his garments, he could hold back no longer. "What are you doing?" he cried out.

"Why, it is very simple," Zusia responded calmly. "When I was poor you never invited me. The only thing that has changed since then is my clothes. Therefore, I assumed you must have invited my clothes to dine with you. So I was feeding them." (Hassidic tale from Marc Gafni, *Soul Prints*, p. 238 New York: Simon and Schuster, 2002)

The present public discussion about education does nothing to address the sickness that is at its heart. It only deepens and prolongs the character of education as an instrumental form of human activity, one that is fixated on the extrinsic results of education in the form of grades, point averages, test scores, graduate rates, college admissions, and so on. The lack of any real concern with the human quality of the educational encounter must inevitably result in the corrosion of student attitudes toward education—apathy, disinterest, cynicism, and deceit. We get what we have asked for: students who are, at best (when they are not entirely turned off to the whole business), trained to focus not on the intrinsic experience of learning itself—the joy, power, and transformative nature of ideas—but only on the payoff in the form of a transcript, resumé, or diploma. The classroom becomes merely a form of menial labor where one puts in the necessary hours in order to get a "paycheck." The paycheck here, of course, is the grade for a course. Education has become nothing but schooling, an obstacle course to be crossed to get on with the rest of ones life. Each class, subject, grade level, and so on become not much more than rungs on a career ladder to be got over speedily and with minimum effort, to move on and up. There is little that is felt to be intrinsically valuable about each of the stages themselves. So much so that it hardly comes as a surprise when we read that a state like Minnesota is considering dropping the entire 12th grade. The process of education feels more and more like a necessary evil to be endured and survived, one that must be dealt with in ways that call on the least expenditure of students' intellect or emotion, as long as it ensures successful passage to the next stage of their lives, whether this is college or a job.

To experience what we are doing as nothing more than a vehicle to get us to something else alienates us from the present, and teaches us to view education as not much more than a passport to some future state or opportunity. It not surprising that after so many years of this kind of behavior, many of us find ourselves pursuing religious or spiritual practices that might enable us to become more "mindful" of our lives: looking for ways to be present and alive to where our lives are now, rather than always "living" in some future and promised state. As I have found when I have raised this issue with my undergraduates, the main emotion associated with the classroom is that of waiting. When I have suggested that the emotions associated with real learning ought to be excitement, inspiration, joy, pain, confusion, struggle, and surprise, I am usually met by a sense of disbelief. Few can remember ever having had such feelings as a consequence of any classroom experience (except perhaps the pain of a poor grade, or the joy of a successful test result!). What we now witness is that schooling with its attention to extrinsic results has become everything; education and its concern for our life's engagement with ideas that might provide insight into who we are and how we are living hardly exist.

REDEFINING THE CRISIS

We need, I believe, to transform our vision of education from this "result-centered" view with its individual alienation, and disengagement from authentic learning, to one that is understood in a radically different way. In the latter, education becomes a vehicle for that most human of all concerns—the quest and struggle for lives of meaning. Such a vision might speak to the real crisis that faces our children as they grow up in this world: not that of falling SAT scores or poor test results in reading or arithmetic, but that of a culture that is increasingly unable to offer young people the possibility of meaningful and purposeful lives. The fact that the crisis of education came to be defined and described in the way that it did is a strange and interesting tale. It is one I do not attempt to explain here. Others, such as Gerald Bracey,[1] made it clear how the oft-repeated pronouncements about precipitous declines in academic achievement, or major downward shifts in things like SAT scores, ability to read or be numerate, or our academic standing vis-à-vis other countries, seriously exaggerated or distorted the reality of any changes that had actually taken place in educational performance in this country. Indeed, according to these observers, the changes that actually occurred during the past 30 or so years in students' achievement levels and academic abilities were modest, at best, when all of the complex variables that influence our computations are factored in. Whatever purposes the "pumped up" crisis in academic achievement served, it certainly drove out the last vestiges of a more progressive, student-centered approach to teaching left over from the 1960s and 1970s. It also deflected attempts to define our crisis in education in some very different ways. The "manufactured" educational crisis turned our attention from the mounting anxiety that there was something deeply at fault with the dominant set of meanings and values that were determining how our kids viewed the world that they were growing up in. The crisis of meaning and values that emerged among the young in the 1960s and early 1970s needed to be either suppressed or given a new interpretation. This meant "re-presenting" or "re-telling" the 1960s experience as one that was all about drugs, sex, rock and roll, and violence. It told a story, repeated constantly by our media and many of our political and religious leaders, that omitted how the youthful energies of the period were directed toward confronting an ugly war, resisting the dominant role of money and materialism in our society's values, and working to change the many forms of social injustice that blighted the landscape of our nation. A time of unprecedented concern for public and political issues among the young, and an unprecedented outpouring of interest in socially responsive activities, was to become seen as a time of little but mindless mayhem and hedonistic excesses. Of course, the radical nature of young people's perceptions and concerns in that period also meant pressure on schools to make learning more connected to what was happening in the world outside the classroom. It led to the demand that education be more relevant, more encouraging of critical attitudes, and more inclusive of students' own experiences. In a way, the turn toward a much more rigidly defined and results-oriented approach to education fitted perfectly with those who sought to stem the ethos of a more questioning classroom focused on questions about what was actually going on in our society and in our world. This "top-down" view of learning with its emphasis on getting the one correct answer to whatever might be asked certainly made for a much more conformist, "one-size-fits-all" approach to learning. It also tied in well with the increasing presence of a conservative moralism that cast our nation's cultural problems as the result of too much sex, drugs, and rock and roll among the young. From this point of view the obvious crisis of meaning in this nation required, in response, more of that old-time religion—discipline and management of the young and the dangerous libidinous energies that had been released in the 1960s. The crisis of meaning would be dealt with through more discipline, through a more rigidly defined set of expectations for what needed to be learned in school (expressed, ultimately, in what became the juggernaut of standardized testing, and the demand that learning means nothing if it cannot be converted into results that fit a uniform set of wrong and right answers), and through the imposition of a far more controlled and coercive regime of permissible behaviors in our schools. After Columbine, and the other eruptions of violence on school campuses, this discipline became almost draconian, with zero-tolerance policies that made no distinctions between kids carrying aspirin to school and those with hard drugs, or between squirt guns and real weapons. Of course, the natural feistiness and recalcitrance of adolescence has meant that high schools and middle schools provide a running commentary on kids' refusal to simply conform to rules. The daily newspapers provide a continuing account of conflicts around locker searchers, pushing the limits on what can be published in school newspapers, disputes over clothing, the demand for clubs addressing the needs of sexually marginalized youth, legal suits filed by students and their parents because of the suppression of First Amendment rights, and so on.

One thing we may say for sure is that the attempt to squelch the crisis of meaning in America can only result in temporary or limited successes. Perhaps more to the point, the attempt to siphon off the crisis into directions that offer only phony palliatives will ensure the return of what has been denied. Neither manufactured crises that do little more than distract us nor policies that do not get at the real issues will enable our children to truly prepare themselves for the challenges that they will inevitably have to face. The struggle for a meaningful life requires an education that will be at once intellectual, emotional, moral, and spiritual. It must deal with what it means to be a human being in all of its complexity. The shallowness of our present educational concerns will do little to prepare young people for the difficult years that are ahead of them. The challenge is very great, and our willingness as a nation to fiddle while our house of meaning disintegrates seems boundless.

THE POVERTY OF THE SOUL

When Mother Teresa visited the United States to receive an honorary degree it is reported that she said, "This is the poorest place I've ever been in my life." As John De Graaf and his fellow authors point out in their wonderful book *Affluenza*,[2] she was not talking about our extraordinary abundance of material goods or monetary wealth. She was, instead, talking about "poverty of the soul." Whether we educate in the classroom, in our communities, or simply in our homes, we cannot ignore such poverty. For our children's sake we must confront this reality, however threatening it may be to our assumptions about our country and its values. If, as

Naomi Remen[3] has said, meaning is the language of the soul, then we must face the fact that our market-driven culture corrodes not just the structure of durable and authentic meanings that might give significance to our lives, but the very essence of our humanity. With an intensity that has no previous parallel, our lives exist under a barrage of messages that endlessly repeat and drive home a view of the world that emphasize money and wealth, celebrity, sex, status, and the possession of material things. To grow up in America (and, we need to add, increasingly throughout the world) is to be socialized into a culture where nearly everything of significance derives from the values of the marketplace. It becomes harder and harder to separate the value of anything from the price it commands. Quite simply, the market has become the primary source of meaning and value in our world. Consuming is, in a very real sense, our religion, and it is linked to the very definition of who we are and how we live. It is the focus of much of our energies, hopes, and passions. John De Graaf and his collaborators made the point clearly:

> Since World War II, Americans have been engaged in a spending binge un-
> precedented in history .... We now spend nearly $6 trillion a year, more
> than $21,000 per person, most of it on consumer goods , which account for
> two-thirds of the recent growth in the U.S. economy. For example, we
> spend more on shoes, jewelry, and watches ($80 billion) than on higher ed-
> ucation ($65 billion). On a five-day shopping trip to Paris the wife of
> Florida Governor Jeb Bush spent $19,000, though she reported only $500 of
> it to U.S. customs. But she's not alone in her passion for shopping.

> In 1986 America still had more high schools than shopping centers. Less
> than fifteen years later, we have more than twice as many shopping centers
> as high schools. In the Age of Affluenza (as we believe the decades sur-
> rounding the Second Millennium will eventually be called), shopping cen-
> ters have supplanted churches as a symbol of cultural values. In fact
> seventy percent of us visit malls each week, more than attend houses of
> worship.[4]

Our capacity to consume is intimately bound up with the sense of being an accepted and effective member of the community. Citizenship, which used to be about public participation and expression, is now more about the "freedom to consume." Perhaps that is why nearly all of our national holidays have become sale days, usually associated with frenetic shopping opportunities, and our major religious holiday, Christmas, is a time of increasingly frenzied buying. Our public squares are now malls (often with fake names like "Town Square" or "Town Center") in which the public activity is really the very private one of buying for oneself or one's family. Indeed, in our "themed" malls, shopping has become the culture's primary form of entertainment or recreation. And as we have become more and focused on the private business of buying, so support for public expenditures on our schools, housing, transportation, and other social needs have become increasingly hard-pressed.

The credit card has become an important, even a key, marker of having become an adult member of the society. Today, along with letters of acceptance to college come the credit card applications, which, in a strange twist of logic, link the encouragement of youthful debt to adult responsibility. Whatever it is that our schools teach, the most powerful messages that shape the values and aspirations of our kids lives are found in TV, movies, magazines, the internet, and in advertising, which relentlessly emphasize fame, success, and money. It can hardly be surprising that American teenage girls rate shopping as their favorite activity. Social acceptance, popularity, and attractiveness, we are reminded endlessly, come from what one owns or, more particularly, what can be shown or flaunted. We learn quickly (how can it be otherwise when this message is on every billboard, magazine ad, and TV commercial?) that my worth as an individual is represented by the car that I drive, the shoes I wear, the makeup I put on, the clothes I wear, the electronic equipment I have purchased, the places I have traveled, and so on. Individual worth, it is drummed into us by the advertisers, is connected to the way I look and the impression I make on others. Respect is commanded by the show we can put on, not by the interior qualities of our humanity. This is a message that is understood well by our kids. It is made clear by the acute awareness of the product labels of the clothes they put on, or the gear they own. For the makers of jeans, or the stores that sell them to adolescents, there is the constant jockeying to make themselves into today's indispensable or "cool" label. Success is always about show, and it is always about the creation of invidious distinctions. In other words, it is a statement about having something that demonstrates a certain kind of social superiority. At the very least, it makes clear the fact that I belong and am accepted into (or, at least, acceptable to) a particular social group or clique.

The world of consuming is a world of never ending concern with appearance, measuring up, and comparisons with others. It is also, therefore, a world of anxiety where one is always having to strive to ensure that you are not falling behind or losing acceptance. And it is a world of permanent discomfort; I could look better, have more, be around the right people, or do more admired things. This is a context in which fear and jealousy are never far from the surface. Although surveys indicate that in the United States admitting to such emotions is often denied, envy and competitive feelings are never far away. Yet it is hard to deny how much the endless consumer drive is stimulated and supported by our looking over our shoulders at the appearance of others. This is certainly apparent when kids kill each other for a pair of expensive sneakers. It is also apparent in the sometimes viciously derogatory relations between cliques in high schools, in which style and appearance are the focus of their relations (this was an important ingredient in the indignity inflicted on students at Columbine, which, in turn, became the rage for revenge).

In the wider culture, comparing ourselves to others is a driving force in the ever-restless drive for new possessions. In her book *The Overspent American*, Juliet Schor[5] noted the critical role television has in spreading notions of what we should expect as our "standard" of living. Indeed, she said, unlike in earlier years when our reference group may have been our neighbors, TV now provides powerful and seductive images of what is desirable or normal. Of course, such images are likely far removed from the real circumstances and resources of people's lives (the spacious New York apartments featured in the sitcom *Friends* or in *Sex and the City*—estimates run from $2000 to $3000 monthly rent—provide telling examples of places to live far beyond the incomes of most people, including the characters in the show!). Nonetheless these images help shape our ideas about the way others are living, and what we too should be enjoying. Schor noted the exponential growth in people's expectations that constantly run ahead of their actual earning power. This produces the paradox that even with increasing income people always feel like they have far less than they would like and need. There, is in other words, a constant sense of deprivation regardless of how much money we seem to have. How often do we feel that what we have is never enough? Someone seems to always have it better than we do? These feelings easily become greed among those at the top end of our income structure, where there is a constant drive to shape tax policies that ensure their access to ever larger quantities of wealth, or in the behavior of corporate executives, who are ready to cheat, steal, and deprive employees of their livelihoods or pensions to add to their already huge chests of wealth. Despite the extraordinary levels of material wealth available to most Americans (certainly as compared to the way most other human beings live in the world), the consumer culture breeds a constant sense of not having enough, or not having the right things. It seems like the "emulation process" as Schor called it, never ends. We can never get enough. And indeed, it is built into the very structure of our economy and our way of life. The market imperative, she said, is always "bigger, better, more," and progress is firmly attached to the belief that we should and ought to have more. It is easy enough to see how products that were once seen as luxuries become rapidly turned into necessities. Our "wants" turn into our "needs." We regularly experience how the novelty of a new item rapidly seems to become tired and unsatisfying. Indeed, this is no accident. This obsolescence is built into the very logic of advertising. We are primed to be always one step away from a sense of dissatisfaction with what is currently in hand. What we have easily turns from being enticing to becoming boring or looking outmoded. This is readily seen in the constant ratcheting upward of electronic gadgets—the constant turnover of new "generations" of computers or communication products, with the promise of ever more extraordinary capabilities and functions (although, in fact, for most people the real differences represent marginal, even imperceptible, changes). Of course, matters of design and packaging are crucial here. Whether in the newest line of computers, cell phones, automobiles, sneakers, or TVs, the latest products must make the "old" ones look dated and unattractive. It is easy to see how this process—the constant turnover and novelty of products—creates the ever-restless and dissatisfied consumer so endemic to our way of life.

THROW-AWAY CULTURE

It should come as no great surprise that this constant search for what is new and different also influences not just our attitude about material things, but also human relationships. The rapid turnover of consumer items and the planned obsolescence of the things we buy produce a "throw-away" culture where nothing, whether material or human, should be expected to endure for too long. Our restless quest for something or someone that seems more enticing and more exciting leads us to be always in search of greener pastures. It is hardly surprising that the material abundance found in consumer societies does not produce a sense of security or confidence about the future. What it does produce is a gnawing feeling of insecurity or uncertainty. There is a pervasive sense of the fragility of the world we have made. Nothing should be expected to last too long before it ends up on the trash heap. The ecstasy that is promised through our latest acquisition is followed by the rapid descent into ennui and dissatisfaction that is certain to come as what we have soon seems to lack the excitement, appeal, or novelty of a newer item or experience. We must expect not just material products but human relationships to suffer the same fate as their initial excitement quickly fades into the boredom of familiarity.

It is interesting that conservative critics of contemporary attitudes toward marriage, which, they say, often lack an enduring commitment by partners, do not look at the way such behavior mirrors values so thoroughly encouraged by the market. Advertising today, as the social critic Zygmunt Bauman[6] noted, emphasizes the pursuit of optimal experience. It is not enough for something to be good or useful; it must promise something that is awesome—something that is no less than sublime. Indeed, at least for the more affluent members of society, there is a sense that life must be lived to its full potential, and in as fully stimulating a way as is possible. In this sense there is the pressure to find the best and the most exciting of whatever is around: the ultimate Chinese restaurant, the most exotic vacation, optimal health and vitality, the most intense orgasm, the most alive sound system, and so on. A visit to the local bookstore provides plenty of evidence to support Bauman's point. Everywhere one looks are books that point us in the direction of not just being okay and living a decent life, but of being rich, of having the perfect marriage or children, of living without illness or pain, with bodies that are perfectly shaped, "peak" religious experiences, the most sumptuously prepared meal, the most fabulous getaway, and so on. The "everyday" is not good enough; it is a waste of one's earthly existence. We need to make every situation, opportunity, and experience an "ultimate" one. And flipping through the magazines in the supermarket checkout line, or watching the innumerable talk shows on TV, provides an endless cavalcade of experts willing to provide us with the knowledge and information about how one can live optimally.

What does all this do to our psyches? In contrast to all of those perfectly shaped, emotionally satisfied, materially secure individuals living lives rich with perfection and excitement, our own lives appear deeply flawed and inadequate. For many, the perpetual struggle to achieve the optimal state becomes a perpetual let down which in turn produces depression, anger, or a gnawing sense of constant envy—why can't I live their life instead of mine? The rate of clinical depression in the United States today is 10 times what it was before 1945.[7] Widespread addictions to drugs, both legal and illegal, as well to alcohol, allow people to dull the ache of dissatisfaction and frustration about the course of their lives (strange how rarely we talk about this aspect of our addictive culture). We cannot forget that the core dynamic of the consumer world is the way we are encouraged to constantly compare ourselves with others. How do I acquire what others appear to have? The consumer world is one that relentlessly reminds us that we lack what another has, and that if only we could fill this lack, our lives would become a great deal happier or satisfying. We have become individuals who are increasingly driven by feelings of unfulfilled desire, and a jealousy for what others appear to possess. It can hardly be doubted that in such a world, anger, frustration, and even rage are never far from the surface. The more we emphasize the gap between those who have the secret to optimal living and the rest of us with our limited lives, the more the latter feel stupid, guilty, or angry for their deprived state. It is hardly surprising that when the streetlights go out, or the backs of those in authority are turned, many of us waste little time in taking advantage of the situation and grabbing some of what we desire.

Market values dehumanize human relationships. Here is not the place for entering into a discussion about whether we have any more effective or viable way to organize our economic life. It is clear that in the 20th century we witnessed some terrible attempts to create revolutionary alternatives to capitalism. At the same time, we in the United States have learned to see the issue of capitalism in black and white terms and, as a consequence, gloss over the important variations that exist in the world as to the extent that market values are permitted to dominate and shape people's lives (we have only to think of the way countries in the EU deal with issues like unemployment and poverty as compared to the way we do in the United States). The important issue for us today, I believe, is to understand what it means for a society's values and meanings to be so thoroughly permeated and influenced by the marketplace. We need also to face up to the schizophrenic way we approach the matter of values. Few of us, for example, would willingly acknowledge just how much our culture is shaped by personal competition and envy. Perhaps this implies something good. Most of us share a moral or spiritual awareness that has taught us to abjure the idea of human relationships that rest on invidiously comparing ourselves to others. We know that this cannot be the basis of healthy, supportive, and caring bonds between people. And, however much we are drawn into seeing others as the object of our jealousy or competition, it is probably reasonable to assume that a part of each of us desires a very different kind of relationship with our fellow citizens and human beings. The same is true in terms of the way that market values relentlessly focus our desires and interests on money and the materialistic. At some level, most of us know that having and owning more stuff does not lead us toward more satisfying and contented lives. Perhaps this is the reason that our places of worship draw the extraordinary numbers to them each week as we seek to remind ourselves of this knowledge and find a way to affirm its truth with others. As we enter more completely into this universe of consumer desires, the bookshops fill up with more books offering ways in which we can transcend this materialistic world and focus on more meaningful or satisfying ways of living.

Still, however hard we try, it takes more than a visit to church or synagogue or early morning meditation to deprogram ourselves from the insidious voices of the consumer world. Those of us who are parents, for example, know the power of advertising and consumer appeal to children and adolescents. Television is arguably the real "educator" of our children. Measuring the amount of time alone that kids sit in front of the TV tells us a great deal about its power to shape attitudes and desires. Juliet Schor showed that the more TV a person watches, the more he or she wishes to spend. She went on to say that the likely explanation for this is that watching TV inflates our sense of the normal, of what it seems reasonable to expect in terms of our material possessions. Of course, this sense of what one should expect is often only remotely related to what one can actually afford. It is no wonder that life in our consumer-driven society is one of increasing indebtedness. John De Graaf and his colleagues noted that each year more than a million people—up from 313,000 in 1980—file for personal bankruptcy. This, they said, represents 1 in every 70 Americans, a number that is more than the number graduating from college.[8] Indeed, it is no accident that one of the major shifts in consciousness associated with the rise of the mass production of commodities was the erasure of the puritan virtues of frugality and fiscal discipline—"cutting one's coat according to the available cloth." Debt came to be redefined as credit. It became a necessary and perfectly acceptable thing to spend far more than one took in. Indeed, the whole economic system with its outpouring of goods produced far more saleable items than most people could actually afford to buy. Thus it became vital to the survival of the system that people be encouraged to purchase far beyond their actual disposable incomes. Installment buying, leasing to own, and purchasing on credit all made possible a revolution in consumer expectations. Today we are implored to hold five or six credit cards and to spend freely on anything that catches our eye or our fancy. And it is certainly the case that with a credit card in hand individuals do indeed become far less constrained about what they buy or the experiences they assume are available to them. Of course, such freedom leads many into the pit of debilitating debt with all of its misery and anguish. Consumer counseling has become a growth profession.

The sociologist Daniel Bell[9] noted that along with credit and the phenomenon of unrestrained consumerism came other effects on consciousness. For example, there was the expectation of immediate gratification of desires. Why wait till tomorrow, warn the ads; life is short so why not indulge oneself now (regardless of the cost!)? Every whim and wish can and should be satiated, and with credit one need not postpone gratification till tomorrow. Such thinking required the transformation of the Protestant or Puritan mentality, which valued self-denial, and induced guilt as an internal mechanism of control. Buttressed by "third-wave" psychology with its emphasis on self-actualization ("being all one can be"), and the need to root out from one's psyche the tendency toward the denial of ones needs, especially those connected to our sentient life, the past three decades have witnessed an amazing shift toward the validation of pleasure as a guiding principle in our culture. Of course, not all of this should be seen as bad. It has fueled the idea that the desire to live well is the right of ordinary people, not just the rich. It has reduced the psychic misery of guilt in terms of our desire for sexual pleasure. It has undercut the hold of lives conducted along the principle of self-denial and self-abnegation. The latter points have been enormously relevant to women's lives, as they have, in recent decades, sought to legitimate their expectation to live fully and pleasurably. At the same time, we cannot avoid the more deleterious implications of these changes in mentality. Our culture is one in which people become more and more monetarily stretched. The cycle of work and spend more and more controls working- and middle-class people's lives, as we must work longer hours and days to keep up with our spending. According to Juliet Schor, between 1973 and 2000 the average American worker added an additional 199 hours to his or her annual schedule—or nearly five additional weeks of work per year. Rather than producing freedom, the culture of material abundance produces an increasing sense of running in place, with all of its frustrations and often just sheer exhaustion. There is the widespread sense that we have of "never getting ahead"—of having to work harder to keep up.

The emphasis on the pleasure principle produces a hedonistic culture in which we have no responsibility beyond the immediate satisfaction of our desires. These desires are defined in terms that are overwhelmingly materialist and lead us to become gluttons in the use and abuse of our natural resources. The consumer world is one of astounding waste in the way that we voraciously chew up and spit out the precious natural resources that are available to us. Styles, fashions, and fads mark the consumer culture, as things that are at one moment "hot" rapidly lose their appeal and become replaced by the next wave of things that catch our eyes. The affluent world is one in which the disposal of waste becomes an increasing problem, as the detritus of consumer living fills more and more available space. Indeed, as available space in the developed countries is exhausted, we turn to poor countries as places to dump our ever-expanding garbage piles. In many ways, in our escalating greed for more and more stuff, the "silent" victim is the earth itself, which must be plundered for resources to keep this insanely profligate process moving forward. In *Natural Capitalism*, Paul Hawken and Amory and Hunter Lovins demonstrated the extraordinary cost of all this in the use of the earth's resources: " Industry moves, mines, extracts, shovels, burns, wastes, pumps, and disposes of four million pounds of material in order to provide one average middle-class family's needs for a year."[10]

Meanwhile, back on the ranch we seek larger homes and more closet space to accommodate the things that increasingly clutter our homes. Indeed, we ourselves are expanding—becoming supersized—as we take in larger and larger portions of food in our restaurants creating, in turn, the need for larger vehicles to accommodate our increasing body size. "Space" planning and expertise is another growth profession. But the expectation of immediate gratification of desire has implications that go beyond credit cards and unrestrained wants in regard to material items. It also spells a way of life in which the immediate satisfaction of wants takes precedence over other values—responsibility, obligation, and a concern with long-term commitments. The consumer mentality is one of short-term perspectives; it is embodied in the teenager for whom the pleasure of sex obscures any concern for health risks or pregnancy. It is also reflected in the behavior of corporate executives for whom the major concern is the generation of short-term profits, or consumers for whom the enduring environmental affects of our wasteful lifestyles on future generations are something that can be ignored. In the pursuit of profit, fast food traders persuade young people to eat in ways that produce an unprecedented scourge of obesity that is horribly destructive of decent health. What matters is simply how much money can be amassed right now. All of this spells human behavior without the constraints of moral responsibility or a concern for future consequences. As the bumper sticker says, "If it feels good, do it." A beer ad declares "Make every day a weekend." Interestingly, it has often been conservative critics who have articulated the sense that the culture has become irresponsibly selfish and oriented to immediate wants rather than long-term responsibilities—although they typically shy away from seeing the connection to the marketplace and the greed for money and wealth. Still, one can detect the way that the usual left/right divisions of politics are confounded by this crisis of meaning.

CHILDREN AS A MARKET

Researchers have also made it clear that young kids are especially prone to the difficulty of disentangling reality from hype when watching TV advertising. The authors of *Affluenza* noted that a child may see a million TV commercials before he or she reaches the age of twenty: "There is more time devoted to them now—the average half-hour of commercial TV now has eight minutes of commercials, up from six two decades ago. And there are more of them—faster editing (to beat the remote control clicker)."[11]

Channels like MTV have entirely erased the line between programs and selling, although the phenomenon of "infotainment" is becoming more and more the norm throughout the culture. Items seen on TV by kids assume a magical aura that guarantees both their delight and power. No matter how hard consumer groups have tried to pull the plug on advertising aimed at young children, manufacturers resist any curbs, knowing the power they have to manipulate children's fantasies and dream worlds. Indeed, recent deregulation of the media has reduced the responsibility of broadcasters to be something more than peddlers of commodities.

Teenagers, especially, are the focus of an extraordinarily powerful process to stimulate their desires as consumers. Whether through TV, movies, magazines, or the ever available MTV, the message conveyed is always one that ties, or more accurately exploits, young people's concerns about sexuality, appearance, and social acceptance to the purchase of consumer items. Teenagers represent the largest consumer market in the country. This market is the object of a relentless campaign to convert the anxieties and dreams of young people into the taste for new fashions, cosmetics, cigarettes, fast food, music, or entertainment. Perhaps nowhere else is the pressure of the consumer world revealed so fully in its amoral character. Nothing is off limits here in terms of efforts to seduce the interests and desires of young people to exchange their money for a product of dubious value or utility. The advertising campaigns by tobacco companies to attract young people—especially those in minority communities—to smoke are documented in all of their greed and lack of social regard. The readiness of clothing outlets to do whatever it takes to sell their line of jeans is apparent (the soft pornographic campaigns by Calvin Klein or by Abercrombie and Fitch reveal that when it comes to selling to teenagers, anything that might attract attention is permissible). Reality television shows like *Elimidate* and *Joe Millionaire* have provided a new level of tastelessness in pandering to the sexual interests and romantic fantasies of adolescents. Of course, here we must pay special attention to the influence of the commercial media on the lives of young females. Feminist critics provide us with a devastating account of the way that girls—at a younger and younger age—are being taught to see themselves in the world. Magazines, movies, TV, video images, and so on conspire to produce a world that relentlessly emphasizes appearance and sexiness as the primary modality of girls' appeal and worth in the world. Although many girls now claim a hipness to the manipulations of marketers and their images, the increasing obsessions concerning weight and appearance, the desire to be ever thinner, the readiness to use clothing in ways that flaunt sexuality, all reveal the continuing power of the marketplace to shape female adolescents' concerns. Young girls are earlier and earlier inducted into a world in which the female body becomes the primary battleground for one's identity and sexuality. It is world stimulated, coaxed, and shaped by corporations in which enormous profits hang in the balance. Profit, not social responsibility, is their primary concern.

In all of this, we can see the process that the philosopher and social critic Herbert Marcuse drew our attention to many years ago. Commercial items, he said, compel us because they are made to stir in us a powerful emotional, even erotic, pull. In other words, in the consumer world of meanings, products are made to appeal to buyers not simply because of their use value, that is, the things they actually do, or the service they provide. Instead, they come to represent for us a means to fulfill some much more fundamental human need or concern. They become associated in our psyches with the possibility of love, social acceptance, fulfillment of sexual desire, acquisition of power and status, youthfulness, and vitality. In this way the object or thing takes on much greater significance for us than what it actually is. It becomes invested with emotional powers that—so we are promised—transfer to, and even transform, the human being who possesses it. This is, indeed, a kind of magic in which inanimate objects can change who we are and how we relate to others (as well as how others relate to us). As an example, we might notice the current enormous appeal of sport utility vehicles (SUVs). These vehicles are now the best selling form of private transportation in the United States, and enormously lucrative items for the automobile companies. Their selling appeal comes from how they appear to fulfill for us a number of fantasized human attributes—being adventurous, control over our environment, power and self-sufficiency, virility, and strength. Although the $50,000 Land Rover is most often found loaded up with kids on their way to after-school activities, or getting food items from the grocery store, its hold on the imagination is connected to its image as a rugged explorer of the wilderness, mountain ranges, or back country. If life is mainly a pretty prosaic business, ownership of an SUV allows us the immediate fantasy of escape and excitement. Of course, in selling them in this way, their demonstrated extravagance in fuel consumption and their danger to others on the road because of their size are obscured. Of course, we dare not forget that the extraordinary gas demands of this vehicle add to our overreliance on Middle East oil, with all of the political and military implications that go along with this. When considered in these terms, it becomes apparent that these toys are an expensive fantasy that adds to the cost and insecurity of our lives.

Elsewhere, we might think of how coffee is now sold as much more than a drink. In the hands of the advertisers it becomes the means to create intimate moments in a world where the increasing demands of jobs and the frantic pace of life leave us little opportunity to come together with our partners and share uninterrupted moments of emotional connection. We might also consider how soft drinks are used to evoke youthfulness and vitality (disregarding, of course, that they are major contributors to our obese culture). In short, amid the clutter of a world with its surfeit of material goods, advertisers struggle to gain our attention by turning wants into needs through the process of linking what we buy to our much deeper human concerns and drives. To purchase a product, we are taught, is to make us more lovable, sexy, socially effective, or successful. How else are we to explain the relatively recent proliferation of company logos on the things we wear or use? The ubiquitous swoosh sign of Nike, for example, is an immediate form of identification, telling others something about who we are, what we value, and the company we keep. Sneaker brands have immediate identification with race or with other social grouping. Fashion labels immediately convey to others the rung you occupy on the social ladder. Although students in my classes typically deny the power of advertising to shape their desires or interests, they almost always know the labels of the clothes they are wearing or that of others, and can readily indicate the social status of different labels. Of course, this is no great surprise. The type of cars we drive, the places we vacation, the furnishings in our homes, the shoes we wear, the places we shop, the colleges we send our children to, and so on are a running statement on how successful we are and how much respect we expect to be accorded by others. In short, labels and logos are about a lot more than who makes a particular product—they are a moving indication of your place in the pecking order. They also are a constant reminder that who we are depends on what we can afford, that our value as human beings is reflected in and reinforced by what we can buy. And of course all of this occurs in a way that makes the process insidious and without any significant conscious recognition.

WEALTH ANXIETY

When the stakes are so high, it can hardly be a surprise that people are ready to sacrifice so much of their time, energy, and creativity to ensure their worth and recognition in the eyes of others. They will also lie, cheat, steal, and kill to gain this recognition. Although we rarely acknowledge it, in a society that places so much emphasis on success and its connection to money, it is surely to be expected that one of its consequences will be high levels of crime and violence. This is compounded by the extraordinary degrees of social and economic inequality that we have in American society, which mean that many individuals are foreclosed in their ability to participate, at least through legal means, in the process of consuming. The authors of *Affluenza* made the extent of this inequality clear:

> In spite of America's image as a cornucopia of plenty, where the shelves of supermarkets are always fully stocked, ten million Americans go hungry each day, forty percent of them children, and the majority, members of working families. Twenty-one million other Americans keep hunger from the door by turning frequently to emergency feeding programs such as food banks and soup kitchens. On any given night at least 750,000 Americans are without shelter and nearly two million experience homelessness during the course of the year. That's the bad news. The good news is that nine million Americans own second homes. America's housing shortage might really be a distribution problem.[12]

The relentless reminders that the "good life" means the capacity to buy and spend freely produce anger and frustration in those who have been excluded from this through the deeply unequal distribution of wealth and income. Nothing has made this clearer than the consequences of hurricane Katrina, in New Orleans. Of course, it is not just the poor who are driven to antisocial behavior to have a "piece of the pie." Consumerism means that whatever we have feels like it is never enough. However well off people appear to be, there is always the sense that we ought to have more. For most of us no amount of income is adequate. We always seem to spend more than we have, or arrive at the end of the month with little or nothing in our bank account. There is always someone else who has it so much better, whose home is so much nicer and whose automobile is so much more attractive. This constant sense of lack makes many resentful of the money that must be given up in taxes that are ostensibly for the public good (rather than for private spending). It also makes us resentful and suspicious of others who seem to have got more than they deserve (typically the poor rather than the rich, who, we are encouraged to believe, are "fleecing" us). It drives us to "cut corners" or even to cheat when we feel no one is watching and we can get away with it, like on our taxes or on business expenses. It feeds our preoccupation with get-rich possibilities and TV fantasies about average Joes whose lives are transformed by extraordinary luck and good fortune.

The drive to always want more is ultimately sustained by the way things seems to promise us happiness. After all, we are constantly looking and comparing ourselves to others because of our belief that those who are successful, and have more, must also live happier lives. Of course this is not a rational matter. Most of us know, at some level, that material things don't guarantee happiness—that life's most important qualities can't be bought. Even MasterCard acknowledges in its ads that the most important things in life can't be bought, that they are "priceless." Paradoxically, Hollywood provides a continuing hymn to the idea that true love and happiness can't be bought. Still, we are bombarded by messages that contradict this enduring wisdom. Indeed, there is a way that every commercial can be understood as a small parable in which all of our deepest human needs can be addressed and realized through the things we buy. There is, so we are encouraged to believe, something out there in the marketplace that can help fill every human desire. Built into this parable is also the constant assertion that some dimensions of our lives are amiss. There is always some part of us that does not feel right, which results in our current state of distress, boredom, or anxiety, or sense of inadequacy or lack of respect. Indeed, we are surrounded by this constant refrain; we are deficient, inadequate, unattractive or lacking in some important dimension that needs to be made right. Of course, in creating this sense of deficiency or lack we can be far more effectively induced to desire something that, hitherto, might have seemed irrelevant to our lives. One consequence of being subjected to such messages is to turn us into people with a great deal of insecurity and uncertainty about our self-worth. Our lovability, our sense of value, and our confidence about our abilities and effectiveness are always depicted as in a precarious or questionable state. We are made increasingly fragile by this permanent assault on our sense of well-being and agency, with the warning that we are in need of a multitude of ever-changing consumer goods that can assure our attractiveness or respect. In light of this, it is easy to understand why the most popular shelves in the bookstore are the ones that promise to alleviate this constant sense of inadequacy and anxiety about who we are—that can lead through the techniques of therapeutic or spiritual practice to a place of self-acceptance and personal tranquility. The consumer culture, whose logo is the smiling face, might be better represented by the churning stomach.

A CULTURE OF HAVING, NOT BEING

A culture that manages so effectively to insert a material object into the place of human needs has profoundly reshaped the way in which we seek meaning, purpose, and satisfaction in our lives. Erich Fromm[13] suggested that our culture is one in which "having" had become much more important than "being." What he meant by this was that in our culture we had misguidedly come to pursue the possession of things, rather than the quality of lived experiences, relationships, and activities. So, for example, people sought jobs not as a vehicle for doing useful and satisfying work, but primarily as a means to earn more money. High school and college students show an increasing tendency to think of careers in terms of how much they pay rather than the promise of doing good and creative work. Many students have told me this was their reason for choosing a business degree or going to law school. Weddings become an occasion to spend huge amounts of money on showy parties that have little to do with declaring and celebrating loving commitments. A recent best-selling book urges Jewish parents to "put God on the Bar-Mitzvah invitation list" as a metaphor for getting back to the ritual's real spiritual significance. We mistakenly believe that the more we fill up our lives with things we can possess, the more satisfying our life will become. The psychologist Richard Ryan pointed to the many studies that make it clear that material wealth does not produce happiness. In the human species, happiness comes from pursuing intrinsic goals like giving and receiving love. He said, "Extrinsic goals like monetary wealth, fame and appearance are surrogate goals often pursued as people try to fill themselves up with 'outside-in' rewards."[14]

In America we talk about "getting" or "having" an education, a formulation that reflects our concern, not with the human quality of the experience (how much did we think, imagine, create etc.), but with what piece of paper do we possess at the end of the process. All of this emphasis on things and possessions takes us away from what it might mean to encounter life in an authentic way. We come to believe that the path to lives that are joyful and nourishing to our souls runs through the marketplace of things, where we can exchange our life energies and intelligence for the fetish of inanimate possessions. The intrinsic beauty, wisdom, and satisfaction of how we might live and engage our world are lost in the frantic struggle to get and have more. It is, as Oscar Wilde once said, a world in which we know the price of everything, but the true value of very little. In the end, this materialism defines not only the value of what we do. It defines who we are as human beings. Each of us becomes, in the eyes of others, things ("consumers," human "resources," "human capital") that are to be leveraged for their usefulness to us. Others become simply vehicles to the fulfillment of our own interests or desires: means to our ends. One is only of value to us if he or she is able to add sufficiently to our bottom line, make us look good by the way they appear, satisfy our sexual desires, and so on. In other words, our interest in other human beings is entirely instrumental. Martin Buber, the great philosopher, distinguished between human beings relating to others in two different ways: as a "thou" or as an "it". In the former we regard the other in the fullness of his or her humanity—as a precious and infinitely valuable being. In the latter, a person has become nothing but an object, one that is viewed in terms of a very limited set of capabilities that might make him or her useful or of service to us. It is easy to see how a world that has put the acquisition of things at the very center of our social existence also produces human relationship in which people are themselves viewed as things that can be bought, sold, and disposed of as our own needs dictate. We see this every day in the ruthless way in which workers are thrown out of work as companies figure they can make more money by relocating to somewhere that would increase their profits. There is, here, little concern for the terrible destruction that this does to the lives of individuals, their families, and their communities. We see it, too, in the sweatshop conditions in which so many people labor around the world—long hours of exhausting work in conditions that are damaging to the physical and mental well-being of human beings. We see it in the exploitation of thousands of women who are forcibly used in the slavery of the sex trade, coerced prostitution, and pornography. And we see it in the abuse and exploitation of so many children who work in fields and factories under brutal and violent conditions, or who are forcibly recruited to mercenary armies.

Of course, we probably don't have to go far from our work places or communities to see human beings treated as "it." We may only need to look around and question whether all those who live and work in our towns and cities, and whose children attend our schools, are treated humanely and compassionately, or whether they are mainly regarded as tax burdens, means to a quick profit, or a liability to educational leaders who want to demonstrate their schools' success in the latest round of standardized tests. Perhaps we do not even have to look at others' lives. The feeling that we live in a world in which each of is treated in manipulative and instrumental ways edges closer to all of us. We feel the vulnerability of living in a world where so many of us feel we are used and then easily disposed of, or where we must learn to market or sell ourselves, or where we must concern ourselves with the management of our appearance and the impression we make on others. No matter whether it is in the workplace, in the care of those who are charged with taking care of our health, in the legal system, or even in our intimate personal relations, there is the same sense of vulnerability as human relationships feel more predatory and manipulative. In a world so pervaded by calculating and instrumental attitudes, who can I really trust or rely on? Will I be treated as a person, rather than as a thing to be used to satisfy another's greed, desire, or need for control?

SCHOOLS AND THE CRISIS OF MEANING

We must ask ourselves, then, whether schools prepare children and young people to face the crisis of meaning that increasingly engulfs our lives. The short answer is that they do not. Not only do they fail to address this crisis, but they add to it in a number of ways. Briefly, I want to sketch out here some of the things that schools do, or do not, that fuel this crisis. In subsequent chapters I return to the concerns raised here and elaborate on them. My intention is to look more deeply at the ways schools contribute to the crisis of meaning, and also to offer a way of re-envisaging education's place and purpose in the contemporary culture. How and what should education do in a culture whose moral axis is now, so blatantly and destructively, one of materialism, money, show, unbridled individualism, and celebrity? I suggest here five ways in which schools are a part of the problem, rather than the solution.

1. The Culture of Selling

First, we need to recognize just how much the culture of selling has invaded the school space. In one sense this is hardly surprising, given what I have just said about the continued expansion, into all areas of our lives, of the influence of the market. At the same time, it is a profoundly disturbing change in the manner and extent of the way that our children's values are being shaped. Schools have now become primary vehicles for drawing them into the culture of possessions and materialism. They have become important sites for shaping and manipulating their assumptions about the role of corporations in every area of our lives from candy bars to pizza, and from care of the body to nuclear energy. Alex Molnar is a writer who has studied this phenomenon in depth.[15] He noted, for example:

> It was not long before a commercial wave broke over the schools. In homes across America, parents may have discovered that their daughters and sons had been given a "Gushers" fruit snack, told to burst it between their teeth, and asked by their teacher to compare the sensation to a geothermic eruption (compliments of General Mills). Children were taught the history of the potato chip (compliments of the Potato Board and the Snack Food Association). Adolescent girls learned about self-esteem by discussing "good hair days" and "bad hair days" in class (compliments of Revlon). Tootsie Roll provided a lesson on the "Sweet Taste of Success." Exxon sent out a videotape, "Scientists and the Alaska Oil Spill," to help teachers reassure students that the Valdez disaster was not so bad after all. And Prego spaghetti sauce offered to help students learn science by comparing the thickness of Prego sauce to that of Ragu.

Molnar points out that the attempt to mine children for commercial advantage is neither new nor surprising, given the fact that elementary school children are estimated to spend around $15 billion a year and teenagers around $90 billion. Henry Giroux,[16] another prominent education writer, suggested that with so many public schools strapped for cash, schools have begun to lease out hallways, buses, restrooms, lunch menus, and school cafeterias as billboards to advertise everything from Coca Cola to Hollywood films. Channel One offers to provide schools with $50,000 in electronic equipment if they will agree to broadcast a "ten-minute program of current events and news material along with two minutes of commercials." Giroux noted that "corporate culture targets schools not simply as investments for substantial profits but also as training grounds for educating students to define themselves as consumers rather than multifaceted social actors."[17] Of course all of this promotion of such things as junk food, soft drinks, and high-priced sneakers raises profound ethical problems about the abuse of parental trust by educators. More shocking is the fact that the widespread practice of surrounding young people with messages, images, and activities designed to sell to them in this supposedly protected space hardly raises an indignant voice among those entrusted with our children's lives. The school is becoming an extension of the mall, and we are, it seems, expected to see this as an entirely acceptable aspect of the "education" of young people. It is clear that the crisis of meaning is not something "out there"; the school itself has become a morally compromised environment.

2. A Capacity to Question

Second, it should be clear from the things I have already said that any attempt to educate young people about the influence and effects of the marketplace on our attitudes, desires, and interests requires a commitment to developing their capacity to question and think in a critical way about the culture. I have already noted just how much school is dominated by an instrumental mentality (it's all about grades, test scores, point averages, SAT results, and diplomas) that takes students far away from the point of any real education, which is, at a minimum, to enhance our ability to think and to question. Thinking and questioning refer here not to how smart we can be at playing the school "game"—figuring out what we may need to "beat" this quiz or exam, or convince a teacher we know something that we actually think very little about. I am talking here, instead, about enhancing students' ability to question deeply the motives, purposes, dynamics, values, and effects of our way of life. What does it mean to live in a society in which material possessions are so central to how we live? How did our society come to be this way? How does the emphasis on status, success, and wealth affect us emotionally, spiritually, and in terms of our physical health? Who are the winners and losers in this kind of world? What are the implications for the environment and the earth of our unrestrained pursuit of material wealth? These are, of course, only a sampling of the kind of questions that might arise in classrooms concerned with teaching young people to think critically about our crisis of meaning. Yet I believe that to a large extent they are questions that we do not ask now. Our classrooms are overwhelmingly places where there is a stultifying deadness in regard to teaching kids to question their world. Our obsession with getting the right answers on quizzes, tests, and exams encourages in young people a mindless conformity in how they think and seek answers to questions. To take seriously our responsibility to educate at this time means that we will have to encourage young people to ask those dangerous questions about the meaning and purpose of the world in which they will spend the remainder of their lives. There will, it is certain, be many in our society who would bitterly resist an education that takes seriously its mission of educating young people to think, question, and challenge in this way.

3. The Hidden Curriculum of Status

Third, we need to understand the way that school educates our children into the culture of status and success that is an integral part of a culture that worships at the altar of celebrity. We need to keep in mind here the fact that what we learn in school is much less about the content of the curriculum (math, English, social studies, etc.), than about the content of the "hidden curriculum." The latter is the name that educational theorists give to what we teach young people through such things as the social relationships in a school, the values that are implicit in what we do (such as the importance of competition), and the things that we emphasize in the day to day life of a school (such as the importance of technical knowledge vs. aesthetic expression). It is in these implicit, informal, and often unstated aspects of school life that students are most influenced. It's interesting that we spend so much time talking about the curriculum rather than the things that actually have the most impact in shaping what kids value and assume about their world. In this context, one of the most powerful lessons of schooling is the tremendous value placed on success and status. The motivational energy of education comes overwhelmingly from the inculcated desire to "get ahead" (of course, of the next person), and to stand out from the others in one's class or school. This is taught and emphasized in a hundred ways, from grades to class rank, from the kind of academic track one is in (AP, IB, Honors, general, vocational, special ed.), to athletic prowess, social celebrity, and the recognition of one's college acceptance and scholarship award. It is a process that starts from the moment one steps into a typical classroom and kids are placed in differential groups for reading, or treated by teachers with quite different amounts of respect and value depending on how they look, speak, or perform on assigned tasks. We return to this process later in the book. Suffice it to say now that school is a place that conveys, and endlessly reinforces, the idea that people are necessarily and inevitably to be ranked in ability and worth, and that those who are deemed of most worth are recognized and celebrated (whereas those of least worth are often treated with disdain, hostility, or avoidance). School is one of the most powerful engines of socialization in our culture, one that prepares us for a world that emphasizes the importance of superior status, success, recognition, and celebrity, and the importance of doing whatever is necessary to attain them.

4. Education as a Commodity

The fourth thing schools do, in contributing to the crisis of meaning, is in the way that they treat education as primarily a commodity. I have already talked about the way that more and more dimensions of our lives have become reconstituted as things that are valued primarily in terms of their monetary potential. The issue here is not whether a market economy is a good thing, but whether a market society is. It is apparent that there is now hardly any area of our lives that remains outside the market mentality, in which we see things primarily in terms of their potential to provide a cash return. The value of something becomes more and more synonymous with its dollar worth. Whether we talk about the value of an artistic venture, such as a film, primarily in terms of its "box office gross", talk about trees and forests as valuable essentially because of their exploitative potential as timber, or regard athletes and their teams as mainly lucrative profit-makers for owners and sponsors, the meaning is the same. Monetary return, not its aesthetic, spiritual, or communal meaning, decides something's value or worth. Even love itself is reduced to its most tawdry and dehumanizing aspects in "reality" TV shows that make the most cherished of human relationships one that is about little more than "gold-digging." Education is a primary experience in this regard. We are told, repeatedly, as we grow up, that education's real value is not in its capacity to draw us toward wisdom and understanding, or to make us thoughtful and socially responsible citizens, or to develop our potential as creative and imaginative beings. The overriding purpose of education is that it that provides us with a commodity that we are able to exchange for a place in college, a better job, a promotion, a mortgage, a car loan, and so on. In other words, it is not the intrinsic experience of education that we value—what it offers to us as human beings and as members of a community. Education, instead, is something we "get" if we do what is required of us so that we can then cash it in for the pleasures and relative security of a middle-class life. This is a lesson we learn early on when our parents promise us an especially appealing gift if we can bring home a superior report card, or via the pizza we can "earn" if we can show we have read enough books. It continues into that time when we look for the "best" (i.e., having most status) graduate program that will guarantee us a competitive advantage as we make our way in the job market. No matter the exaggerated rhetoric of educational discourse—realizing individual's abilities and developing them as "rounded" beings, and so on—we all know why we really worry about school, and demand improvements from it. It is, after all, the place where our children's "tickets are punched." The concern we have for ensuring that our children have that ticket is understandable. It is necessary if they are to attain the security and opportunity that any decent life must have. Yet we must also understand what is lost when the value of schooling lies almost entirely in the marketable value of a diploma or a degree. Corporate campuses, technical schools, distance learning, and online universities will ensure that in the coming years anything in education that does not directly translate into job or career purposes will seem more and more irrelevant to schooling. Education concerned with the moral, spiritual, aesthetic, and communal aspects of human lives will likely seem like an ornament from a distant past.

5. A Prophetic Imagination

Finally, schools fail to address the crisis of meaning through the way they neglect to promote a sense of possibility. I do not mean here the sense of personal or individual possibility. That is one aspect of schooling and American culture that is, indeed, promoted with great gusto. "Be all you can be," "realize your dreams," and similar slogans express a central theme in our national ideology, one that is an important source of the creative and entrepreneurial energy that distinguishes this country. It is certainly a ubiquitous message of schools, found on bulletin boards and in graduation speeches up and down the United States. No, here I mean the sense of possibility that is related to the interest and hope in changing our culture in a profound way, so that our world and our nation are more socially just, compassionate, environmentally sensitive, humane, and peaceful. For students to have this sense of possibility, education will have to offer things that are the antidote to the cynicism and self-indulgence that are so much part of popular culture. Possibility, here, is grounded in a concern for the future, but starts with a serious questioning of our present world: what it is we value, and how we behave toward our fellow human beings. However, the capacity for critique is not sufficient. It requires, too, an attitude of hope, strong commitment, and the capacity for imagination and re-creation.

Change is not a gift brought to us on silver platter. It requires that we have the courage and will to persist in the struggle for a better world. These characteristics, as Studs Terkel[18] showed in a recent moving book on the subject, are the universal character traits of those whom we celebrate for their dedication and commitment to making a difference in the world. We will need to ask ourselves what sort of education can produce such human beings. We may certainly assume that some aspects of people's lives and experiences and what these have taught them are responsible for their persistent commitment to making a better world. Change also demands that we have the imagination to see within the present reality other ways of being and acting. The enemy to such imagination is the kind of conformity, moral timidity, and intellectual obedience that is so pervasive in our classrooms today. Walter Brueggemann[19] talked about a prophetic imagination, which brings together determination, and willingness to conceive of our shared lives in radically different ways, as things that are essential to a sense of possibility. David Purpel[20] also wrote about the need for educators in our present culture, with its vulgar excess and waste and unsupportable social injustice, to bring this prophetic stance into the classroom.

The prophetic imagination is also sustained by hope. Without hope we must assume that each day will be no better than the previous one. Life will appear as simply the recurrence of what is already present, and human efforts seem useless. Perhaps encouraging hope is a matter of teaching the history of human struggle with its defeats but also its shining achievements. Perhaps hope is found in the very act of challenging and changing the world, serving others, and getting involved politically as citizens. Or perhaps hope requires a reaching into the spiritual roots of the human condition, connecting to the timeless and mysterious impulses that seem to be present in all the great faiths of humanity, reminding us of the abiding need for justice, for love, and for peace. Educating for hope, I believe, is best achieved when we can blend all these: school as a place that attempts to connect the young to the passions and struggles of past generation, where learning is not just about books but actually engaging in communal healing and improvement, and education is a process of human development that reaches both into our intellects and also into our spirits. In the coming chapters we revisit all these possibilities.

NOTES

1. Gerald Bracey. (1977). *Setting the record straight*. Alexandria, VA: ASCD.
2. John De Graaf, David Wann, & Thomas H. Naylor. (2002). *Affluenza*. San Francisco: Berrett-Koehler.
3. Naomi Remen. (2000). *My grandfather's blessings*. New York: Riverhead Books.
4. De Graaf et al. (2002). *Affluenza* (p. 13).
5. Juliet B. Schor. (1998). *The overspent American*. New York: Harper Perennial.
6. Zygmunt Bauman. (1997). *Postmodernity and its discontents*. New York: University Press.
7. De Graaf et al. (2002). *Affluenza* (p. 72).
8. Ibid. (p. 20).
9. Daniel Bell. (1976). *The cultural contradictions of capitalism*. New York: Basic Books.
10. Paul Hawken, Amory Lovins, & Hunter Lovins. (1999). *Natural capitalism: Creating the next revolution* (pp. 51–52). Boston: Little, Brown.
11. De Graaf et al. (2002). *Affluenza* (pp. 149–150).
12. Ibid. (p. 79).
13. Erich Fromm. (1997). *To have or to be*. NY: Continuum International.
14. De Graaf et al. (2002). *Affluenza* (p. 108).
15. Alex Molnar. (1996). *Giving kids the business*. Boulder, CO: Westview. (p. 167).
16. Henry Giroux. (2000). *Stealing innocence*. New York: St. Martin's Press.
17. Ibid. (p. 95).
18. Studs Terkel. (2003). *Hope dies last: Keeping the faith in difficult times*. New York: New Press.

19. Walter Brueggemann. (1978). *The prophetic imagination*. Philadelphia: Fortress Press.
20. David Purpel. (1989). *The moral and spiritual crisis in education*. Granby, MA: Bergin and Garvey.

Human Nature,
Human Possibility

A rabbi spoke with the Lord about Heave and Hell. "I will show you Hell," said the Lord and they went into a room which had a large pot of stew in the middle. The smell was delicious and around the pot sat people who were famished and desperate. All were holding spoons with very long handles which reached to the pot, but because the handle of the spoon was longer than their arm, it was impossible to get the stew back into their mouths. Their suffering was terrible. "Now I will show you Heaven," said the Lord, and they went into an identical room. There was the same pot of stew and the people had the same identical spoons, but they were well-nourished, talking and happy. At first the rabbi did not understand. "It is simple," said the Lord. "You see, they have learned to feed each other." (Jewish legend)

THE QUESTION OF HUMAN NATURE

For many years now, I have started some of my classes with questions about the existence of human nature. I particularly like to ask two questions: Does human nature exist? And, second, what is it? I always joke that the smart ones would answer "no" on the first question so that they could then avoid having to give any answer to the second question. Fortunately (at least for me), the great majority of students can be relied on to answer yes on the first question, and thus have to volunteer an answer on the second. Actually, I am hopeful that they will take this route, not only because this will ensure an interesting and often amusing discussion, but, and more importantly, this ensures that the class will have an opportunity to "unpack" a very important matter that is related to key issues in my course. You see, how we answer this question about human nature will likely determine our attitude toward the power and relevance of education to affect and change human behavior. Typically students will answer that human nature does exist. I make sure to hold their feet to the fire on this by telling them that this means they are asserting that there is some core dimension of being human that remains the same across time and space. It implies that there are "essential" qualities that all human beings possess no matter where we find them, and regardless of when. Human beings, in other words, for the believers in human nature, are changeless in some key ways across time and space. I make the matter even more problematic for students by insisting that we emphasize the human part of human being, so that the essential qualities they may identify are not to be found in any other species (otherwise why call it human nature?). Of course, this makes things a lot more difficult and restrictive. I have a great deal of fun poking holes in the things that students suggest. For example, students will suggest being egocentric or selfish is an essential dimension of humanness. My response is that as common as this may be among people, it certainly does not cover the myriad ways in which human beings manifest generosity or altruism. Others will offer the desire for survival. Here, too, I suggest that this excludes the many ways that individuals are ready to sacrifice themselves for others—whether, for example, for the sake of the nation, a religious or political cause, or perhaps as parents forgoing their own safety to save the life of a child. What about love, some students will ask. Isn't love found in all cultures? Here I need to remind them of the rules of our discussion. Sure, love is found among many human beings, but certainly not all the time. If human nature means something that is always present then we will have to say that love, as an example, fails badly. Hate, prejudice, abuse, and violence are certainly pervasive aspects of human societies since time immemorial. Even in that most precious of relationships, that of mother and child, there is sometimes disinterest, abuse, even murder. Some students will raise the capacity to think and ask questions. Here I argue that this willingness or propensity to challenge accepted ideas is something rare in human cultures. Indeed, far from being common, it is a phenomenon that has existed only among relatively small groups of human beings in fairly unusual circumstances. Here I like to make a distinction between a human capacity or capability to do or be something, and its actual occurrence or manifestation. This same argument applies to moral reasoning and decision making. I suggest that the actual extent to which people might make moral choices varies greatly. Indeed, what marks much of human behavior is a willingness to make no decision other than to allow others to decide for us. Individualism, in a similar vein I argue, is a fairly recent invention in human history—no more than 500 years old. The issue of language is brought up. Here I sidestep the issue somewhat by suggesting that although it is obvious that only humans have the capacity for such elaborate and complex use of language, it is also not possible to argue that we alone as a species have this capacity. For example, the languaging capability of chimpanzees or of dolphins is well known. What about the desire for sex? Well, I respond, sexual desire varies according to circumstance. Cultures make us, or allow us to be, more intensely sexual, or more ascetic. A religious calling, for example, may cause us to sublimate sexual desire into other forms of yearning. I offer the example of the "Wild Boy of Aveyron," the child discovered in the 19th century in France who had, apparently, grown up alone without human contact. This boy, by the account of those who raised him, did not manifest sexual desire in any way that could be observed.[1] Also, I add, like other children who grow up outside of culture and deprived of human contact, he had lost the capacity for language-making.

I point out that we often refer to human nature when we attempt to explain things that are socially undesirable. For example, we might say that "women like to gossip" or that "men are sexually irresponsible or aggressive," or that "people never have enough money." The same explanation, I offer, is used to explain the existence of war, greed, selfishness, exploitation, the desire to show we are better than another, being ethnically prejudiced, and so on. I jokingly add that although we use our theories about human nature to "explain" the bad aspects of human behavior, we rarely to do the reverse and suggest, for example, that those who act selflessly or generously do so "just because of human nature." It would seem that our common sense reinforces an idea that things that are socially damaging or harmful are somehow part of our essential makeup, and that those things that are socially redeeming or restorative are the human exception, not the rule. Of course, my students are not alone in relying on a theory of human nature to explain who we are and why we do what we do. Perhaps there is something comforting about the idea that human beings have some fixed dimensions to who we are, that these essential parts of us set the limits to how much we can change about ourselves, and offer an explanation of why people seem forever incapable of living up to their best, most caring, just, and loving ideals.

The idea that there is an essential or fixed quality to human nature has a long history. Ideas about original sin, the lustfulness of the flesh, the "animal" versus the divine aspects of human beings, are deeply imprinted in the psyche of us all. They affect how we view children and childhood, our attitudes to play, pleasure, sexuality, and work, and our beliefs about education. Sociobiologists continue to research and assert what they believe are the fixed or unchangeable dimensions of males and females. These usually end up confirming our most blatant prejudices about gender, such as the unalterably promiscuous nature of men, or women's irreplaceable need for motherhood. Today we are subject to powerful scientific paradigms that suggest to us the biological "infrastructure" that governs how we think and act in the world. Physicists in the neurological sciences, for example, "insist that this unseen realm of synaptic interactions must be carefully studied and understood if we wish to truly understand just why the surrounding world appears to us as it does."[2] This invisible world of firing neutrons and neurotransmitters, said David Abram, generates the coherent appearance of the surrounding world that we experience at any moment." He added:

Although very few of us have any clear apprehension of the subatomic world, or of the inscrutable particles that comprise it, we are continually assured by the physics community that this arcane realm is the ultimate source, or fundament, of all that we do apprehend. According to most contemporary physicists, the visible, tangible world glimpsed by our unaided senses is not at all fundamental, but is wholly structured by events unfolding at scales far beneath the threshold of our everyday awareness.[3]

Meanwhile, said Abram, in another set of laboratories, other researchers, molecular biologists, operate on the assumption that the real truth of our natures is to be found in the nuclei of our cells. There the "complexly coded structure of our chromosomes" provides the template for our particular "proclivities, dispositions and behaviors." Abram noted that anyone watching the way researchers are racing to fill gaps in the emerging map of the genome would begin

> to suspect that the microscopic world of gene sequences and genetic interactions somehow determines our lives and our experiences. The ultimate source of our personality—of our habits, our appetites, our yearnings, and our decisions—would seem to be thoroughly hidden away from our ordinary awareness, carefully tucked within the nuclei of our cells.[4]

NORMAL VERSUS ABNORMAL HUMANITY

Certainly, the wish to unlock the underlying secret of the way that humans are—how they think and act, what they desire, and why they are motivated the way they are—has been a continuing fascination among philosophers and intellectuals throughout much of human history. The interest, however, has been of more than purely academic concern. There is always implicit in this search some belief that there is a more normal form of human behavior that those other human beings, with their strange and unfamiliar ways, violate. The latter group usually ends up being described as deviants from what is most natural in being human. It is a mark of all cultures that some form of categorization is constructed that distinguishes the so-called normal people from the outsiders, who are then viewed as a threat to normality. It is easy to see how the distinction between "normal/natural" and "other" has been used to create systems of exclusion, demonization and oppression, and to legitimate the exploitation, persecution, and even genocide of whole groups of people. We might think of the native peoples of this continent who were seen as "savages," people less than fully human. European colonists could engage in genocidal wars against such people secure in the knowledge that their less than human status made such horrors morally acceptable. The enslavement of millions of Africans was given sanction through the pernicious ideology of racism, which gave credence to their supposed subhuman inferiority. Or we could think about the Nazi ideology that chose to view Jews and other groups as less than fully human. Of course, the process of distinguishing human beings in this way has a long and terrible history, which continues unabated into our own era, where people continue to be abused or slaughtered because of some supposed deviancy from the supposedly proper norms of humanity.

In all of this, we need to remember that schools have always played an important role in passing on ideas about who is normal, or at least who think and act in ways that are maintained as proper to civilized human beings. Our textbooks still convey ideas about the "savagery" of Indians. Our history lessons emphasize the supposed superiority of Western and European minds over non-Western peoples, Christianity over other religions. Schools reinforce attitudes about the claimed intellectual inadequacies of Blacks and Latinos (continued differences on testing results have sustained the arguments of those who believe that genetic differences between Black and White children account for differences in results). We know that schools reward middle-class norms in language, vocabulary, dress, attitudes to authority, and behavior, in ways that make working-class or poor kids feel like school is not a place in which they may comfortably belong. School is also typically a place that recognizes Christian holidays as normative (e.g., in the arranging of the calendar). It is also a place in which kids who follow a nonconventional path in their dress, sexuality, or musical and cultural tastes are marginalized and often stigmatized. Of course, as I like to emphasize to my students, none of this should come as a surprise. To understand schools and what they do, we really need to see them as places that are expected by many people to turn unsocialized youngsters into civilized human beings. In other words, the process of normalizing children is central to school's cultural tasks. And ideas about what is normal have always come with the heavy baggage of prejudice, ethnocentrism, and one-sided cultural assumptions.

At this point in the discussion about human nature, some students will turn to me and demand to know what it is that I actually believe. They are usually quite disappointed when I tell them that I am agnostic on this question—I really don't know the truth about human nature. With very rare exceptions, human beings do not appear in the world as culturally "naked," unaffected by language and learned responses. In other words, we really don't know what people would be like if they were not shaped by their social experiences and were governed solely by "natural" determinants. Moreover, I tell them that I am quite suspicious of all those who are quick to claim knowledge of the "essential" qualities of human beings, of the things that supposedly conform to the natural requisites of human behavior. Certainly such claims have supported all kinds of racism and ethnocentrism. They have been used to denigrate the kinds of intelligence demonstrated more often among women than men. Normality is often a straitjacket that restricts diverse and imaginative forms of human practice, tastes, and forms of expression. It is a club that has been wielded, time and again, to repress and censor human beings, and to cajole them into political, religious, cultural, and sexual conformity. I am with Karl Marx in my belief that the one thing we can say about human nature is that it is in our nature as human beings to transcend our own apparent limits. In other words, the extraordinary gift of human beings is that we can, in fact, make ourselves different tomorrow from what we are today. An amazing fact that should give us hope about human possibility! Indeed, if we look around us we can see quite quickly what this really means. Although, for example, we may have, until recent times, assumed that human beings are locked into the rigid distinctions of masculine and feminine (men are viewed as active, rational, inventive, self-sufficient, and dominant; women, by contrast, are passive, emotional, relationship-oriented, and destined to follow), it is clear now, to many of us, just how much such distinctions are the products of upbringing and enculturation. These traits are much less the product of human nature or genetic coding than a result of the things we have learned, and the pressures that have been placed on us to conform to a certain way of being in the world. In other words, the extraordinary changes we have witnessed in recent decades made us see just how right Marx was about our ability to challenge and change who we were told we were supposed to be.

Is there a genetic dimension to gender differences? Possibly so. But it is clear that there is enormous room for reshuffling the traits we have called masculine and feminine. Men can certainly be care-givers and nurturers in the private space; women can certainly be leaders in the public world. Reason and emotion belong to both men and women and cannot be divided up and parceled out in any simple way. Nor does creativity, intellectuality, or inventiveness belong to one gender more than another. When human traits are divided up and allocated to some people more than others, it is usually the case that lurking in the background are issues of power and privilege. Most often it is in the interest of members of a more dominant or privileged group to convince everyone concerned that only they have the more prized attributes. This gives credence or legitimacy to the leading role they play in a particular society or culture.

Perhaps, at this time, no more contentious issue can be found to illustrate the dangers and damage of mistaken ideas about human nature than that regarding homosexuality. Antagonism to homosexuality produces passionate assertions about it being an "unnatural" human practice, that it violates "fundamental" laws of normal human behavior. Characterizing gays and lesbians as sinners is a sure recipe for licensing exclusion, prejudice, inhumanity, and finally violence against this population. (The argument that one can hate the "sin" and not the "sinner" made by some is specious in that it denies the way that our sexuality is so central to our human being, not like an article of clothing that one can slip out of at will!) History has made clear to us the terrible dangers and consequences of such pronouncements, which produce whole categories of people who can be categorized as outside the field of acceptable human attributes. We must certainly expect that casting individuals as somehow less than fully human will result in their being victimized, discriminated against, and subject to brutalizing treatment up to and including genocide. We should also wonder how it is that millions of our fellow human beings can somehow be designated as having "failed" the test of humanness. With what hubris or certainty do some of us take on the role of judging and making distinctions as to who among us should be treated with full respect and dignity, and who less than this? We are also forced to examine the way religious beliefs and commitments become complicit in the persecution and suffering of our brothers and sisters. Yet it is also a positive and hopeful fact of our time that more of us than ever before are able to see and acknowledge just how arbitrary and fluid are our assumptions about human nature. Millions of us are aware of the horrific consequences that have befallen those treated as deviants from the norm or having inferior natures. Feminism has brought widespread awareness of the questionable ways we have tried to "fix" male and female natures. Millions of us now recognize that women are in no way cast by nature as excluded from scientific exploration, political leadership, athletic skill and competitiveness, or artistic brilliance. Conversely, men are not made unfit by nature to nurture the young, to tend the aged, to share the housework, or to be impelled by sensitivity and compassion in human relationships.

All of these claims are not the work of the biological forces in our makeup, but much more the products of history and the social contexts within which we have grown up. We can see, too, that those who have refused to recognize this have usually had some interest or privilege attached to the maintenance of existing social and cultural arrangements. In other words, power and advantage have been sustained by the denial of the shifting and fluid potential of what it means for any of us to be human. To say that something must be is to say that we as human beings can only act and live our lives in one way, and one way only. No alternative is possible to how things are now. Of course, throughout the 20th century, powerful social and political movements have helped break down such a pessimistic view of what it means to be human. Anticolonialism challenged and destroyed the assumptions about the inferiority of people in poor and exploited countries to rule themselves. Antiracist struggles challenged the way we have aligned physical appearance and skin color with intellectual ability and cultural achievement, so that the story of civilization is made into the story of one small segment of the human population. Such racist narratives about human nature have sought to give credence to a whole litany of terrible and destructive charges against people of color, and in so doing have given a spurious legitimacy to the social injustice found in our educational, legal, political, and economic institutions.

EDUCATION AS SOCIALIZATION

Spending this time on inquiring into the matter of human nature is important if we are to understand, at a much deeper level, what it means for us to educate our children. To recognize the extraordinary fluidity and flexibility of being human is to invite us to see education as a force of very great moral and social significance. We are, as educators, from the very beginning, in a world of profound social and existential choices. Our choices have to do with our vision concerning what it means to be human, and in what ways human beings are to relate to one another. If, as we have seen, there are few givens in the nature of being human, then we must call up instead our own hopes, aspirations, and commitments about what it means, or should mean, for our children to live in a human way. We have to choose the narrative that best represents our vision for living good and meaningful lives. Reflecting on the meaning of human nature brings us to the realization that there is little that is set in stone about what we should expect from human beings in terms of their proclivities, dispositions, and attitudes. Although perhaps not everything about who we are is "up for grabs," nonetheless a very great deal of who we are remains to be decided through the way we educate the young.

Obviously, here, education refers to the whole process of socialization that includes all those things and influences that shape how we think, act and relate to the world we live in. This certainly includes school, but it also includes other powerful influences on us, such as the family, peer relationships, religious institutions, popular culture, and the mass media. In this sense, the African proverb about it taking a "whole village to raise a child" correctly indicates that we are shaped as human beings by all those cultural forces that influence the cognitive, social, moral, and spiritual dimensions of who we are. If we are to see education for what it really is—a process that shapes all aspects of our being human (not just those limited spheres of competence like whether we know a certain amount of math or even whether we can read)—then we can understand what it is that John Dewey meant when he said that education shapes a world. In our public discussions about education we typically forget this, as we obsessively focus on whether students have this particular competence or possess that small piece of knowledge. We fail to see that education is about the development of whole human beings. The ability to be numerate and literate, to have some scientific understanding, to possess a degree of historical or cultural knowledge, is only a small aspect of our total education. Perhaps this seems to simplify matters, making the work of education seem more focused or manageable. Nonetheless, in restricting our discussions about education to these very limited aspects, we are avoiding or even denying the really profound nature of what it means to educate our children. We are able to ignore questions that relate to the kind of social outlook we desire for our children, the moral and spiritual ends we truly wish them to cherish, or the forms of human relationships that we wish them to cultivate because they are the most valued. Whether we like it or not, education is always, and everywhere, a process that shapes what it means—or we would like it to mean—to be human. Education is always a process that gives us a template for the moral life and our spiritual quest for meaning and purpose. Of course, this says nothing about whether the template that we employ most often in our schools is a good or bad one, or one that fits the real struggles and concerns facing young people nowadays. Indeed, I believe that the particular messages we convey in our schools about what is socially worthwhile, how we should relate to others around us, or in what we should invest the preponderance of our life's energy do little to address the crisis of meaning that permeates and corrodes our culture. To a large extent, what schools offer our children in moral, social, and spiritual terms only compounds the crisis and provides no adequate solution.

Part of the difficulty is, as I have suggested, that so much of our talk about education focuses on such a small part of what actually goes on in school. It is as if we try to understand what advertising is about by focusing on the particular qualities of the product that is being advertised without analyzing the deeper values and meanings being transmitted through the commercial message (the subliminal sexual images, the emphasis on material solutions to all problems, the encouragement to live in debt, to be heedless of the ecological damage of our endless consuming, and so on). In school such an approach has meant that apart from a few educational scholars few people are aware of what is called the "hidden curriculum." Those who have studied the hidden curriculum[5] believe that it is not just that students learn things in school that do not appear on the "official" curriculum (math, English, social studies, science, etc.). It is that these hidden or implicit dimensions of what we learn are the very things that make the deepest and lasting impression on the attitudes, beliefs, and values of students. I start to make this clear to my students by asking them a simple question: How much from their many years in elementary and secondary school do they actually remember or know? This question is usually met with a nervous or embarrassed silence as they try to actually recall the things that the official curriculum has taught them beyond basic literacy and arithmetic. Someone will be able to recite a poem or a scrap of a monologue from Shakespeare, or name a book he or she has read. Others will remember a geometry proof, some dates from history, or a scientific law. For most students the things they can name and recall from the actual subject matter are quite minuscule—a pathetically small "return," it must be said, on the huge quantity of time required of them in the classroom. But, I point out, this does not mean that school leaves little mark on how they think and see the world. It merely gives emphasis to my argument, and that of others who study schools, that it is the implicit or informal dimensions of the classroom and school that have the biggest influence on students' education. For example, school very successfully teaches students that it is competition (and not love or cooperation) that is the primary source of human motivation. From the very beginning of our schooling we learn that the normal and expected way that individuals relate to one another is through a process of invidious comparison. This is perhaps the most powerful message of all in our education, and one we ignore or reject at our own peril. In the remainder of this chapter I want to look a little closer at this unstated but pervasive message.

CONDITIONAL AFFIRMATION

How many of you, I ask my undergraduate class, suffer from the effects of serious anxiety? All, or nearly all, of the hands shoot up. Is this a normal thing to expect? It is a strange question for most of them. Although many of the students must invest a great deal energy dealing with the effects of anxiety in their lives—ulcers, migraines, muscle spasms, emotional debilities, and so on—few have ever really considered why our culture produces so much anxiety. They simply assume that this is the way things are (and perhaps always were). When I explain that this phenomenon is not something universal in the human condition, and is unknown in many other cultures, they look at me with surprise. What causes anxiety, I ask them. The responses are thoughtful and range from the pressure of keeping up with their studies and holding down a job, to the need to be perfect, whether in the way they look (applying more often to the women) or in their grades. There are, of course, also other issues that create anxiety, such as the fear of not getting a job, and concerns about security. I tell them that although I agree that there are many factors at work in generating our culture of anxiety, my particular interest is on what school contributes to this culture. It is, I believe, a critical part of the anxiety-producing mix.

School people like to say that they value all of the children entrusted to them. Indeed, it is part of the oft-repeated official rhetoric in our society to say that all children are precious and must be treated with care and respect. This sentiment is frequently expressed and reaffirmed in our public discourse, whether by educators, politicians, or civic leaders. Yet if we look more closely at the implicit message of the classroom, we discover something quite different. What holds sway there is not the unconditional valuing of all our children but a process that offers a very conditional kind of affirmation indeed. In sociological terms, schools are primary transmitters of *achievement ideology*. The latter refers to the belief that who we are, and the kind of worth we have as human beings, is not intrinsic to us, but is dependent on the degree of success or achievement we can manifest in the world. Who we are, and how much respect we should expect to receive from others, is in direct proportion to how good or successful we can show ourselves to be at something. So although we may say that all children deserve equal respect, or even that we care for and love all our children, our actions in school most often stem from achievement ideology, and this means treating them in very different ways in regard to how much we value them. If they are anything, schools in America are places that teach children to see and value themselves in very different ways. All schools, no matter what they may say about valuing all their kids, busily construct hierarchies that daily reinforce the moral belief that some individuals are far more deserving of respect than others—whether this is because they read better, get superior grades or test scores, or are part of the "right" social group or admired athletic team.

The world of achievement ideology is one that is divided between the "nobodies" and the "somebodies". Fear and anxiety hangs over all of us, that we not end up in the former category. It is easy to see how this way of thinking has so profoundly shaped Americans attitude toward the poor. The poor not only suffer from a lack of money and resources, they also suffer a lack of respect. To be poor has often meant to be treated as a person who has little worth and whose moral qualities are the subject of constant suspicion. We can see this in the discussions of welfare reform, when poverty and the need to depend on community resources are so often addressed in terms of the moral shortcomings of recipients. The issue becomes how we can "shape up" these individuals so that they stop their irresponsible and indolent behavior. In contrast to most other comparable societies, our attitude in America toward the jobless, the low-income, or the dependent has long been a suspicious and punitive one. Recently, in my own state, a furor was set off when the summer freshman reading assignment at the University of North Carolina was Barbara Ehrenreich's book, *Nickel and Dimed*.[6] The book vividly and movingly describes the lives of women working in low-income jobs, and the sheer drudgery and exploitation endured by those who do this work. Many in this state could not stomach the idea that students at a state university would be exposed to a sympathetic and morally challenging view of what it means to be at the bottom end of the economic and social hierarchy. There were demands that the book be withdrawn, or that a "more balanced' view be presented. It is, of course, hard to know what it means to present a balanced view of suffering, hardship, and exploitation, unless it means an effort to somehow justify the necessity of blatant social injustice, or to blame the victims for getting themselves into this wretched position in the first place! In comparison to other generally affluent societies, our support for those in need has always been meager, and the climate of opinion a frequently hostile one that has been exploited by right-wing politicians. The latter have used the widespread animus toward the poor as a vehicle to garner and construct their own political support.

Our suspicions and hostility are well ingrained in us through media depictions of minorities and welfare dependents, but it is a process that begins much earlier in the ideological conditioning provided through our education. School constantly urges us to "become somebody," to make "something" of who we are—or else! To fail at this task guarantees not only poverty and insecurity, but the risk of becoming invisible. The ultimate "stick" school waves before us is that of becoming an individual of little regard or value to others in our society. This quest is made that much harder by the belief that success and recognition are in limited supply. The scarcity means we have to compete against our neighbors and friends for a share of society's "goodies." This idea is taught to us and reinforced throughout our schooling. The basic message we learn is that although anybody can be successful, not everybody can. We learn at an early age that there is only so much success available, and grasping some of it means we will have to beat out others for the limited amount available. This "reality" is conveyed to us early through that staple of classroom evaluation, the bell curve. This humanly invented artifact conveys to us the powerful fiction that human intelligence and achievement must inevitably fall out in ways that ensure that although some excel, others must fail, or at best be average. My students are constantly amazed by my assertion that this supposed scientific phenomenon (supported after all by numbers!) is actually a story made up by a group of people who, in the early years of the 20th century, were determined to find a way to sort and differentiate human beings, and to do so in ways that showed that some ethnicities were intellectually inferior to others.[7] The bell curve depends on the idea that intelligence can be identified in an objective and measurable way that allows us to compare one person's cognitive performance against another. All of this denies the complex and diverse forms of intelligence possessed by human beings, and the situational nature of being smart (we all know how some situations seems to "make" us smarter than others, and some do the opposite, eliciting a low self-confidence in our ability to solve a problem or express an opinion). There are also the well-established critiques of researchers that throw into question any claims about being able to measure someone's intelligence in an impartial manner, not influenced by one's own cultural assumptions or prejudices. What I emphasize to my students is the bell-curve "mentality," which insists that in any situation (at least in school) everything students do results in them being measured and sorted for success, and supposedly in a fair and accurate manner, and that this success can only be given to a fraction of the students. Others are required to fail or at least do less well. In a nutshell, we must find winners and losers or the system would not be working. (Of course, this is what makes Garrison Keillor's comments on his National Public Radio show about how, in his home town of Lake Wobegon, all the kids are "above average," a humorous parody of the real world, where such a notion would be untenable). Indeed, any standardized test of intelligence or ability that demonstrated students all scoring above average would not be a reason for celebrating a successful learning process, but a time for hand-wringing over poorly constructed tests. Something like this has recently happened in a number of states, where political pressures to ensure rising test outcomes in public schools has produced the strange effect of embarrassment at too many kids doing well! This has generated demands for inquiries into whether the tests have become too easy. All this reminds one of the Chinese proverb about the need to be wary of having ones wishes granted.

THE MORAL ECONOMY OF WINNING AND LOSING

The oft-repeated rhetoric of schools concerns trying to ensure that every child is successful—"leave no child behind"! The reality is that the moral economy of schooling is based on differentiating kids to identify winners and losers. Schools are, sad to say, in the very business of leaving kids behind. It maddens my students that when we discuss the issue of grading I tell them that, no matter how hard and conscientiously they might work in my class, I ought not to reward them all with an A. To do so, according to the prevailing wisdom, would lower the worth of the A's that are received. This is the phenomenon of "grade inflation" that bothers some educators so much. It is a bit like keeping up the price of gold by ensuring that the supply of it is always restricted. It is scarcity that maintains the value of gold. Similarly, what makes one successful in the classroom is about doing or knowing something that only a few others can do or know. If we all understood or knew something, what would be the point?

I try to convey this powerful message, in which success is always about getting something that is denied to others, by reminding students of some of their early experiences in school. Remember, for example, the excruciating manner in which youngsters cover their work so that others cannot benefit from their answers. The competitively charged nature of most classrooms in this culture means that most sharing of information is understood as cheating or copying—not helping ones fellow student. Many students also remember covering over their work as a way of avoiding the shame of an incorrect answer. And it is important to recognize that this is no aberration. In an environment that values success (usually meaning giving the answer the teacher expects) so highly, and the personal esteem that goes with it, incorrect responses quickly become a vehicle for personal disparagement. We learn rapidly in school, and at a very early age, that academic achievement is the currency that marks our personal worth. We learn quickly that the real stake in the competitive ethos of our classrooms is the value of ones identity. It is the child's sense of personal worth that is always on the line. Praise for an assignment well done, or a correct response, is always about something much more significant than the ability to read something correctly or to solve an arithmetic problem. The contingent nature of respect for who we are is the real lesson in our classrooms. Our worth, we learn again and again in school, is not something inherent in our presence as human beings, but something that has to be fought for in a game whose rules ensure that there will always be winners and losers; that some will have their value and presence affirmed, and others will not.

Of course, this lesson fits very well with what is taught in the larger culture. Everywhere we look, our culture is awash in the games of winning and losing, and the celebration and glorification of winners. There is no end of award shows that identify who is the best, and who is to be rewarded and recognized. Everything that can will, sooner or later, be turned into a contest for identifying the best (and the worst). Like no other society in history, we celebrate competitive and antagonistic relationships between people, and engage in finding endless ways to rank people on hierarchies of worth. Although we may at times, in America, talk about the inherent worth of all human life, the everyday reality tells us all a very different story. What is drummed into is the inevitability and desirability of a moral economy in which a few win and a much larger number lose. Life, for all of us, is made to be a constant struggle to join the lucky few, or to deal with the pain and humiliation of not making it. Our language makes it clear that success and worth are only achieved through the fact of beating out others. In school we learn "to get ahead" or to "get a head start." For the most part we seem blithely unaware, as we talk about leaving no one behind, that the classroom or school is set up to do just that! Schooling is a process designed to sort out the winners and losers. It is all about that. There is little time in school that is not, in some way, about evaluating, grading, or measuring students in a process designed to pit them against others to see who is better or worse. This process is never simply about ones ability or prowess in a discreet activity or subject area. The issue is never merely about whether you are better at reading, science, or algebra than your neighbor. It is always in some way connected to the affirming—or denial—of one's worth and value.

Young children rapidly intuit this when they are allocated to ability groups in first grade or even, nowadays, in kindergarten. They know that being in the "Bluebirds" or in the "Robins" group signifies much more than a certain level of academic competence. It is also a measure of an individual's worth. How could it be otherwise when our culture is one in which achievement or ability is so clearly tied to the extent that we respect or value someone? It is a process of selection and labeling students that continues throughout our schooling. The academic sorting practiced by most high schools is always much more than recognizing differences in aptitude or interests among students. Honors, Advanced Placement (AP), IB, general education, vo-tech (vocational–techanical), and special education classes are all significant markers of the way we measure human worth. It is hardly surprising to me that when I ask my students to write about their school experience and its meaning, what they mostly focus on is the need to "prove themselves." Whether this refers to academic achievement, or making the cheerleading squad or athletic team, the quest is always to overcome the same sense of injury or perceived threat to their self-respect. For not a few students, the constant reminder of mediocrity or failure in school instills a sense of shame that becomes a gnawing sense of self-doubt or low self-esteem they carry with them into adulthood. For others, school becomes a focus of alienation or even (as we now know in our post-Columbine world) rage, as it appears to deny an individual's integrity and value. More insightful commentators have understood this connection as they have sought to make sense of the violent episodes in our schools. For most students, however, schooling produces psychic wounds that leave many individuals emotionally more fragile or crippled, as well as unlikely to risk being intellectually assertive. The paradox of the relentless emphasis on succeeding is to make schools places that are socially conformist and mentally timid. One of my graduate students, reflecting on her own education, poignantly expressed the damage that the relentless evaluation does to students' capacity to be assertive about their own ideas and interests, or honestly self-reflective about themselves:

> This constant outside evaluation lesson is particularly insidious, I believe, because it tends to render children unable to fairly and honestly evaluate themselves because they internalize the evaluative views of others. ... From as early on as I can remember in my schooling, I was hyper-aware of other people, particularly teachers evaluating me. ... I garnered praise from my teachers for such behavior and apparent learning, and from that point on I was addicted. To me, outside evaluation was a positive thing; it made me feel good about myself and superior to those others who did not receive the same or comparable praise that I did. My adaptive strategy to this outside evaluation was to do everything I could to keep this praise and positive feedback coming.

The student went on to describe the strategies she developed to maintain, at all costs, this positive evaluation. This included avoidance of tasks that she knew might be difficult or too challenging for her. It also meant a readiness to create a false persona that "did not reflect who I truly was, but one that would cause others to view me as admirable—a leader, a go-getter, and so on." This persona, she added, was her "ticket" to move on in the game of education. Movingly, she concluded:

> I learned the lesson of constant outside evaluation well, almost too well. Although this outside evaluation was mostly rewarding to me throughout my schooling, it also had a negative effect on me in my quest to become a whole and healthy person. ... I have noticed in myself an obsessive need to continue to have the positive regard of others. I struggle with trying not to flaunt my schooling successes in front of others, and I am constantly battling the desire to have every utterance or piece of work of mine "graded" by others. Learning to self-evaluate in an honest and fair way is exceedingly difficult after so many years of others evaluating you.[8]

It is especially pernicious, I believe, that this sense that of having to hustle to gain a sense of personal worth is conveyed as the only real game in town. In other words, we teach children to believe that these competitive relations between themselves and others are the inevitable, as well as the fairest and most desirable, way in which human beings can relate to one another. Indeed, we learn that it is what made America great! Competition comes to be understood as an expression of our human nature. Anything else, it is said, violates our normal human tendencies. Even as my students share the pain, frustration, anguish, or even anger of this need to constantly prove their worth through besting their friends and fellow students, they will, paradoxically, make the argument that no alternative set of human relationships is possible or even imaginable. They have learned well the message of the hidden curriculum. Its power is daily reinforced through what Elizabeth Dodson Gray called the "culture of separated desks."[9] The typical school classroom in America is a place where students are expected to pursue their tasks in isolation from their peers. School, she noted, is the place that values the "long-distance runner": the individual who, in constant competition or comparison with his or her peers, is able to distinguish herself from the others. He or she is the one who is able to succeed at the constant process of doing the required work, performing well or at least adequately in the endless round of tests and examinations, and accumulating the points and grades that have come to represent education. Gray described the process this way:

> We conceptualize an education as a solitary and autonomous experience. To sit as a first-grader at a separated desk in one of our school systems is as solitary an experience as for a runner in a track event to put his or her feet in the blocks and take their mark. We are to start running our own course, start learning our letters and math by ourselves, start competing with others for grades, start better jobs in the real world that come after the educational world, the real world of adulthood.[10]

Of course, she added, this educational model allows for little or no cooperative work. Learning, knowledge, and understanding are viewed as the achievements of individual and autonomous actors. Each of us runs our own course in competition with others, and any act of helping or sharing with others is defined as "cheating." It is a process, she noted, that strongly reinforces what are thought of as typically masculine social values—individualism and self-sufficiency—at the expense of learning that is a shared or collaborative venture. Each person is to look out for his or her own success, and to jealously guard the pieces of information or knowledge that give an edge in the zero-sum game of classroom achievement. Even as adults, many of us painfully remember the need, as young children, to cover our completed classroom assignments with our hands, either to ensure that others should gain no advantage from our assumed knowledge or, worse, to guard against classmates seeing incomplete or erroneous work. We may remember too, as young children, the competitive vying for the teacher's attention with our waving arms and oohing and aahing sounds, as we sought to win praise for a correct answer or response. Perhaps we also remember the shrinking souls whose hands rarely rose in the air, and who spent much of their time in the classroom feeling foolish and out of place. For these students, looking to others for help violated the competitive and individualistic moral code of the classroom. It meant risking identifying oneself as incapable, stupid, or a cheat. The shame and embarrassment of such moments remains seared into our memories long after our school days are done.

Those of you reading this may feel, at this point, that I have unfairly ignored other more laudable motives that guide people in their relations with others. Don't we also teach children in school the importance of sharing and helping others? Doesn't our culture also offer numerous examples of the fact that we also value those among us who are not the most successful? Are we not a people that also seek to lift up the lives of even the lowliest among us? Do we not teach our children the importance of charity, of giving to others out of care and compassion, of cooperating as members of a team? The answer to all these is certainly yes. In a sense we could only feel anguish at what I have just described as a culture that exaggerates winning, getting ahead of others, and measuring individual worth by how successful one is, if we had a sense that such values violate some deeper moral imperative. Our religious traditions, however corrupted they might become by the "gospel" of wealth and status, still remind us of the importance of caring for the least among us, and the need for unconditionally affirming the value of each and every life. They remind us of *B'tselem Elohim*—that we are all made in God's image. Nor can we entirely forget the rhetoric of our democratic creed, which reminds us, as a nation, about the equal worth of each citizen.

Our moral condition is, at the very least, schizoid—emphasizing invidious comparisons between people, but also, too, the beauty and worth of each human being. However much schools seek to pin badges of fame or shame on students, to differentiate our children on hierarchies of worth and recognition, most teachers are motivated by something more when they choose to teach. We need to see their

sincere desire to cherish each student before them. Their language of loving
children, and wanting what is best for them all, should not be dismissed as empty
cant. It means that those who seek to work with young lives are in touch with
something other than the usual calculus of how we measure success in schools. So
much at odds with the public language of performance, ranking, and measurable
achievement, the language of care and love for all children speaks to an altogether
different moral and spiritual outlook. It is one that radically breaks from our
society's dominant emphasis on differentiating individuals on hierarchical scales
of achievement, and instead seeks to affirm the sacred commonality of
unconditional worth found among all our children. It is to see all our children as we
would want others to view our own—unique and irreplaceable beings that no scale,
test, or evaluation can do justice to. Of course we know that when we walk into a
classroom for young children, often much effort has gone into shaping an
environment of care, respect, and mutual help among them. Teachers and principal,
in that school, work energetically to try to create a culture of loving community, in
spite of all the pressures to make school a competitive hothouse for a
performance-driven education.

Certainly, even as parents, we are forced to inhabit contradictory moral
universes. When our children enter the world they do so "trailing clouds of glory."
Effecting not much more than the basic bodily functions, we typically view them as
miraculous creatures of ineffable beauty and immeasurable value. We ask nothing
from them other than to breathe and exist. This is quite enough for us to be filled
with delight and awe. Later, however, we move back into the work of creating
hierarchies of success; "if you get good grades I will reward you with ... " We
become the proud parents of the smartest/prettiest/most talented (and so on) child.
We carry bumper stickers that say "Proud Parents of an Honor Student." Our love
as parents becomes more and more conditional on what our kids do in a very
competitive world. There is a great deal of sickness around this. We have seen the
"beauty pageants" for 5- and 6-year-olds in which parents put unbearable
expectations on small girls to dazzle the judges with their contrived sexuality. We
have seen, too, the parents at sporting events screaming at kids and umpires as if the
value of their whole lives is at stake. We know the overanxious parents pushing
hard to get their children into classes for the gifted or other academically advanced
tracks. We are aware of the "gourmet babies" whose parents dare miss no
opportunity through which their offspring may be stimulated to be all they can be.
Although we may all love our kids, this love comes at a higher and higher price.
Parents pass on to their children the frustrated hopes and needs that have been
incurred in their own lives. Through the hoped-for achievements of their offspring,
they often seek a vicarious healing of their own wounded egos and insecurities.

A society that makes success and achievement the price to be paid for our sense
of personal value has created a psychic monster in which we each must exert a
never-ending effort to shore up the fragility of our own, always-in-doubt,
individual worth. Even after we score a success, the moment feels short-lived. We

experience the need to do it again and again. Often the most fragile students, I have found, are the ones who are used to getting straight A's. God forbid they receive something less—they feel shattered out of all proportion to the reduced grade. Our society insists that we should never feel too emotionally secure or comfortable. We are driven to keep proving our worth. And we justify this with the belief that only such insecurity will produce the creative and entrepreneurial energy that makes America so productive. We dismiss other ideas about what might motivate human creativity and inventiveness (such as the joy of innovation, or the satisfaction of serving others). No wonder our bookstores are filled with book after book, and endless magazine pieces, that promise how we can become "our own best friend," or feel okay about who we are right now, not in some promised future land of success or perfection. It perhaps explains also the enormous fragility of intimate relationships, as we are driven to seek that "special someone" who will love and accept us just as we are. Although the larger culture is a place of endless judgments about who we are, how we appear, and what we do, our love relationships, we hope, might offer a respite in this relentlessly competitive world. Yet as Christopher Lasch pointed out in his brilliant *Haven in a Heartless World*,[11] the larger competitive culture seeps into even our most intimate relationships, and we find ourselves frequently wondering whether there is someone better—richer, more attractive, more compatible or exciting—out there for us. It is difficult indeed to escape the world of invidious comparisons—a world of endless self-doubt and restless striving to reach the safe shores of unconditional acceptance and love.

A WORLD OUT OF BALANCE

We have learned from our discussion about human nature that not much about us, beyond our physical state, is predetermined or immutable. As we have discussed, we all exist in a world where we find ourselves the subject of very different, even contradictory, moral, social, and psychological pulls. We know what it means to be endlessly judged but also the meaning of unconditional acceptance. We understand the meaning of being pitted against our neighbors for respect and recognition. But we also know that other human possibilities exist in which our relationships are about cooperation, care, and compassion for others. We are very familiar with a world in which only a few win. But we are also aware that good communities are ones that seek to ensure that there are no losers. Of course, my students will argue that competition provides them with a great deal of pleasure and stimulation. This is certainly the case. Nothing here is meant to deny the enormous fun and excitement that comes from participating in or watching sporting events or other forms of competitive entertainment. My argument here is not to somehow nullify competition, as if that were even possible. It is that we have allowed this particular form of human relationship to overwhelm and subsume other important ways in which we may relate to one another. We have created a world that is morally, spiritually, and emotionally out of balance.

Students will sometimes say to me, after I have presented them with these kinds of choices, that however desirable it is to create a world where we are all affirmed, respected, and supportive of one another, such a world is "pie in the sky." Such a vision is too much at odds with the way things are in the real world. I tell them that they may well be right. Still, as educators our job is to make choices—not on the basis of what seems most feasible, but because of what seems to compel us morally and spiritually. Education requires a courageous willingness to affirm, in our work, what appears to us as the right path—to discern in the flux and multiple possibilities of human attitudes and behavior those dimensions of how we are that offer a path toward what we believe is a better world for the next generation. We are not here, I emphasize, to merely be what Henry Giroux has called "clerks of the empire"—employees of state bureaucracies who merely rubber stamp how things are or have been in the world.[12] Our job is to light the candle of possibility: a possibility not removed from the reality of people's lives but found right there among the clutter and mishmash of our daily experiences. Such experiences tell us that there is much that unnecessarily fills us with anguish, pain, and anger. Yet that is not the whole story. Love, caring, cooperation, and mutual support are also always, and everywhere, a part of the human condition. As human beings, and as educators, we cannot rely on nature or normality to tell us how we or our children should be. We will instead simply have to make choices about what we wish to nurture and encourage in the young lives before us. That will include the need to right a culture sinking under the oppressive weight of our addiction to competitive and success-driven forms of human relationships.

As we embrace the existential or choice-making dimensions of educational work, we turn to pragmatic matters. Can we pry ourselves, and more particularly our children, loose from the world of competition and comparisons? Although I believe we need a radical redirecting of our culture's values and norms, I also understand that the change will most likely happen over a long time and through a million small efforts. Schools are not typically sites of revolution. But we need not wait passively for change to happen. There are things we can try to do. First, educators and parents are responsible for encouraging a critical awareness among our students of the damaging and hurtful effects of a culture that puts so much emphasis on winning, and judgments about an individual's worth. We can help students understand something about the hidden curriculum and the way it produces painful feelings of inadequacy and worthlessness among some kids, and a sense of smug superiority among others. And we can affirm the importance of seeing the unconditional value in all human lives. We must be willing to ask the uncomfortable questions about what it would mean for a society like ours to construct a culture that ensures that everyone is treated with dignity and worth. To do this requires not just posing difficult, even painful questions about the nature of school and the larger society. It means also encouraging students to develop their imagination so as to envision social relationships that are not based on competition and ranking. How would things look and feel if we related to one another through unconditional and loving acceptance? What would it mean for us if our schools and classrooms were much less concerned about grades and point averages, and all the other ways we devise to identify and distinguish winners and losers?

There are, in addition, other things we can do. We can, for example, encourage more opportunity for peer learning in the classroom, where those more able in some area or activity are urged to help those less able (of course, without any feelings of superiority). We can support and encourage more time for cooperative learning, and projects in our classrooms where students work together on joint tasks and assignments. Wonderful ideas around this have been developed by innovative educators like Mara Sapon-Shevin.[13] We can also press for more time in the school day in which students are engaged in nongraded work—where we can learn the pleasure of creativity or learning disconnected from showing how good or smart we are in comparison to others. We can support and expand activities in the curriculum that are about giving to others, through work in the community that improves the life of our fellow citizens Such "service learning" should not turn into another grade-producing or resumé-enhancing activity (something to show colleges how "well-rounded" we are). We need to teach that such learning is its own reward, that it reflects the wisdom found in all our faith traditions that life's greatest rewards is in giving freely and generously to others.

Beyond all of this, we need to try to create learning environments in which grades and test scores receive less attention and significance—classrooms that are much less centered on the question, "what d'ya get?" This means emphasizing the joy and significance of the act of learning itself. Of course, as we have indicated in this book, this is to go against the whole instrumental direction of education in our society. It is not an easy proposition and it is one that requires courageous and visionary leaders who have become alert to the current degradation of education. Such leaders will need to be willing to articulate a different moral agenda for the education of our children that is not always about competition, winning, doing or being better than others, and creating hierarchies of success and failure in our schools. They will, instead, need to be the harbingers of a transformed culture that seeks to genuinely affirm the worth and value of every human life. We need not expect that our small efforts alone can shake the moral and social order. Nonetheless, each of us, parent, teacher, principal, or community member, has the capacity to add something to the much larger tide of change that is so desperately needed in our world.

NOTES

1. Roger Shattuck. (1980). *The forbidden experiment: The story of the wild boy of Aveyron*, pp. 33–37, 65. New York: Farrar Straus Giroux.
2. David Abram. (2003). The eclipse of the sensuous. *Tikkun, 18*(5).
3. Ibid. (p. 35).

4. Ibid. (p. 35).

5. Among the many writers who have written about the hidden curriculum are David Purpel, Henry Giroux, Maxine Greene, Jean Anyon, Peter McLaren, Phillip Jackson, Michael Apple, and C. A. Bowers.

6. Barbara Ehrenreich. (2001). *Nickel and dimed*. New York: Henry Holt.

7. See, for example, Stephen J. Gould. (1981). *The mismeasure of man*. New York: Norton. Also see Joe L. Kincheloe, Shirley R. Steinberg, and Aaron D. Gresson III (eds.). (1996). *The bell curve examined*. New York: St. Martin's Press.

8. Kristan Morrison. (2004). *Progressive educators' assumptions, structures and practices: Critical pedagogy and the Albany Free School*. Unpublished doctoral dissertation. UNC at Greensboro.

9. Elizabeth Dodson Gray. (1989). The culture of separated desks. In Carol Pearson, Donna L. Shavlik, & Judith G. Touchtone (eds.), *Educating the majority: Women challenge tradition in higher education*. American Council on Education.

10. Ibid.

11. Christopher Lasch. (1977). *Haven in a heartless world*. New York: Basic Books.

12. See, for example, Stanley Aronowitz and Henry Giroux. (1993). *Education still under siege*. Toronto, Ontario: OISE Press.

13. Mara Sapon-Shevin. (2004). *Lessons in peace*. Syracuse, NY: Syracuse Cultural Workers.

4
vvvvvvv

In Search of Community

On the first day of the new school year, all the teachers in one private school received the following note from their principal:

Dear Teacher:

I am a survivor of a concentration camp. My eyes saw what no man should witness:

Gas chambers built by learned engineers.

Children poisoned by educated physicians.

Infants killed by trained nurses.

Women and babies shot and burned by high school and college graduates.

So, I am suspicious of education.

My request is: Help your students become human. Your efforts must never produce learned monsters, skilled psychopaths, educated Eichmanns.

Reading, writing, and arithmetic are important only if they serve to make our children more humane.

Any attempt to address the crisis of meaning in our society must certainly be concerned with the need for community. We have, in the previous chapters, looked at the way our culture, and schools in particular, create a world in which we emphasize competition, separation, and isolation. It is not surprising that so many people feel alone and disconnected from the society in which they live. And it is no shock that there is a growing hunger for communities where people can feel recognized and needed.[1] This is not a problem that we face only here in the United States. It is clear that there is, in many countries and places, a yearning to feel a part of something that is larger than the very small sphere of our private lives. Whether this takes the form of a resurgent nationalism in some situations, religious communities with almost a tribal identity elsewhere, or groups that unite people behind the commonality of race, ethnicity, or geographical region, it is quite clear that our atomizing and fragmented world is producing alternative forms of human relationships that give individuals the feeling of being part of something that transcends their own limited lives.[2] It is, I hope, clear from what I wrote in the last chapter that the "culture of separated desks" must surely produce human beings who feel an emotional dis-ease with their lives. The price of worldly success in our materialistic, consumer-driven, competitive world is increasingly experienced, even by those who have done well by it, as being spiritually too high. If we are to educate a new generation so that their lives are richer and more purposeful than our present dominant values would allow, we must ensure that the desire for, and the capacity to build, meaningful communities is an integral part of what education is all about. For many in our world this desire to find our way back into deep connection and engagement with others who can share our dreams, hopes, and concerns is the most pressing issue of our time.

A PARENT'S DILEMMA

Several years ago I had deep personal reasons to reflect on this issue.[3] My daughter was approaching a transition point in her education, and it confronted me with the very questions and issues I am concerned with here. As I struggled with the issue about what kind of high school my daughter was to attend after her elementary and middle school years were over, I tried to sort out some of the complexities and dilemmas that, I believe, continue to confront parents. These speak to the meaning and place of community in our complex and increasingly diverse society. They are issues that do, of course, concern all of us as citizens in a democratic society. They are the same kind of issues that emerge around questions of home schooling, ethnically based schools, and religious or parochial schooling. I would like to return here to some of my thoughts and reflections at that time (now about 7 years ago) as a way of uncovering and clarifying what it should mean for us to affirm the importance of community in the lives of our children, as well as our own lives.

I remember well thinking that the fifth grade at my daughter's B'nai Shalom Day School had arrived far more rapidly than I had wanted. And I would now have to seriously confront my own commitments to public education, and to Jewish education, and along with this, my ambivalence about private schooling and the privileges of social class. And I would have to think a lot more about the rootlessness that besets so much of postmodern America versus the comforts and security of the private community offered by my daughter's Jewish day school. Although I was concerned with the bigger moral, spiritual, and social issues (part of what we academics get paid to do!), as we are here, I also tried not to forget that in the end there was a real life at issue here: in this case, my 11-year-old daughter Sarah and where she should spend her sixth grade, and the grades after that.

We lived in Greensboro, North Carolina. The Jewish community there exists as a very small island in an overwhelmingly dominant Christian milieu. Although, for us, this city provided a comfortable and safe place to raise our child, to grow up Jewish there is certainly a minority experience. However, I might add, in today's somewhat more cosmopolitan world, it was far from the culturally marginalizing and politely silent experience I had, growing up Jewish in England in the 1950s. Now the local TV stations wished us a happy Chanukah, and the downtown Christmas decorations were referred to as a "Festival of Lights." The Jewish school my daughter attended offered kindergarten through eighth grade. It was, in many ways, a lovely institution. It provided a warm and nurturing environment where Jewish holidays and the Sabbath were richly and joyously celebrated, and the Hebrew language was in daily use. Its Judaism was of the nondogmatic kind, and it affirmed the vision of *Tikkun Olam*—the healing and repair of the world. Sarah certainly found much delight and meaning in being educated there—a place that sustained her spirit, not oppressed it.

In choosing this school, I wanted my daughter's heart and mind to be shaped by an experience in Jewish tradition that would give her lifelong connection to our cultural and religious traditions. I make no claim that there wasn't something selfish about this decision. Such an education would ensure my continuing ability to recognize an important part of my own self in my daughter's being (a natural, if not always laudable, part of most parents' desires). Indeed, the decision was richly rewarded; she absorbed not only some of the knowledge and culture of Jewish life but, more significantly, its emotional texture and feel. She sensed its importance and its beauty. Because of the school, the joys and significance of Jewish life belonged not just to the private, weekend or evening sphere of family life, but also to the arena of a larger shared community. Jewish life existed for Sarah not merely in the home or synagogue, but vibrantly, in the everyday world of her daily existence. Jewishness became more than an abstract set of ideas and, instead, the living vehicle through which my daughter could construct her identity and articulate her ethical and spiritual commitments. Such an education was a matter of both the heart and mind, and only an environment that was flooded with the resonance of Jewish memory and experience could nurture it. I knew that this deeper sense of value about Jewish life was not available in the larger Christian (although public) world. It required a context in which it was integrated into a community's daily practice—one that drew from the moral and spiritual meanings of her people's historical wisdom. The "thick" texture of Jewish life—the pervasive sounds of the Hebrew language, the smell of challah bread on Friday, the Chassidic melodies or niggunim, the *benching* or blessings after eating—was the curriculum on which was built a self that would contain an enduring joy and commitment to Jewish life.

Of course, the appreciation for this marvelous education was, for me, always mixed with some trepidation. I knew, for example, that the intensity of this experience held the potential danger of a *shtetl* consciousness—that is, a parochialism or narrowness that shuns anything foreign or different. Such a mind set is one that has distrust of anything not Jewish, and a dogmatic belief about having the right answer to each and every question. All of this is too familiar in our world of growing religious orthodoxies, with their intolerance of other faiths and cultures and their unquestioning conviction about their own correctness. Actually, B'nai Shalom worked hard at developing a sense of responsibility and concern for others in our world, and at celebrating the values of human connectedness. Still, the school was a sheltered community separated from much that confronted other kids. Its selectivity as a Jewish and predominately middle- and upper-middle-class institution ensured that it was a secure and cohesive community that was appealing to many parents for precisely that reason. It was a gated community that provided a privileged and protected space for their cherished offspring.

THE EROSION OF PUBLIC LIFE

This all provided me cause to ponder hard regarding my decision. In my struggle to decide the fate of my fifth-grade daughter, I was mindful of the desperate need to sustain the promise of public life in this country. The withdrawal of the middle class from public institutions is the certain vehicle for the demoralization and decline of those institutions. The turn toward more individualistic lifestyles and privatized institutions promoted by conservative governments over the 20 years, as well the consumerist culture, has turned the public spaces increasingly into ones of neglect and decay. Whether in health care, housing, transportation, or education, the story is one of double standards—where publicly provided institutions or systems are synonymous with the poor, and where standards are increasingly inferior as compared to those found in the private domain. In wrestling with whether to send my daughter to public school, I felt compelled to weigh my own moral responsibility as to whether I am to be part of the flight from our public world to the safety and privileges of a private, middle-class institution. My own commitment to a progressive vision of society demanded from me a commitment to those public institutions where we may share, at least to some degree, our lives and resources with those who inhabit economic, cultural, or racial worlds quite different from my own. It has been ironic that those conservatives who have often been the loudest in their condemnation of the decline of community and the need for an ethic of social responsibility have pursued agendas that have sought to allow the standards and ethics of the market place to exert ever more dominance in our social, economic, and cultural lives. In working to ensure a world in which private interests and profit are less and less hindered by responsibility to the larger community, the free-marketers have helped create a society that more and more resembles a predatory jungle—a place in which each individual concerns him- or herself with personal needs and interest, not those we hold in common.

Sadly, it is often only when cuts are made to services or benefits that are felt directly by individuals that we are awakened to what is happening on a broader level. The effort to privatize Social Security is another representation of this, as an "all in it together" form of social insurance is replaced by the mentality in which we each must take care of our own futures as aging members of society. Meanwhile, a bunker mentality spreads that calls for a social ethic of each for him- or herself; individualism, separateness, and isolation frame our disposition toward the rest of the world. All of this has been given added impetus by corporate behavior, with its proliferation of layoffs, downsizings, and closings, and the greedy, selfish, and often illegal actions of executives and managers. It is a world that has mocked any notion of obligation or commitment to workers, consumers, or the general community. Nothing really counts here except the hunt for immediate profits. Public accountability has been a barrier to be subverted by whatever means necessary. Yet in spite of all this, I believe that there is still a deep hunger for communal life and the public good in America. Despite the shift to the Right, large majorities continue to affirm the importance of protecting our environment, maintaining investments in public libraries, schools, and cultural resources, and ensuring the availability of health care for all.[4] Even the concern with protecting the "flag" is, I believe, an expression of the concern for community (although this is often a community that tries to stifle critique of government and free debate of national policy). Behind all of it can be heard a cry for a society in which our shared concerns, not just our private interests, are honored, and where there is a strong sense of the public good instantiated in our civic world and in our social institutions.

The political discourse that has sought to achieve these ends is not without its own conflicts and contradictions. It is clear, for example, that many people subscribe to the notion of smaller, less wasteful government, but also support a state that ameliorates the failures, hazards, and dangers of the free market. In this sense the state is, paradoxically, both the focus of much popular anger and also the repository of much of our needs and aspirations as a community. It irks us with its costs and intrusiveness, but it also instantiates our collective responsibilities and obligations. For all its flaws, the state embodies some notion of a shared purpose; its ultimate client, we want to believe, is the public good and the national community. Perhaps this paradox helps explain the anguish and anger around the question of supporting "our" troops when they are off fighting a war. For many, whatever the reasons for going to war (whether it is legitimate national defense, or the attempt to further enrich corporate interests or assert political power), the soldiers risking their lives are part of the national "family" and as such need to be given our full emotional support. Obviously, for others, whatever the sacrifices of these men and women, the legitimacy of the war they are fighting cannot be ignored. And those who object to the war are easily painted into the corner of being insensitive and unsupportive of those who share our national community.

PUBLIC SCHOOLS
AND THE DEMOCRATIC COMMUNITY

Aside from these issues of peace and war, perhaps nowhere has the struggle around the question of community been more contentious than around the institution of public education. Indeed, all of our societal schizophrenia around questions of the private and public, equity and the distribution of wealth, democracy, and capitalism are in evidence there. In its most ideal rendering, public schooling represents a space where all of our children may be educated: a place where the rights of citizenship take precedence over the privileges or disadvantages of social and economic life. Understood in this way, public education becomes a crucial element in the making of a democratic community. Public education brings together in one setting (so it is hoped by those who argue for such a vision) all children, regardless of background, so that they may acquire the sense of belonging and the cultural literacy that are the requisites for full participation in this community. It is well documented that public education falls very far short of this ideal. For many children, and their parents, the schools reflect the same racial and other social inequalities that divide the rest of our society.[5] Indeed, schools often reinforce the terrible obstacles to real and full economic, cultural, and political participation in this society. Sadly, of course, the reality of public schools has always been a long way from its democratic promise. The fundamental ideal of a place where the offspring of all citizens might meet and come together as a community has always been upset by the harsh realities of privilege, inequity, and racism. The historic struggles to eradicate the effects of a segregated system of public education are well known. Less obvious have been the continuing pernicious effects of class and race in maintaining schools vastly different in their resources, funding, expectations of students, and educational climate. Jonathan Kozol,[6] among others, vividly documented the horrendous conditions that beset schools in poor and underfunded districts, producing debilitating and demoralizing environments for kids. This reality, which undermines and belies the public school as a vehicle for promoting a civic community, mirrors the increasing polarization of wealth and opportunity found in our wider society. Urban schools, with their violence, high dropout rates, and low morale, exist as altogether different institutions from those in suburban areas that function as conduits to good colleges and economic well-being. Social and economic apartheid like this is quite clearly incompatible with any meaningful idea of a democratic community.

Social and economic privilege and exclusion are not the only problems that faces us as we seek community. One of the most difficult and perplexing issues that confronts educators is the growing awareness that such a community does not mean sameness—indeed, sameness or uniformity has usually killed the energy and involvement of many students who see their own lives and experiences far removed from what schools attempt to teach them. There is an increasing recognition of the ways that education has denied the contribution and presence of many kinds of people; whether because of class or race or ethnicity or gender or religion or nationality, it has become clear just how much we have ignored or invalidated the knowledge and traditions of others—those who fall outside the majority norms of the culture. As educators we have come to see how this process demeans and silences our students, as the classroom becomes a place that is quite foreign to their homes, neighborhood, or community.[7] It takes only a cursory look at many schools to see how education affirms the knowledge and experiences of some young people, and silences and marginalizes that of others. In this regard, the emergence of a multicultural awareness in our schools is an important and liberating phenomenon. It is certainly a mark of progress that children are being taught to question the notion that "Columbus discovered America" or that the West was "opened up" by European settlers, with all of its ethnocentric assumptions about the meaning of civilization; it is progress also that history, social studies, and English are beginning to be taught in more expansive and inclusive ways. Still, even where there are good-faith efforts, multiculturalism too often becomes trivialized—a matter of feasts and fiestas. It offers a very superficial appreciation indeed of what difference has meant to communities often denigrated or excluded by those in the mainstream of society. Yet whatever its limitations, these efforts represent real cracks in the wall of cultural prejudices and assumptions that have confronted generations of young people, shutting out or silencing those whose language, traditions, history, beliefs, and experience seem to exist on the margins of the society we live in.

So here the consideration over my daughter's schooling takes another turn. For quite apart from my concerns about forsaking our world of public spaces and institutions, there are other dilemmas. Even where difference is celebrated, I know that the texture of the particular cultures presented by our public schools is usually shallow. For my daughter, some mention of Chanukah, or reading a book on the Holocaust, hardly comes close to matching the ethnically rich, joyful, evocative, and full experience that is available to her in the limited enclave of her parochial school. Only in that environment does Jewishness become a form of life that colors moral expression, gives texture to historical commemoration, offers the time for soulful reflection, and adequately celebrates the days and seasons of the calendar.

GROWING UP IN AN UNCERTAIN AGE

The issue for me as a parent is not today (thankfully) about giving my daughter the strength and resilience to withstand anti-Semitism, as it would have been in other situations and times. It is about the moral, spiritual, and emotional consequences of our postmodern society. The society we have entered is one in which clear-cut barriers and boundaries in so many areas of our lives have eroded or even collapsed. Our age is one of uncertainty, flux, and ambivalence, in which little seems absolutely certain or fixed.

Who we are seems labile and fluid; borders that once marked distinctions between nations or ethnicities have become porous; personal identities can be reworked and remade; rules and truths appear relative; what we know depends on where we stand, and who the knower is determines what is known; beauty and aesthetic value are a matter of social preference; age-old religious faiths can be melded with traditions that were hitherto quite foreign; and moral values require constant reinterpretation and adaptation to a particular cultural ethos. Even things that hitherto appeared permanently defined, such as gender, now are seen as having boundaries that can be crossed, and sexuality can be bent in many directions. Indeed, our very physical being can now, with the help of cosmetic medicine, be reconstituted and remade.

There is much to celebrate in all of this. The unfixing of boundaries, truths, moral certitudes, and firm distinctions has given us the promise of a world that is more open, flexible, tolerant, and free. Yet there is also a price to pay for our postmodern attitudes—one that has had some traumatic consequences for how we, and especially our children, can be expected to conduct our lives. In this, conservative critique finds a powerful resonance in the anguish and uncertainty of many parents across the political and cultural spectrum. It is, for example, quite clear that the desire for discipline and structure in the raising of the young now hits a powerful chord across a wide range of parents. This desire emanates from the increasing feeling of a world in which a moral and spiritual rootlessness is the prevailing sensibility. For many people there is the sense of having been cast adrift from the stabilities of place, family, and normative communities. The postmodern world is one in which individuals increasingly feel as if they are in exile—existentially and morally afloat in a world that constantly disrupts and dissolves any sense of permanent connection in an enduring web of meaning and community.[8] Indeed, far from acknowledging the pain and dislocation of so much alienation, we are urged by Madison Avenue to enjoy the tumultuous ride. Our culture urges us to always find what's novel, "revolutionary," exciting, and different. In the world of the TV remote our attention span is short; our capacity to switch "channels" is made easy; the options seem endless; and our expectation for immediate gratification is unlimited.

In ways that distort the broad concern for the disintegration of ethical life, and the erosion of the sense of social responsibility, talk of tradition, values, and discipline is mistakenly understood as only the language of the political Right. Yet a world in which all that is solid melts—religious belief, identity, community, jobs, marriages, and more—this is a matter that confronts all of us. Nowhere is this more painfully so than in regard to the upbringing of our children. Daily, all of us, especially parents, are forced to confront the fallout from the postmodern condition—the self-destructiveness of adolescents, suicide, drugs, alcoholism, compulsive dieting, widespread depression and generalized rage, and a cynical detachment from social institutions. However manipulative or distorting it can be, conservative discourse and evangelical Christianity, or other orthodox religious traditions, do speak to the widespread anguish that so many parents feel in these uncertain and confusing times.

For myself (being neither Christian nor sympathetic to the political Right), in this society of disintegration, rootlessness, and shallow spectacle, my daughter's Jewish schooling offered, I felt, a sense of real and durable meaning not easily found elsewhere in the culture. Here was the hope of nurturing an identity grounded in the Jews' long history—a history rich with the struggles for a world of justice and freedom. Here, too, was the possibility of transmitting what it means to be a "stranger in the land"—developing personalities empathic to the pain of exclusion and human indignity. Jewish "memory" roots us in a temporal community of unbelievable human tragedy, suffering, courage, and the will for communal survival. Such history makes powerful claims on the living—an insistence on the vision of *Tikkun Olam,* the repair and healing of our world: to act as if we ourselves had experienced the bondage of Egypt and were impelled to seek the end of all forms of human enslavement (something we are still engaged in). Far from the Disney World theme park in which history is shown as amusement and spectacle, or the dreary recitation of remote facts in the typical high school history class, Jewish pedagogy offered history as the long struggle for spiritual and physical survival. Becoming aware of, and learning to identify with, this history provided a student with a compass through which to orient his or her life around a powerful moral and spiritual vision. History was about much more than things that had happened in the past. It became a living guide to the present, and the way to find significant purpose in our lives. Such purpose could be found through our participation with others in a community that sought to make our world a more just, loving, and compassionate one.

The spiritual sensibility forged in this historical awareness is one that continually demands that we create and recognize boundaries—distinctions within our world between ways of living that express the sacred and those that are profane. Judaism is a religion of everyday life that constantly seeks to make sacred the ordinary, taken-for-granted acts of daily existence. Those of us who grew up in Orthodox homes know the rigidity and frequently stultifying nature of *halakhic* (or orthodox) Judaism. Yet at the same time, one can find here a powerful rejoinder to the dehumanization and degradation of our common world—one that insists that we seek to make holy human life and behavior, as well as the whole environment that makes life possible and sustains it. Certainly Judaism, like all religions, can become dogmatic and reified: a series of mindless rituals and practices. Yet I also could see, within my daughter's education, the importance of a spiritual ambience that provided a set of deep, some might say ultimate, meanings to children. Such meanings pointed to the limits, boundaries, and obligations that would structure our relationship to the world as one of respect, consciousness of the needs of others, and responsibility toward them. Without this structure, human life can only become predatory, uncaring, and destructive. There are, of course, many routes to this kind of spiritual being (sometimes religiously based and sometimes not), but its importance to the education of our children cannot be ignored. The future of our civilization, and of the earth itself, is in the balance. We cannot leave the ethical and spiritual developmental needs of our children to the glitz, superficiality, and materialism of the popular culture. Sarah was fortunate that the ambience of her school was one with a strong sense of celebration and festivity—one that sought to teach the young something about experiencing lives of joy, wonder, and appreciation. It is, I believe, in this synthesis of communal identification, social responsibility, and joyful mindfulness that we can find the beginnings of a meaningful response to the rampant cynicism and disconnection of our culture.

Of course, the school was much less than perfect: too bound up in competition and individual achievement, and too concerned with grades and test scores—like most other schools. And it was too cautious in questioning the injustices of our world, or developing a critical mind that challenged the assumptions that undergird the way our society functions. But beyond the need for our young to be educated to enable them to question and challenge their world (the lifeblood of a democratic culture that I return to in the next chapter), there is a need for a sense of hope and possibility that things can be changed, even radically transformed. Without this sense, one may ask, why bother? And this sense of hope, I believe, happens best in an environment where we feel a deeply shared sense of connected fate. For Jews, there is our long history of struggle in a harsh world of brutality and oppression, and yet, in spite of this, there is the continued hope for a better world. Without this communal affirmation of the possibility of change, there is, I think, little emotional capacity to act in the world—at least not where acting means trying to transform the moral character of our lives and the shape of our society. There is only disconnected apathy and cynicism—the world of the young so well reflected in a host of Hollywood movies specifically aimed at the youth market. These are not easy times. Educational communities that might offer this sense of connectedness and sharing, around a common set of moral commitments and spiritual purpose, are not easy to find or sustain in this time of uncertain vision, and where the seductions of the dominant culture are so strong. Yet the need to find a place in which our commitments are shared, and our identities confirmed, is the necessary ground for lives in which we feel inspired and moved to contribute to the repair and betterment of our world. However imperfect the institution, I was consoled that my daughter's educational experience provided her with some of the resources she would need to become a moral, spiritual, and social agent in the world.

DIMENSIONS OF THE LOVING COMMUNITY

For those readers who may be interested, my daughter stayed at her Jewish school till the completion of eighth grade. She then transferred to a public high school. She is, at the time of writing, a freshman at Brandeis University, where she plans to major in Jewish studies. I have traced this personal journey because I thought it would help to illuminate what it might mean to be concerned about issues of community and identity in the education of young people. I hope that I have made it clear just how important nurturing a sense of belonging to a community should be as we think about our vision for education—a vision that speaks strongly to the need for meaning and purpose in our lives There are, I believe, terrible social and personal consequences when a society places such a disproportionate emphasis on individual goals and success as we, in the United States, now do. It is only through community that we are able to meet those three dimensions of human existence that are essential for our well-being, and we ignore this at our children's, and our own, peril.

In the first place, the community provides the means through which we may receive the recognition of our presence, and affirmation of our value, in the world. I am disturbed at how often students in my classes will declare that they believe, and hope, that this sense of personal value is something they can attain on their own. In other words, they have learned to see the need for others to recognize and affirm them as a sign of weakness or inadequacy. Their goal is one of emotional self-sufficiency. I point out to them that such a quest flies in the face of what it means to be human. I say to them, we are "made" for relationship. The need for others who provide us with the mirror through which we come to know who we are is a quintessential aspect of our humanity. Far from a weakness, it marks the inseparability of individual lives from our social bonds and connections. The philosopher and social critic Cornel West noted that "our identity is who we are in relationship." I tell my students that what ought to be cause for celebration and joy—that we are, as human beings, bound to one another for the very basic need of affirming that each of us is wanted and needed in the world—is regarded by some of them as something scary and unreliable. It is, I continue, a sad commentary on the culture that we live in, and on their education. So many of their social interactions are competitive dog fights to show who can outshine the other. So many of their relations with others are shaped by the sense that there is a winnowing out going on as to who will get the kudos and who will be ignored. It is hardly surprising, I continue, that relationships are viewed not as the source of affirmation, but as an unreliable, even dangerous, venue in which to risk their emotional well-being. Most of the students love to watch those so-called TV reality shows where groups of young adults are brought together to vie with one another: to show who can survive the longest in an aggressively competitive environment. Such shows deliberately provide a forum to demonstrate the utterly deceitful, insensitive, and hurtful ways in which people act as they seek to satisfy their own selfish wants. For many of my students it is this image of how social groups interact that provides an apt metaphor for human relationships, rather than the community that seeks to positively affirm the presence and value of all who are present. Perhaps the voyeuristic pleasure in watching these shows is in the way they provide an opportunity to share in a kind of vicarious "community" of sufferers, in which we can reexperience with others what it feels like to be abused or put down in this way. Perhaps, too, we can experience some guiltless satisfaction at our feeling of loathing for the despicable conduct of the eventual winner. Despite all of this, it is interesting that when my students are asked about the kind of schooling they would like to create for the youngsters they will eventually teach, their answer is almost always the kind of schooling that resembles the loving community—a place where all children are fully recognized and their unique presence unconditionally valued.

Second, communities that are serious about this unconditional valuing of all who they comprise (is there any other kind of real community?) must also be places that ensure that they provide care and support for everyone. Compassion is inseparable from real community. To recognize all within a community is to be cognizant of the different needs that each child or individual brings to the table. In this sense, communities are much more than declarations of words. They are places that share and distribute resources so that everyone, to the maximum extent possible, has what he or she needs to realize his or her full possibilities. Meaningful community, in other words, cannot be separated from social justice. Material issues are often paramount here—adequacy of food, clothing, medical care, transportation, and so on. In the case of a private school there is the thorny problem of who can afford to attend, and how one community's needs affect, or pull resources, from others. At all schools there is the need to assure the availability of truly adequate educational resources to all students. The varying circumstances of each individual must be addressed so that no one falls short of what he or she needs to thrive. For educators, this issue of the unequal economic and social circumstances of students and their families certainly casts a dark shadow over our hopes and desire to see the school as a genuine community. Community is both a place that asserts the fundamentally equal value of all lives, and, at the same time, a place that compassionately addresses us as beings with differences that must not be treated as sources of humiliation or unfair disadvantage. Perhaps (and despite its disingenuous practical manifestations) the idea of legislation that seeks to "leave no child behind" resonates with this appealing vision of America as a compassionate community that cares for all its young members, including those who have had least. Of course, we must always remain on guard against the misuse or exploitation of these noble sentiments for political gain. But these are issues I leave for now. I return to them later in the book, when I discuss more fully the issue of social justice and our vision of education.

The third dimension of community is one that provides the sense that we are on a shared journey—a journey of the spirit that provides us with resources to form a compelling vision for meaningful lives. Unquestionably this is the most difficult dimension in the search for community—especially in the context of education. I know from my own experience that among educational administrators there is a growing awareness about the importance of caring and supportive environments for children (an awareness that I believe has grown with the increasing number of women in the field of educational administration). Indeed, especially at the younger age levels, there are schools that do some wonderful things to promote the sense of being a caring and loving community. But the notion of schools being communities of meaning is a much more complex and challenging proposition. It is one that immediately raises questions about the fundamental purpose of education, and also questions about cultural and social values. What are our goals as educators? What is it that we wish to convey to our students about living purposeful and meaningful lives? Do the usual school goals—better attendance, more quiescent behavior, improved grades, higher test scores, more students going on to college, and so on—represent an adequate configuration of purposeful goals for young lives? Is it possible to seriously address questions of meaning and purpose without challenging our larger values as a culture? And would not such reflection inevitably take us into the thorny territory of morality and spiritual matters? The short answer to all of these questions is, yes. A school that seeks to become a community of meaning must certainly find itself addressing the kind of things that are now, for the most part, ignored or buried under the weight of accepted and conventional educational concerns. It means having to embark on a difficult path of reflection—one that demands courage, honesty, and imagination. It certainly requires leadership from those who understand that we need a very different vision for what it means to lead a purposeful life that takes us far from the banal conformities of money, career, and success that are so very inadequate to the existential and social crises facing humanity in the 21st century.

When we say that something is meaningful we are making a statement about connections. Something becomes meaningful to us because it seems to connect things together in our minds. It is as if we have drawn lines between the dots and spaces in a newspaper photograph so that we perceive it not as a set of separate and formless marks on a page, but as a whole, related image that tells an intelligible story. Another example is the lines that comprise a television screen image, which when viewed up close become unrelated visual effects but at a distance make up a connected whole that conveys something we can relate to as a familiar image of our sensible world. There is something that seems to be innate in the human drive to find or make meaning. It seems that we are, in some way, compelled to take the separate and nominally unrelated fragments we encounter in our world, and find ways to connect them together so that they can be understood as whole and related phenomena. Indeed, it seems as if we cannot rest or feel satisfied until things are seen in their entirety as a form whose threads reveal some interrelated story or narrative. Meaning, or at least the search for meaning, compels us; the incoherent, the dissonant, and the fragmented leave us disturbed and troubled.

In a parallel way, when we say our lives are meaningful it is because we feel ourselves to be connected to some larger worldly or cosmic purpose. We see our lives' energies expended in some way that furthers the possibilities of others' lives or, perhaps, some larger historical movement or universal process. Purpose or meaning represents the ability to transcend what is, inevitably, our own small and insignificant space in the scheme of things, and to see our own finite being as part of a much larger story. It is a story that might tell of our connections to family, religious community, ethnicity, nation, or to the earth and the chain of life itself. It might place us in the struggle for a more just world or for more compassionate and ethical lives. It might also, of course, tell of conquest and domination of others, of glorious empires, of blood and race, or of being God's elect or chosen collectivity. Whatever form this transcending narrative takes, this quest for meaning compels us. It is the quintessential human capacity—a need, we know, that if not adequately responded to will produce in us a sense of futility and despair about our lives. To say that life is meaningless is to declare that there is little purpose in the energies we must expend to live. This is the spiritual death that precedes our physical death. One does not need a degree in clinical psychology to recognize how filled our world is with the casualties of this condition: depression, anxiety, "burn-out," inertia, and apathy are all its manifestations.

The more we live, think, and act in individualistic ways, the more we live in ways that separate us from others, the more shrunken is our sense of meaning. Lives that exist in spheres of narrow or egoistical pursuits can only produce a diminished sense of purpose. We have come to recognize that it is the widening and deepening of connections among human beings, as well as to the natural world that is our ultimate home, that augments the meaningfulness of our lives. The more we can see and experience our lives within their web of connections to others, the more purposeful our existence is felt to be. To recognize these connections is to fill us with the sense of wonder and appreciation for life; it also galvanizes us to fight against those forces in our world that act in ways that threaten or destroy these life-giving relations. Cultures that are predicated on encouraging the drive for self-interest and self-gain must be seen as cultures in crisis. They are cultures that are pushing human beings toward lives of spiritual emptiness and despair. In an earlier chapter I tried to describe this crisis of meaning in our culture. The relentless emphasis on individualistic goals and ambitions, the endless pursuit of private wealth and material acquisitiveness, the constant competition with others in our professional and personal lives that undermines trusting relations with others, can only produce a greater and greater sense of alienation or disconnection from others. It is a culture of shallow meanings that provides little that speaks to, or nourishes appreciation of, more enduring or compelling purposes in our lives.

THE SEARCH FOR COMMUNITIES OF MEANING

In the face of this, there is no more significant function for education than to provide a space within which meaning and purpose can be discerned. The emptiness of our culture gives particular urgency to this task. In my daughter's education I have described something of what I believe is the enormous importance of belonging to a community of meaning within which one can begin to appreciate a moral and social purposes to our lives that transcends the limited, frequently damaging, concerns of the dominant culture. Such a community becomes the link between the concerns of one's own life, and the struggles of a larger group of people to spiritually and physically survive. The community enables us to see our own life as something much more than an isolated, brief moment of consciousness, simply here to satisfy our egoistical wants. Within this community of meaning I can see my own life as a continuing link in a chain that connects me to countless others who have felt similar responsibilities, perceived and attended to similar challenges, and experienced, celebrated, or commemorated familiar events and moments with similar rituals. The community of meaning replaces the self-absorbed human being with one whose concerns are focused on the good of others. Instead of separation and detachment from other human beings, it offers the richness of mutual support and shared purposes and goals. Finally, it provides a vehicle for realizing that the deep sense of meaning in our lives comes not from the results of any short-lived spasm of personal ambition and gain, but from joining with others in continuing the work and struggles of previous generations to better the human condition. Some have argued that this community of meaning is nothing more than an act of human imagination. Of course there is truth to this. Yet it is clear that human existence demands precisely this exercise of imagination, because without it there can be no moral life, and no enduring sense of connection to others is possible. The real issue is not imagination—we humans cannot live without it anymore than we can live without food. No, the issue is what kinds of tales we tell about who we are and how we ought to live. The stories we live by determine just what kind of world we will inhabit and how we will treat each other.

It is an interesting phenomenon of recent times that schools (along with many other organizations and institutions) are more and more drawn into the idea of developing, for themselves, mission statements that lay out the creed and the goals of the institution. In terms of developing what I have called here a community of meaning, this is, I believe, a good and helpful step forward. It does imply that those who come together to work within an educational setting will attempt to articulate some shared, binding vision that animates everyone's plans and actions. Such a vision does not attempt to supply detail or specificity to every aspect of the complex life of a school. It does, however, usually try to provide an overarching social and ethical framework within which each person can attempt to give some larger sense of meaning and direction to what they do. It provides a template against which teachers, administrators, and students may ask themselves how they contribute to the broader goals and purposes of the institution. Sadly, however, these mission statements more frequently resemble the banalities of a Hallmark card, rather than offering a strong and compelling statement that gives purpose and direction to our everyday work. And, like the cards we buy, they are more often filled with soothing words that are carefully chosen to conform to conventional wisdom rather than challenging the dominant meanings and values. As I have tried to argue in this book, to talk seriously today about questions of purpose is to confront the spiritually empty and morally corrosive effects of our consumer culture and the many forms of human degradation and suffering that blight our world. To evade this challenge is to turn our mission statement, as well anything else we attempt to do concerned with finding meaning and purpose, into a bland mush that supplies us with little that really sustains or energizes us. It represents a refusal to engage, in a serious way, with the critical concerns that face us, and our children, at this moment in history.

If we are to be serious about creating our community of meaning we will, perhaps, have to see ourselves also creating, what the theologian Sharon Welch called "communities of resistance."[9] Such communities, she said, provide the social, moral, and intellectual support needed to challenge the dominant values and ethos of our culture. The pressure of cultural and ideological conformity about what our children need to be concerned with and pursue in their lives—good colleges, lucrative careers, affluent lifestyles, money, good looks, and so on—makes it a difficult struggle to sustain an alternative view of what is important, and how we should behave and treat one another. In my daughter's school it was clear how much division really existed in the school between the education of the "heart" and the education of the "mind." The former attempted to convey to the students the wisdom and understanding, derived from long Jewish experience, about the importance of *Tikkun Olam*—of repairing and healing our world through social justice, treating every human life with dignity, providing compassion and respect for the stranger, and the importance of nonviolence in resolving conflicts. The latter typically meant something very different, with its emphasis on individual success, personal achievement, and its attention to hierarchies of status and reward. Cultural dominance, or hegemony as it is sometimes referred to, ensured that the latter values were preeminent in the school. Parental anxieties, although sympathetic to the education of the heart, ensured that the school did not stray too far from the culture of individual success. It is clear that to sustain a community of meaning that offers a real alternative to the values and meanings that currently dominate our culture will require parents and educators whose concern about the moral, spiritual, and social development of young people is truly central to the vision of the school. Such a community will knowingly and courageously articulate a vision that offers a significant alternative to the present direction of both school and society, and will work to ground their everyday work in this vision.

Of course, the latter may seem like a very far-fetched possibility at this time of intensifying concern with tests and academic performance. We can be in no doubt how difficult it would be to develop such schools with these transformative goals in the face of all the political, administrative, and ideological obstacles. Still, I am writing here about the longer range and broader struggle that all of us, as parents, teachers, teacher-educators, and citizens, must consider if we are to have a sense of the direction we need to be traveling, and the issues that we must raise if we are to engage in what Rabbi Michael Lerner[8] calls a politics of meaning in our culture. It is important to remind ourselves that our time is one in which communities of meaning that seek to resist and challenge where our world is going have had, and will continue to have, an important influence on many aspects of our lives. And even where they do not achieve all their goals, they are affecting our world in important ways. We can see this politics of meaning at work in numerous important social movements from antiracist and civil rights struggles to those virtual global "communities" fighting for a more democratic, equitable, and environmentally sane economic and political order. Each represents a challenge to the way we define our values, priorities, and concerns as a culture. Perhaps this helps us understand better the push for separate Black schools in our society. Those who advocate for such schools have in mind not only raising the poor achievement of many African-American children in our public schools. There is also a wish to create more "Afrocentric" educational environments for students that can redress the debilitating cultures that so many Black kids find themselves in at school—cultures that have a devastatingly destructive effect on their sense of self-worth and personal efficacy. More than this, Afrocentric education celebrates the generative vitality and creativity of the African and African-American heritage, and the contributions, so often ignored, both to American life and to world culture. It provides a very different picture of Africa and African civilizations than the jungle images so endemic to European and North American literature and popular culture. Instead, it offers a history of the rich and vibrant African cultures that slavery and colonialism destroyed. It provides a community of meaning in which members of a younger generation can see themselves as the current bearers of a history that represents an extraordinary story of physical as well as spiritual and social survival. They can come to appreciate the moral, political and spiritual power of the Black struggle for human rights and social equality—a struggle that has provided inspiration to other oppressed groups worldwide. And students can learn about, and celebrate, the traditions and practices that have sustained and nurtured this dream. This has included a social gospel in which Christianity is understood as the re-enactment of a community's struggle to escape the bondage, suffering, and degradation of enslavement and racial subjugation. It has meant communities that have survived through a remarkable history of collective support and solidarity and the "other mothering" of Black women who saw their kinship group as extending to the needs of all children within this community. And it produced the rich legacy of artistic and cultural creativity that has provided America and the world (and continues to do so) with images of consolation and survival, as well as insurgency against the oppression of the body and soul. All of this becomes part of an education that must urgently address the moral, social and spiritual development of a generation of Black youngsters who have "bought into" the dominant individualistic dreams of wealth and celebrity, or the fantasies of power through thuggish violence and underworld scams. Education here is for the mind, heart, and soul of a younger Black generation whose conventional education has offered too little in the way of shared meaning, ethical purpose, and spiritual sustenance.

In a parallel context, too, we can understand the struggle over bilingual education as something that represents much more than a discussion about the best way to teach English to non-native speakers of the language. For some in the Hispanic community the issue of the use of Spanish among students of Mexican-American or Puerto Rican origin represents a claim that this is a matter of the preservation not just of a language but a way of life. Bilingual/bicultural education, as it is called, means the opportunity for students to learn the heritage, history, traditions, and the contributions to humanity of this group. Of course, as with Afrocentric education, the educational community is seen as one that can nourish the pride of a people whose culture has been excluded or marginalized by the dominant Anglo society, and to better understand the way their lives have been shaped by the economic, cultural, and political forces that have worked against them. Such a community can empower students to overcome or resist the discrimination and injustice they will encounter through a positive sense of their past history and a renewed sense of the cultural, social, spiritual, and political values they share.

We can think, too, of others who have struggled to see education as the work of a community of care, support, and meaning. Quakers created and sustained a remarkable legacy of independent schools that, even today, offer environments that nurture students in the values of critical thought, independence of mind, an obligation to speak "truth to power," the importance of human freedom, social justice, and individual dignity. Quaker schools have continued to provide spaces that encourage young people to understand democracy, not as words on the page of a civics textbook, or abstract and legalistic-sounding declarations, but as a living and vibrant form of communal living in which each person is expected and encouraged to be a thoughtful and articulate participant in the deliberations and decisions of a community. Not least, Quakers have seen their schools as seedbeds of moral and social regeneration in a world of economic injustice, social exclusion, and material waste and irresponsibility. And they have continued to be centers of advocacy for peacemaking in a world so enamored with violence as forms of personal expression and as means to resolve conflict. It is hardly surprising that graduates of Quaker schools and colleges are disproportionately visible and active in movements of social change and transformation.

Of course, in all these schools (as in my daughter's), there is also the expectation that the education will ensure high academic achievement. The concern that students' moral and social development be matched with equal success in the conventional tests of education is, I believe, a serious tension in the pedagogic focus of these schools. Quaker schools typically draw students from educated, professional family backgrounds, and there is the expectation that, whatever else they might learn, students will get the grades and SAT scores that will enable them to move on to the country's more prestigious colleges. Schools for African-American students, by contrast, must deal with the history of an education system that has failed to ensure social and economic mobility for this group. So the argument is made that providing an affirming psychological environment and a curriculum that speaks to the lives of Black students will also enable them to overcome the disaffection and alienation that produces their poor intellectual performance in school.

Elsewhere we can identify the struggle for schools that speak to the meanings, values, and traditions of indigenous peoples and, in so doing, seem to resist this split between educating the mind and spirit. Both here in North America and in many other parts of the world there is a rising movement that demands schools that teach something other than the values and priorities of modernity to the children of native peoples. Educational advocates for such people argue that for too long, schools have been unchallenged conduits for values that stress that human development flows in one direction only—toward the concentration of economic power and higher growth; the maximization of profit at the expense of all other human concerns; an emphasis on cultural uniformity and standardization throughout the world; and an attitude toward the earth that turns it into inert matter and sees all life forms as mere fodder for the industrial process. Indigenous education demands schools that offer a very different moral and spiritual view of the universe. They start with the importance of teaching a reverence for all of nature. They reject the anthropocentric picture of the universe which puts "man's" concerns and needs at its center. Instead, the earth is viewed as a living organism, which must be treated with respect alongside all living creatures. Indeed, the earth and all living species are typically seen as emanations of a single spirit that fills the universe. We humans are indebted to all of these life forms for our own existence, and must live in ways that show our respect and gratitude to them through a careful and sensitive use of the earth's resources. We must see ourselves, at best, as stewards of nature, not its masters. Indigenous communities continue to fight to retain rights to the land and resist the appropriation of their mineral and natural resources by multinational corporations. The economic changes they have been subjected to have meant the loss of land, unemployment, growing poverty, and environmental destruction and contamination. They have had also to resist the erosion of ancient tribal traditions. The "Macdonaldization" of the world's cultures has meant the absorption of ancient tongues, beliefs, and forms of life into a single consumer-oriented market and culture. The economic and cultural consequences of this uprooting of a people's ways of life have resulted in social and psychological breakdown; violence, alcohol, and drug addictions; and high levels of suicide. For these groups, education rooted in their communities of meaning has meant the attempt to reground the lives of young people in a way of life that can provide a renewed sense of understanding, pride, and commitment in the culture and language of their people. And it attempts to nourish the hopes and vision of younger tribal members in their struggles to provide a viable and sustainable way of life.

CLOSED COMMUNITIES OF MEANING

Of course, there are others who define their educational work in terms of a community that nurtures or defends moral and spiritual meaning. Conservative Christian communities, as is well known, have withdrawn their children in large numbers from public schools, claiming the need for an education that cannot be found there. They certainly view their education as an important vehicle for shaping their community of meaning. These meanings are seen as a way of inculcating a set of moral, social, and religious beliefs that are oppositional to the cultural values that shape public life in America. In place of what are viewed as the relativistic moral values that are now dominant in American life, these Christian communities educate their children in the belief that there are clear-cut and certain rights and wrongs. As a result of this turn toward relativism there is, it is believed, permissiveness in the way we bring up kids that leaves them without a sense of ethical direction. They argue that life in this country is increasingly guided by the pursuit of short-term pleasure and immediate gratification. There needs to be, they say, a return to the traditional values that elevated the importance of work, responsibility, perseverance, and obligation. And the importance placed on change, novelty, and indulgence in our lives has produced a generation that has little sense of self-discipline or commitment. Their critique of American culture certainly resonates with many parents. Indeed, it is interesting that there is a good deal of overlap with the critique of consumer culture that is found among those on the political left with whom they do not ordinarily share much sympathy. At both ends of the political spectrum there is a belief that our culture feeds an overemphasis on materialism, an exaggerated concern with the self and little sense of personal responsibility. The conservative approach to education stresses, without apology, the need for strict discipline and respect for authority—the importance of "tough love" that imposes a rigid structure of behavior and consequences on young people, who, it is believed, must learn that appropriate behavior depends on the ability to control the sinful, immoral, and socially destructive dimensions that are always a part what it means to be human.

It is not hard to understand the relevance of these kinds of communities of meaning, and what they offer educationally. In a world that does indeed face a crisis of moral and spiritual meaning, they offer an understandable appeal to many parents in anguish about how to bring their kids up without falling prey to the problems of drug addiction, alcoholism, sexually transmitted diseases, teenage pregnancies, and self-destructive behavior. Yet there are serious problems with the education that is offered by these conservative Christian communities. Some of these problems, I should add, take us back to questions and concerns that I raised in regard to my own daughter's educational journey. There are, for example, the dangers of communities that approach the world with an unquestioned certitude. For every issue and problem there is a sure answer whose validity is vouchsafed by the sacred text. The price of such certainty is a refusal to fully open oneself to the contrary views, ideas, and knowledge of those different to oneself. Such an opening, it is believed, can only produce a "contamination" of one's worldview. In this sense, those who have views and opinions different from one's own are a threat to the correctness of the knowledge we share with others in the group. This is contrary to democratic ideas about truth and understanding, which assume that the best answer is that which emerges through the open encounter of different ideas, where each is allowed to make the most persuasive and plausible case that is possible. Conservative communities are, in this sense, prone to be closed communities that limit their engagement to others who are like them, and have little openness to others who think differently about the world and are possessed of ideas, experiences, and values that are dissimilar. Such communities are unlikely to encourage students to become too critical, or to challenge the accepted beliefs of the community. The goal is much more likely to be a conformity to, and reinforcement of, the prevailing ideas and knowledge. Such a view of education seems oppositional to a democratic worldview, which requires the cultivation of minds and hearts open to the challenge of new or different ideas, and students ready and able to exercise a critical intelligence that is unafraid to question the accepted, even hallowed, beliefs they encounter.

The problem of being closed is, of course, certainly not restricted to conservative religious communities. We have to see this as a problem, or potential problem, of all communities of meaning. All such communities are entered into, and sustained, by a degree of single-minded commitment to their rightness. And there is a short line from genuine conviction to total, undoubting adherence. The history of ideological and religious movements can leave us in no doubt that one generation's subversion of the dominant truth quickly becomes the next generation's blind loyalty to the "emergent" truth. The sad result is to view those who hold other ideas as a threat to oneself and one's fellows, and to view these others with suspicion, fear, and not infrequently hate.

Conservative educational communities also demonstrate another dimension of this separation from others that I raised earlier in the chapter. It is hard to deny that some, perhaps many, of these schools were created as a way to escape the racial integration of public schools. In this sense, such schools express a narrow notion of community far from the ideal of the diverse cultural, ethnic, religious, and economic mix that one can find in the public school world. They are like gated communities that seek to keep out anyone who does not resemble the accepted members of the community. Of course, it is not hard to discern the psychological impulses that lay behind such behavior: fear of those unlike ourselves and a sense of threat that comes from difference. There is also a desire to escape the undoubted troubles and problems that beset some of the world of public education—violence, classroom disruptions, insensitive bureaucracies, low academic expectations for many children, inadequate facilities or resources, and so on. The increasing movement toward these private academies reflects the increasing drive to deal with our needs and concerns as a nation, not through the means and institutions of the broad society, but in ways that address only limited and restricted groups of citizens. Communities are no longer about enhancing the general welfare of the society, but taking care of one select group or another. There is, indeed, a growing desire to take care of our own by withdrawing from the larger society into particular and selective institutions that may effectively address what "people like us" need. These, not surprisingly, do little for our neighbors who are unable to afford or gain admission to this more exclusive group of people. We can see this happening in health care, where, rather than a broad universal form of coverage that would apply to all citizens, there are increasingly wide differences in the kind of insurance available (if it is available at all). In social security there are proposals for "opt out" programs for those who can afford to risk their income as seniors playing the stock market—a process that would draw money off from the general pension fund. And we can see it also in the appeal of voucher programs for educating kids. Here the promise is to those parents and students attending inadequate schools that lack resources, quality teachers, and the expectations for achievement found in better off neighborhoods. Such students will be given the chance to attend more successful private or parochial schools. Unfortunately, there is a sleight of hand at work here. It is as if we can fix our public problems by privatizing them. We are asked to believe that inadequate resources, and the low expectations and hopes of kids growing up in impoverished neighborhoods, can be banished as problems by simply having the kids attend other schools. Private schools work well precisely because they are able to be selective as to who they admit. If all the previously excluded kids now had access to these schools the private advantage would no longer exist. They would have become de facto public institutions. Private answers to public problems imply, by definition, favoring a few over the many. The private is always about addressing some people's needs more than others, ensuring that one community receives privileges not available to others.[10] In the end we must decide what is the community to which belong: the narrow or exclusive one, or a broader and less restrictive one that includes adults and children whose ethnicity, economic background, and language, among other things, represent a greater human diversity reflective of the whole society to which we belong?

EDUCATIONAL LEADERSHIP

So what is to be done? A valuable development is in the fact that some of the more forward-thinking university programs that prepare educational leaders have begun to shift their emphasis from teaching administrative skills to the importance of individuals being capable of articulating an ethical and social vision for their schools. This entails potential educational leaders defining their work as something other than line managers who can fill the output prescriptions of those above them in the school bureaucracy. The changing definition of the educational leaders' role is a potentially radical one. It asks them to see the school as a community that must, with the help of all those who are stakeholders in it (teachers, staff, parents, and students), define a mission for this community that speaks to the moral, social, spiritual, and intellectual development of those they teach, as well the organizational culture they wish to create for themselves. From my own experience working with students in such a program, there are many wonderful, as well as difficult, challenges associated with this project. There is the need, for example, for students to actually begin to think about education's purposes far beyond that of raising test scores or keeping order. Students must think a lot more deeply about what an educational community is about, and, in particular, about what are the broader and deeper purposes of education. Most students realize that such questions are, in the end, really not "educational" questions at all, but moral, social, and spiritual questions. They come to see their work as, in some way, always about responding to the two fundamental questions articulated by the late educational theorist James B. Macdonald: what does it mean to be human and how should we, as human beings, live together?[11] Considering such questions does not come easily to school administrators and teachers who have typically been called on to think in only the most pragmatic and instrumental ways. The recognition that the work of education is always deeply implicated in our philosophical, moral, religious, and cultural thinking is something society has sought to deny as it focused on only the most shallow, vulgar, and conventional goals for our public schools. Yet in my work I have seen how these potential school leaders begin to understand that to engage in the task of making school a community of meaning can have no real significance unless there is this opportunity for all concerned to reflect on education in its fullest purpose and possibilities. Of course, there are enormously difficult and challenging implications to this process that many students are quick to recognize. How does a diverse and complex community reach some kind of consensus on the meanings it wants to shape its children's education? Can we, as a culture, find a sufficiently common ground of ethical and social values to enable this process to reach agreement? My short (not always entirely satisfying to students) answer to this is that, whatever the difficulties, we must attempt to engage these issues. No challenge could be more important to a free society, in an era when there is such an extraordinary crisis in our society's values and meanings. It means we must face for ourselves, and our children, the full impact of the commercialization of our culture, and its addiction to destructive levels of competition, individualism, and the pursuit of personal success. Educational leadership in this context is something much more than keeping the wheels of the school machinery humming; it is to assume the role of a catalyst for encouraging a community's serious deliberations on what are the most compelling and meaningful goals for their children's education. The educational leader becomes someone with the insights and courage to help others formulate a transformative vision for this school and its community,[12] and of course, someone who has the determination to fight for this vision in the face of the many contrary pressures that exists to undermine it. I have no illusions about the difficulties—some would say impossibility—of following this road. Here, however, is not the place to address all of the complex challenges of taking on the role of a transformative leader. Others have addressed this in ways much better than I can do. Still, I am sure that to abdicate this responsibility is to simply write off schools as sites that can offer our children anything that can speak to the yawning abyss of meaning in our society. It would mean schools continuing with business as usual in a time that cries out for radical change in the goals and purposes of education.

However much we seek a community of meaning for ourselves, or our children, my hope is that, in this chapter, I have highlighted the danger when such communities seek to be exclusive and sealed off from interaction with others' ideas, identities, and influences in the world. Although such communities offer security and safety for their members, they are also sure to contribute to the fragmentation, intolerance, and divisiveness of our world. They become, in the words of Zygmunt Bauman, neo-tribal communities that are locked into their own sense of authoritarian truth and self-contained arrogance. One thing that has become all too evident in what is described as our postmodern world is that human identity is never shaped within one single circle of influence. We are all made in an overlapping series of social and cultural circles that affect us in a myriad of ways.[13] Much as some would like to view who they are as the result of a very circumscribed and limited field of influence, this view only serves to maintain a mythic sense of our own purity (something that serves essentialist explanations of racist, fundamentalist religious, and authoritarian explanations of who we are). The truth that applies to everyone is that all identities today are a hybrid mixture. We are all, in some way, a patchwork quilt of complex origins, with our beliefs deriving from multiple sources, and living in a world where even the most isolated of us is likely to find him- or herself exposed to an extraordinary range and diversity of influences. This much is undeniable. What we have to decide is how we are to deal with this reality. Our choice is whether we live in ways that deny the complex weave of our relationships with others, as some would prefer, or whether we acknowledge how much we are part of others' lives, and honor how much we owe much to others for what we have and who we are. The decision we make here is very important indeed. To accede to the former view means to pursue the neo-tribal view of community and its concern to try to purify our world of the presence of others. Others are seen as an intrusion, threat, or contaminant of our world, and our need is to shut them out as much as possible from influencing or interacting with us or our children. Our only responsibility for others derives from our hope that they might eventually become more like us. It is easy to see the reflection of this view in anti-immigrant feelings, hostility to gays, or the English-language-only movement. The second view is a quite different one. Although we may see ourselves as part of a particular community that is important to our sense of purpose and our well-being, we also recognize ourselves as members not of this one community alone. Our lives are seen as inextricably connected to others, and this means we have debts, obligations, and responsibilities toward all these others who are, in some way, a part of our lives.

My sympathies are certainly with the latter view. We must not forget, for example, that our world extends much further than to those who are near and familiar to us. Those who live on the other side of town pay taxes to support the public amenities we want; they work and provide products and services that are necessary to our world; their children grow up to assume responsibilities that directly impact the quality of all our lives. Of course, it is not simply those on the other side of town who are implicated in our lives. The quality of life in our own small sphere is deeply enmeshed with the lives of countless others across our nation whose work, political participation, civic engagement, and cultural contributions shape the quality of life for us all. Now, as never before in human history, what happens in our neighborhoods and cities, as well as in our nation, is dependent on things that happen globally. In an extraordinary new way, time and space have become compressed so that economic developments, political events, cultural innovations, and intellectual advances rapidly affect and impact all our lives, no matter if they occur on the other side of the world or in far-away places. In this new global condition, borders and boundaries have become increasingly permeable: Disease, terrorism, and environmental deterioration are international conditions that affect us all. The huge flow of migrants across borders, of people looking for a better life for themselves and their families, increasingly disrupts our notions of who truly belongs where, what the relationship is between citizenship and identity, and who is to be treated as an integral part of our communities. All of this, I believe, points our work as educators in the direction of providing young people with a much more complex vision of community and belonging. We must educate them so that they see themselves as members of multiple communities that are linked and overlapping with one another. Young people will need to understand their lives as one where they become comfortable with the crossing of cultural borders and inhabiting diverse social contexts. Their own identity consists of a number of different allegiances, multiple spans of concern and responsibility, and overlapping fields of cultural identification and consciousness. We need to convey this sense as a source, not of anxiety and fear, but of celebration and of possibility.

Such an emerging consciousness implies a whole new importance to the teaching of foreign languages, which is, of course, the precondition to communication with others on a more level and respectful basis (as opposed to our expectation that everyone ought to talk to us in English!). It also implies a curriculum that is deliberately aimed at increasing understanding of other cultures and ways of life, and without the arrogance or condescension that this often carries. It also means that we need to have a more sensitive and critical awareness of our own culture so that we can begin to see the kinds of assumptions we bring into our interactions with others, and also how our "own" culture is always and everywhere deeply influenced and shaped by the experience and expressions of others. It speaks to the need for education to facilitate greater opportunities for travel and cultural exchanges (something that is happening in higher education). Finally, however, this larger consciousness is one that is predicated on an expanded sense of moral responsibility, one that harks back to the ancient wisdom of indeed being our brothers' and sisters' keepers. Our teaching must, in this global age, help to breach the walls of insularity and indifference to the lives of others. Our strong communities of meaning, while nurturing a secure and confident self, must also be vehicles for enhancing our sense of responsibility and concern for those who live across the economic, social, cultural, linguistic, and religious borders, which are within our nation, as well as across our world.

NOTES

1. Robert D. Putnam. (2000). *Bowling alone: The collapse and revival of American community.* New York: Simon and Schuster. Also, Robert N. Bellah et al. (1985). *Habits of the heart: individualism and commitment in American life.* Berkeley: University of California Press.
2. Zygmunt Bauman. (2001). *Individualized society.* Cambridge, UK: Polity Press.
3. These reflections first appeared in an article in *Tikkun* magazine in 1996 (vol. *11*, no. 6).

4. Robert B. Reich. (2002). *I'll be short*. Boston: Beacon Press.

5. There are numerous books and articles that address and elaborate this claim. A recent clear and accessible one is Joel Spring. (2004). *American education*. New York: McGraw-Hill.

6. Jonathan Kozol. (1991). *Savage inequalities*. New York: Crown.

7. Gloria Ladson-Billings. (1994). *The dreamkeepers*. San Francisco: Jossey-Bass.

8. Michael Lerner. (1997). *Politics of meaning*. Philadelphia: Perseus Books.

9. Sharon Welch. (1985). *Communities of resistance and solidarity*. New York: Orbis.

10. Zygmunt Bauman. *Community: Seeking safety in an insecure world*. Cambridge, UK: Polity Press, 2001.

11. I first encountered these two questions in this context in the work of the educational theorist James B. Macdonald, whom I was privileged to work with for a short while before his untimely death.

12. Among those who write about educational leadership in ways that speak to this is Thomas J. Sergiovanni. (2000). *The lifeworld of leadership: Creating culture, community and personal meaning in schools*. San Francisco: Jossey-Bass.

13. Amin Maalouf. (2000). *In the name of identity*. London: Penguin Books.

5

Banality of Evil

When the Baal Shem was faced with a particularly difficult challenge, he would go to a certain place in the woods, light a sacred fire, meditate in prayer, and the challenge would be met.

When his successor, the Master from Mezerich, was faced with a similar challenge, he would go to the same place in the forest. There he would say, "We no longer know how to light the fire, but we have the prayer and that will be enough." And the challenge would be met.

When his successor, the Master from Sassov, was faced with a similar situation, he would say, "We no longer know how to light the fire, and we have forgotten the prayer, but we know the place in the woods." He would go to the sacred spot and the challenge would be met.

Finally, however, in the fourth generation, a great challenge arose, and the Master from Rishin, successor of the earlier generations, was called to action. "We do not know how to light the fire," he said. "We have forgotten the prayer. We do not remember the place in the forest. What shall we do?"

He put his head down in defeat, only to lift it a moment later. "We shall tell the story of what they did!" he exclaimed.

So he sat in his chair and told this story. And the challenge was met. (story by S. Y. Agnon retold in *Soul Prints* by Marc Gafni. New York: Simon and Schuster, 2001, p. 217)

I teach very few classes where I don't, at some time, refer to the events of the Holocaust—the genocidal murder of the Jewish people by the Nazis. Although the

92

Jews were the greatest victims of the Nazis, it is well known that many other groups were also victimized: homosexuals, gypsies, Slavic people, political opponents of the regime, and others. This event, for me, is the emblematic phenomenon of the 20th century—the bloodiest century in human history. I tell my students that no teacher should teach if he or she has not reflected, in a serious manner, on the meaning and significance of the Holocaust. In it is to be found all of the greatest dangers that continue to confront civilization. My lesson always starts by some reading or depiction of the horror of what took place in Europe a mere 60 years ago. Of course, no description can come close to rendering what happened—the great chroniclers of the Holocaust, like Elie Wiesel, are the first to admit that their writings only give a hint of the full suffering endured during this period. Still, I feel we are duty bound to remember, and describe to the best extent that we can, some of what occurred. If we can convey at least a fragment of the pain, loss, and brutality, it will be worthwhile. In some strange way we can give some shred of meaning and dignity to the lives of those who perished through our efforts to remember and pass on to a new generation some of what occurred in those terrible times.

But I will be honest about why I continue to teach about this in my classes on education. It has much less to do with remembering. I am much more concerned with the present and the future. There are, I am convinced, powerful lessons that must be learned from what may seem to many as historically remote events that continue to speak to the issues that we must address today. I start by asking my students how it is that the Nazis could have done such terrible things to innocent human beings—how they could have signed on to commit such atrocities against men, women, and children for reasons that appear so senseless. There are the usual responses about psychopathic individuals gaining political power. A few students might ask what it is that Jews did to create this situation. Some students, usually African-Americans, will quickly relate to the capacity of people, acting under the influence of racist ideology, to murder and brutalize others. There are always students who will raise the issue of evil motives in the hearts of men and women. Of course, accusations of evil lead to some difficult discussion about what exactly is the meaning of evil, and which individuals act out of its influence. How, I ask, do we know who are the evil people in our world—are they clearly differentiated from the rest of us?

I lead my students through these difficult, and never fully answerable, questions. Toward the end of the discussion I suggest to them that explanations that identify a small group of individuals as somehow responsible for the genocidal murder of millions are much too simple, and too easy. It lets off the hook the countless ordinary people who participated in small ways in these events: those who ran the trains that delivered victims to the concentration camps; those who helped produce the poison gas that killed children; the thousands of bureaucrats who checked identities to see who should be included among the imprisoned; teachers who agreed to segregate, and later exclude, students from their classrooms; those who guarded the camps; and, finally, those who said or did nothing to protest what was happening, or to help the victims. This, after all, was a process of mass murder that required the skills and energies of untold thousands of accomplices, not including the millions of others who acceded to what happened through their silence. Central to my concern here is not the careful calculating evil inclinations of some Nazis, but the unthinking obedience of so many others. It is this immoral thoughtlessness that I consider the source of so much suffering, both then and now. The defining characteristic of this behavior is found among those Nazi leaders who were tried at the Nuremberg War Crimes Tribunal shortly after the end of the Second World War. Those on trial each repeated that famous mantra about how they were simply following orders, doing what they were told by those above them in the chain of command. It is something we have, chillingly, heard again recently at the international court in The Hague from those Serbian soldiers who stand accused of genocide and "ethnic cleansing" in Bosnia and in Kosovo, and among American soldiers accused of mistreating prisoners at the Abu Graibh prison in Baghdad or at Bagram in Afghanistan. Most famous, I tell my students, is the case of Adolph Eichmann, the person who was placed in charge of the Third Reich's plans to annihilate the Jewish people. Eichmann was brought to trial in Jerusalem in 1960 after Israeli agents found and kidnaped him from his hideaway in Argentina. His trial, which occurred when I was in my early adolescence, filled the news in England where I grew up. The testimony of the witnesses exposed most of us, for the first time, to the full, gruesome horror of what happened to Europe's Jews. I remember being riveted by the news reports. It was the stuff of my nightmares, knowing that but for the chance of my grandparents having disembarked in London, rather than some other European port, after fleeing Russia and Poland, my parents too would have disappeared into the back smoke of Auschwitz. The question that gripped me, as it did many others, as we listened to the reports of the mass killings, the gassing, the crematoria that "processed" millions of bodies, the medical "experiments" on live victims, the brutality against children, the torture, beatings, hunger, forced marches in freezing conditions, and so on, was a straightforward one: How could this have happened? How could human beings have done such things to other human beings? Eichmann's answer, like that of so many others, was simple: "I was following orders." It was an answer that stayed with me, reverberating in my mind, both then and, increasingly, as I grew older and continued to reflect on the Holocaust and how it had happened.

Years later I came across the book *Eichmann in Jerusalem* by the famous political philosopher Hannah Arendt.[1] Arendt, herself a Jew whose family had perished in Germany, attended the Eichmann trial and wrote about it in a series of articles for the New Yorker magazine. These articles subsequently became a book. She describes there how she felt facing this man who had been responsible for so much suffering and horror. This individual, she thought, who organized the killing of six million human beings must be some kind of demonic being. Yet when she eventually saw him sitting in the dock in the courtroom, the wizened old man reminded her more of her grandfather than of any satanic figure. And here, for Arendt, was the key to the terrible events of this time. For Eichmann, the mass murders that he so coldly and methodically carried out were much more about carrying out the orders he received—whatever they happened to be, rather than the fulfillment of any political or ideologically driven vision. Like so many others, Eichmann did what his superiors told him to do. Indeed, he described well how his schooling and his military training taught him that the good citizen is exactly the one who does what he is told. A blind obedience was the hallmark of good citizenship. His story was the story repeated *ad nauseam* by too many killers and torturers in the 20th and now the 21st century. Arendt coined the memorable phrase the "banality of evil" to capture the mind set of those individuals who lent their participation to some extraordinarily terrible undertaking without any great motive, short of simply doing what is asked of them. They do their part without giving much real thought or reflection as to what is the end result or consequence of their actions. For Arendt this banality of evil was far more terrible than identifying a few psychopathic or malevolent individuals who were responsible for these awful events, for at the heart of this human catastrophe were ordinary people, minding their own business, but agreeing to do things without the restraint of consciousness or conscience.[2]

MINDLESS LEARNING, THOUGHTLESS LIVES

Of course the United States is not Nazi Germany. The latter was a society with a short history of democratic institutions and a deeply rooted culture of authoritarianism. It was a society that had been wracked by the severest economic and political crises, and a devastating military defeat. The United States is a society with deeply rooted democratic values and a rich history of civil disobedience and courageous struggles for human rights and social justice. Yet there are lessons here that even these differences do not erase. The famous Milgram experiment in the 1950s showed that American adults could be led into the same direction of mindlessly following the orders of those in positions of superior authority, and agreeing to inflict pain on others for no justifiable reasons. I share with my undergraduates the story of the My Lai massacre. Almost none of them know anything about it. They are horrified to learn that American soldiers in Vietnam were capable of following orders and murdering hundreds of innocent men, women, and children without justifiable cause, and did it with barbarous behavior. Our discussions take us into the way that Japanese-Americans were interned during the Second World War. And, of course, we dwell on the acceptance, for so long, of the brutality and horror of slavery and racial apartheid in the United States. We consider some of those things that we have recently witnessed, such as the Rwandan or Darfur genocides, that seem to have drawn relatively little attention or outrage (perhaps because these horrors took place in Africa). We reflect on those atrocities we accept in our own society and in the world, without too much questioning or opposition: the persistence of poverty, hunger, and homelessness in the United States; the terrible inequities in the distribution of material resources in the world; the millions with AIDS who are condemned to death because of the expense of medicines; the sexual slavery of children and women in Eastern Europe and the far East; the economic exploitation of workers in our farms and sweatshop industries, the widespread abuse of migrant workers; or the thousands of children who die each day because of the lack of food or the availability of basic health care.

My students are quick to recognize their own ignorance and insensitivity. They readily grasp that the banality of evil comes in different guises. Almost all agree that their schooling had taught them little or nothing about what it means to question or challenge the injustices or unnecessary suffering in our nation, or in our world. What they do learn in school accords well with what many observers of our classrooms have said over the years. Most schooling in the United States teaches young people little about thinking critically about their world. The classroom is mainly a place where kids, in order to succeed, learn about finding the "right" answers to the teachers' questions, and to respond successfully to their tests and assignments. It is, perhaps, the central lesson of the hidden curriculum.[3] The classroom is a place where we learn to play the game and fill in the blanks or the bubbles in our homework or classroom tasks. Standardized tests feed a standardized form of learning in which conformity of thinking is the rule. There is an absence, as many observers have made clear (and many teachers acknowledge), of anything resembling a culture of critical thought in most American classrooms. There is little that goes on that encourages young people to engage in a form of education that encourages them to think about, or question, the assumptions and beliefs that surround them. And, certainly, there is little that is about awakening their consciences so that they might feel the call to challenge or resist the inequities or the inhumanity in our world. Indeed, it is probable that for many adults in our society such an education would be regarded as a dangerous and unwanted anathema.

Each year when I address the participants of the North Carolina Governors School—a summer program for a select group of the state's most creative and academically talented high school seniors—I confront them with a list of questions that speak to the injustice and irrationality of our country and our world:

- Why is half of the money of the money in the world that is used on weapons, spent by the United States?
- Why does the United States, which represents 6% of the world's population, consume 60% of the world's resources and half of its energy?
- Why do women make up 70% of the world's 1 billion poor people?
- Why do one-third of the world's people have no clean drinking water?
- Why does a half of the world's population live on less than $2 a day?
- Why does one-third of the world's population have a life expectancy of less than 40 years?
- Why is the financial wealth of the top 1% of Americans equal to that possessed by the bottom 95%?

- Why do 25% of the children in the United States live below the poverty line?
- Why do 40 million Americans have no health insurance?
- Why do only 50% of American citizens vote in a general election?
- Why do we spend more on advertising than on public education each year?
- Why do we have the highest proportion of people in jail of any developed country, and why are 75% of these Black or Brown?
- Why is consumerism such a central part of our nation's culture and lifestyle?
- Why is there is there so much stress, depression, and anxiety among the American population?
- Is there a conflict between corporate power and influence in the United States, and our democracy?
- Why is there such widespread dislike and distrust of the United States around the world?

After presenting these questions, I ask the students whether they have addressed or thought about these questions as part of their schooling. The truly shocking response to my question is that, even among this group of select students, almost none had seriously addressed the issues and concerns that are implicit in these questions, in any of their classes. Their answers speak volumes as to the way that schools typically offer little that might teach young people about the need to think and engage the truly important questions that confront our nation and our world. The classroom, these students told me, is rarely, if ever, a place in which individuals are required to grapple with issues about war, poverty, the growth of economic inequality, violence, sexism, homophobia, the addiction to consuming, our society's wasteful and destructive approach to the environment, or the threat to democracy posed by corporate power and the growing concentration of wealth.

Far from a site that nurtures the critical spirit of thoughtful engagement with the injustices, violence, pain, and wastefulness of the world we live in, school has become an important transmitter of Arendt's banality of evil. It is a place that, with rare exceptions, cultivates a willful ignorance or avoidance of our responsibility to be questioners of the status quo. It is not too surprising that a recent survey of high school students showed that 20% of the respondents thought that the government should not allow the expression of unpopular opinions and 40% thought the "bill of rights went too far in its freedoms." Over the many years of teaching I have come to see and hear from students from all over the country on the failure of public and private schools to teach individuals to think critically. The courage and intellectual capacity to challenge assumptions and beliefs is subordinated to the kind of timid instrumentalism we have talked about in earlier chapters. Being successful at school has little if anything to do with challenging and questioning accepted ideas and beliefs. Indeed, the reverse is often the case. "Good" students are usually the ones who have learned best to play the game of finding the "right" answers to the questions that will guarantee them the highest grades or the most praise from their teacher. This is, of course, a talent that has little or nothing to do with the capacity to being individuals who know how to interrogate received truths. One student at the summer program described the process of becoming a "good" student (by her own admission, she was one) as learning to act like a "brick in the wall." It was mainly, she said, about learning to conform, either through the fear of failure, or the seduction of the status rewards that success would bring. After listening to what I had to say, she responded by saying that the high achieving students that were sitting in the hall around her were not there because they had learned to exercise their power to think and question in any real way. They were there, she said, because they were obsessive about the prospect of getting into the best colleges and doing whatever that demanded. Knowledge, for these students, had very little to do with empowering them to become thoughtful or sensitive members of society. It was, instead, merely the stuff that one needed to remember or manipulate in order to play the game of schooling. Perhaps this is the reason that so many of my undergraduates, after years of treating knowledge in this instrumental and detached way, actually resent my invitation to them to approach learning as the opportunity to call into question the things they read, hear, or are told. For many this approach to education is an unsettling and disturbing experience. Indeed, for some, it is reason to become downright angry with me. We are not here to think, they are saying. Just give us the correct answers!

EDUCATING FOR DEMOCRACY

I will say that by the end of my lecture to this "elite" group of students there is usually quite a furor in the lecture hall. There are a number of reasons for this. For some there is the sense of betrayal about an education that has taught them so little about what it means to be thoughtful human beings. For others, there is a pent-up fury at how cynical the process of schooling has become, and how little it spoke to the important issues that faced them and their generation. And, of course, for not a few students, there is anger at me for suggesting that there was anything wrong at all with a process in which they had invested so much time and energy, and from which they expected great rewards. For me, the great tragedy is that today, in all our talk about improving education, there is almost no concern with a critical education, and its responsibility to inculcating the values and attitudes that are essential to a vibrant and meaningful democratic culture. The detachment, ignorance, and cynicism that are so rampant among students in regard to what their education is about are sad testimony to this fact. It is also a loud call to us to transform the goals and purposes of education.

Although we do talk about schools imparting to young people the importance of being "good citizens" this usually refers to students following the rules, and generally doing what teachers instruct them to do. Sadly, this conformism is often the way character education is defined by school leaders (of course it doesn't have to mean this). Responsible students are usually regarded as those who are active participants in school activities and programs, playing sports, attending after-school clubs, serving on the school council, and so on. It is rarely about democratic citizenship, at least not in the terms that I have talked about it earlier. When I am working with teachers and school administrators, I always consider it important that we spend time reminding ourselves of the meaning of democratic values. So I will ask them to list what are the values, beliefs, and dispositions that they think inhere in the idea of *homo democraticus*—the democratically inclined individual. My graduate students enjoy the challenge of this task. They will energetically consider this question and return with a lengthy list of attributes. Typically, it will include the need for tolerance; a willingness to be cooperative; a belief in equality; participation in elections; the rule of law; a concern for the community; and the need for compromise. Although I congratulate them on their work, I also remind them of the absence of something that is crucial to the meaning of democratic life. It is a startling fact that most times what is absent from their lists is the importance of a critical intelligence or consciousness among citizens. Is it not the role of education in a democracy, I ask, to cultivate the Socratic art of questioning? Was not the very essence of a democratic culture one where citizens had the willingness and capability to challenge the things that were being presented to them, to unearth its basic assumptions, and to ask the question—who benefits most from keeping things the way they are? To challenge the veracity and basis of what those in authority are telling us is at the very core of meaningful democratic life. This can be, of course, a dangerous and disturbing thing to many people, both those who directly benefit from the way things are, and those for whom change of any kind is threatening to their sense of order and stability. But democracy and the capacity to pose subversive questions are two sides of the same coin. If Eichmann, Calley, and the many others who blindly followed the orders of their superiors had been exposed to this kind of education, perhaps there would have been fewer innocent casualties in the 20th century.

Why are teachers, I am compelled to ask, so reluctant to embrace this aspect of democratic education? Perhaps there is the fear that encouraging students to think more critically will also encourage them to challenge the teachers' own authority. There is also the concern that classrooms that emphasize the importance of questioning what is said will become more contentious places. This, too, will create more problems of control for teachers. Also, learning that is less about getting the right answer than asking the right questions, is not really compatible with the kind of education that puts so much stress on the "one size fits all" kind of thinking that dominates our curriculum and modes of assessment. The latter is clearly about an intellectual conformity, rather than the need for a cognitive process that values any kind of dissonant or divergent thinking. Nor can we doubt that the present political climate has made the challenge of a democratic education that much harder. The prospect of an endless war against terrorism has created a mood in the United States that is much less conducive to those who might question or challenge our cultural values, or the interests that hold sway in this society. The "Patriot Act" which has greatly expanded the government's powers to police dissident views and activities, is certain to chill the free expression of contrary ideas and values much as the McCarthy hearings did in the early 1950s. Feelings of threat and insecurity are always a damper on a society's openness to views that challenge the status quo. These are real concerns that speak to the need for deep changes in how we train (or perhaps select) prospective teachers. None of this, however, should allow us to deny the importance of recognizing the full meaning and implications of what it means to educate young people to becoming citizens in a democracy. Whatever the difficulties and concerns associated with such a goal, we need to remind ourselves about just how much more dangerous it is to bring up a generation who will passively conform to the powerful, seductive, and ultimately destructive messages of our culture, and who are unable to challenge or deconstruct the view of the world that says that the way things are now is the only real possibility open to us.

Of course, unthinking acquiescence to authority now takes very different forms from those that led to Holocaust. But we need not be in any doubt that the present forms of moral and social blindness have consequences that could not be more serious for our lives and our children's future. Teaching our children what it means to think critically, to question the assumptions that govern our lives, and to have the capacity to challenge injustice and inhumanity, and the need to wage war, as well our environmental destructiveness, has never been more important. Indeed, it is no exaggeration to say that our future as a species hangs in the balance. We see all around us the damaging and deadly effects of selfish and shortsighted human behavior. And there can be no more important goal for education than an aware, thoughtful, and alert citizenry. Indeed, nothing highlights our present denial of the threats to decent and humane life in our country, and in the world generally, more than the fact that such a goal for education rarely if ever appears in the "official" expectations of what our schools should achieve. Even the rhetoric of preparing young people for their active participation in a democratic society has been eliminated from the public discourse on schooling.[4] Today, few people suggest that education has something to do with preparing kids to be active and engaged members of the human community. Even fewer are heard suggesting that we need to rethink the curriculum in the light of our democratic and citizenship concerns. Indeed, it is a strange fact that the core curriculum of American schools has hardly changed in the past 50 years, despite the seismic changes in our culture. We might look, for example, at the ways we are preparing—or more accurately, not preparing—young people to deal with the powerful influence of the media in shaping our imagination, values, assumptions, and desires. Certainly it is impossible to deny the extraordinary influence of the mass media in shaping our identity, relationships, and the view we have of the world. In many respects the media function, in the words of one commentator, as a "propaganda of integration". In other words, they help shape conformity to the particular ways we make sense of things.[5] Being aware and independent in our thinking becomes immeasurably harder in the face of the enormous power wielded by the "culture industry" to shape our minds and our desires. The issue is far more complex now than whether or not we are simply capable of resisting immoral commands. What is at stake is our very awareness as to the way our ideas and attitudes are determined by forces that are much harder to see, and that come in forms that provide us with entertainment or pleasurable diversion from the tensions and stresses of our everyday lives. In a very real sense we live in the "one-dimensional" culture that was described by the social critic Herbert Marcuse,[6] where imagination, expression, and the things we hope for and dream of are more and more inseparable from the images projected by Hollywood and Madison Avenue.

I am always amazed, for example, by the number of students in my classes who are insistent that they remain unaffected by advertising, even while they confess to their preoccupations (sometimes to the point of illness) with the size and shape of their bodies, or their rapt awareness of the brand identities of the clothing, electronics, sneakers, and automobiles that they, or others, own. I have to labor, as a teacher, to show how television and other media are a pipeline for conveying an ideology that sifts and selects for us a particular way to make sense of our world and our lives. For almost all these students (despite years of formal education), it is an ideology that has remained unseen, unexamined, and, to a very great extent, accepted by them. Any ideology works best when the view of the world it contains becomes simply an unchallenged, commonsense part of people's reality. It is especially hard to challenge or question those things that seem natural, or simply a given part of our lives and world. When this happens we become unable to recognize that how we make sense of the world is not a particular view of how things are—one that, in all likelihood, serves some people's interests more than others. Instead, we intuitively come to believe that this is simply and unalterably the way things have to be. It is what we mean when we say to one another, "Get real!" This is how it is, and you need to adjust to it! This is an extraordinary threat to democratic life, with its promise of change, and the capacity of ordinary people to reshape how things are. We are all subjected to a barrage of powerful images that shape our understanding of the world, tell us what to believe, and set priorities and directions for our lives, images whose very pervasiveness makes it hard to question or challenge. It is, after all, a world in which Coke is presented to us as the "real thing."

TOWARD A CRITICAL MEDIA LITERACY

Through the media we are offered an America that is suffused with images of violence and crime, and cities that are almost always places of risk and danger. In this world the Black male is, again and again, identified with drugs, guns, and threatening behavior. Most other minorities—Asian-Americans, Mexican-Americans, American Indians— are hardly visible at all. It is overwhelmingly a world in which White males are presented as the possessors of authority, intelligence, and expertise. It is a world in which people are continually made happy through the things that they can buy. And we learn, again and again, that things can help us fulfill all those basic human needs—for peace of mind, good health, youthfulness, friendship, and intimacy. It is a world that shows very little of the everyday life and struggles of working-class people, but instead elevates the centrality of the rich and the famous. Enormous emphasis is placed on women's bodies and their physical attractiveness to men. Sexuality is disproportionately associated with violent behavior, as well as with selling almost everything. Nurturance and care of others are overwhelmingly women's work and responsibility. Life's meaning is typically to be found in romance and falling in love. This is especially so for women. Youth is worshiped and aging disdained. Competition and aggressive behavior is pervasive and given very high value. Gay and lesbian relationships are rarely shown, and when they are it is usually as a vehicle for humor. In this world, wars are generally celebrated, the military are heroic, and America is represented as the "greatest" country in the world—a land of freedom and progress. It is generally assumed that our political interventions in other countries are motivated by the desire to bring democracy and freedom to other people (not the desire to ensure states that are acquiescent to this country's corporate and economic interests). Very little about the rest of the world enters into this "reality" (indeed, whole continents, such as Africa or Europe, rarely appear in either drama or news!), and little attention is given to the way American military and economic power is perceived by other nations. Environmentalism is presented as another special interest, usually associated with overzealous middle class youth, out of touch with working class concerns. Extraordinary attention is placed on getting money, and the realistic "bottom line" for what we do is the capacity for making a profit.

Of course, there are counterimages to the picture of the world that is drawn for us by the media: counternarratives, as they are sometimes called. There are portrayals of the experience of minority groups and their histories; depictions of the lives of men and women that run against the social, economic, and political grain; satires of our cultural and political life; critical reporting on our country that does not glorify and celebrate who we are in relationship to the rest of the world; and opportunities to consider other, less materialistic, more spiritual or moral, ways of how we might live our lives and be in relationship with others. We are, of course, not a totalitarian culture or society. We cannot forget that through our culture have continued to run powerful currents of resistance to the dominant values, beliefs, representations, and structures of power. Such resistance has flowed, for example, from the pain of racial injustice, from economic exploitation and hardship, or from our nation's failure to live up to its noblest beliefs about peace, freedom, human dignity, and individual worth. Through music, dress, and language, young people have constantly found creative ways to disturb and contest the staid and conventional mores of their parents. Such resistance has ebbed and flowed through our history, bursting forth with great energy at certain moments like the 1930s or the 1960s. And, of course, challenges to the status quo have, indeed, brought important changes to all of our lives. We only have to think about the civil rights movement, or the women's movement, to recognize that people, acting together, have challenged and changed fundamental aspects of our society. Recalling such history is an important part of an education that is concerned with energizing young people with a sense of possibility, rather than apathy or cynicism, about making change in our world. Today we can, for example, see within rap music and hip-hop culture powerful forms of critique concerning the world that confronts many young people. One of America's greatest social critics, Cornel West, noted in his recent book *Democracy Matters* that

> The fundamental irony of hip-hop is that it has become viewed as nihilistic, macho, violent, and bling-bling phenomenon when in fact its originating impulse was a fierce disgust with the hypocrisies of adult culture—disgust with the selfishness, capitalist callousness, and xenophobia of the culture of adults, both within the hood and the society at large.

West asserted that although hip-hop culture has become tainted by the very excesses and amorality it was born in rage against, the best of rap music still expresses, more clearly than any past expression in the past generation, a "profound indictment of the moral decadence of our dominant society."

Although resistant forms of expression offer important, alternative ways to make sense of things, we must still take very seriously the powerful, and largely unreflected on, ideology that dominates how we generally think and give meaning to our lives. We must still contend with what philosopher Maxine Greene has called our "sunkenness" in the everyday world.[7] By this she means the unconscious acceptance of so much of what looks like reality, something that is especially true of the young. At the very least, we need to appreciate that citizenship today requires a different type of literacy, a critical media literacy that would enable young people to "decode" the powerful messages that shape who they are and how they have been influenced to see the world. We must, for example, ensure that young women growing up in this society are educated so that they can begin to understand the way their identities are constructed by the media and by advertising. Whatever advances women are making in this society, female identity still overwhelmingly emphasizes physical appearance and attractiveness.[8] Young women, in particular, are subjected to a barrage of messages that make it hard for them to freely choose their own goals and ambitions. Indeed, far from being free, they are subjected to a tyranny of influences that instill in them an obsessive concern with their sexuality and the attention of the male gaze. The destructive consequences of this tyranny have been well described by a legion of insightful commentators, many of whom have also provided creative and powerful methods to educate young women so that they may develop the capacity to resist these influences. So, too, do we see the effects of media's influence on the understanding and expectations of male identity. We know that masculinity, too, is presented in terms that limit and circumscribe the capacity for boys to more freely choose the content of their humanity. The constant emphasis on physical power, aggressive behavior, and competitiveness, as well as the suspicion cast over nurturance and sensitivity, limit and channel boys' capacity to define the nature of their selves.[9] Unfortunately, there are fewer vehicles that might educate young men into contesting these constricting and damaging images of masculinity.

It is never been more important to our future that we teach young people to pierce the veil of images that inundate their world. It is incumbent on us as adults to help free them from passive submission to a reality that reflects and deepens the moral cynicism and bloated materialism that marks so much of our contemporary culture. A critical media literacy would help youngsters gain an understanding of the way that reality, or at least what we understand of reality, is now something that is produced or constructed no less than any other product or commodity. When we watch TV, see movies, look at videos or DVDs, log on to the Internet, we are entering a world that is, indeed, a virtual or "made up" place of humanly engineered images. It is a fictional world that appears to offer us a window onto the real world but is, in fact, the carefully crafted product of cultural workers who today employ extraordinary technological and creative capabilities, allied with unprecedented monetary resources. The results are often astounding in their emotional and sensual power, providing images that often seem to be "more real than reality itself" (as the French cultural observer Jean Baudrillard described it[10]). They provide us with experiences that have the power and the appeal to convince us that this is the way things really are, or should be!

The world of television news is, for obvious reasons, especially important in this regard.[11] Television is now the main avenue through which American get their news (fewer people than ever actually read a newspaper or news magazine). Television news presenters stand in front of banks of television monitors and promise to provide us with images of extraordinary immediacy and veracity as to what is actually happening in the world. The information and communications "command posts," they seem to occupy seem to imbue their reporting with an unprecedented degree of authority and scientific accuracy. Yet we need to remind ourselves, as well our children, that the reality offered by television is, too, only a concocted one. Those behind this wizardry sift and select from the endless events and occurrences to decide what they deem newsworthy and what are the priorities among these "stories." They must also organize these events in ways that make their meanings familiar and accessible to the prospective audience. And they must, at all times, keep at least one ear cocked to the audience ratings to see if what is broadcast produces a sizeable enough audience to ensure lucrative advertising revenues. Being literate in this era of 24-hour TV news coverage means ensuring that those who will be tomorrow's citizens are able to pose questions about the formulation and presentation of the news. Such questions must include asking, who owns the giant news organizations like ABC, CBS, NBC, CNN, and Fox? And how does their ownership affect the kind of news coverage they provide? How much do the news networks in this country provide coverage of developments in other countries? What political views get time on news shows, and which ones rarely get heard? Whose voices typically get heard on news shows? What issues are provided abundant time and which ones are not? How does the commodification of news, with its increasing emphasis on entertainment and advertising revenues, affect the quality and form of news coverage?

These are dangerous and turbulent times. Human beings are faced with extraordinary and far reaching challenges. The problems of war, violence, unemployment, poverty, and environmental destruction loom before us. Imbalances in access to food, medicine, economic and technical resources, and education have never been more glaring. Hopelessness among millions of people feed social and religious movements that express their frustrations through violence. Consumer cultures and values can, through the immediacy of television and the Internet, rapidly undermine traditional ways of being that have lasted generations. And the mass media have unmatched power, everywhere on the globe, to shape and influence popular attitudes and beliefs. It is surely an important goal of education in our democratic society to equip future citizens with the capacity, in the words of Henry Giroux, to interrogate the social and human reality that is presented to them through the media. It is, after all, on the basis of this "reality" that opinions will be formed, and political positions arrived at, by those who will vote and be members of our civic community. It is hard to imagine, given the crucial decisions that confront us as citizens, both in this country as part of the global community, how we might continue to ignore or discount the importance of developing the critical intelligence of our young people. To ignore this task or relegate it to only secondary significance is to neglect the serious challenges that face us in attempting to revitalize a democratic culture so that we really address the epochal issues that now face us. And it is to deny the fact that this culture is now one where large numbers of people, including an especially high proportion of young people, feel alienated from having any meaningful input or involvement in the determination of our nation's political life.

THE LESSONS OF CONFORMITY

We need to step back here and remind ourselves that the capacity to think critically, so important to a democratic society, is not something that simply exists without careful cultivation. From the ancient Greek city-states on, it is has been recognized that this capacity must be nourished and stimulated by the right kind of education. Human beings are just as likely to develop into beings that act out of a habitual adherence to what has gone before, or an unreflective acceptance of authority, than as people who ask why we should be expected to believe what is presented to us by those holding privilege or power. Can we be in any doubt, after the history of the last 100 years, that passivity, and the will to follow, have as much purchase on our being as the desire to challenge and change?[12] The impulses to freedom, choice, agency, and self-determination are, in themselves, the product of a human and societal choice. It seems that we have all but forgotten this when we look at the emphasis now placed in our schools on conformity. The leviathan of testing rests like a dead hand over education, squelching in it any impulse toward creativity and independence of thought. The standardization of the learning process—the constant need to search for the one and only true answer—impedes divergent or original thought. Each problem has only a single correct response, and that response is always unequivocally known by those with the authority to set the questions. Students merely have to "discover" what is already known with absolute certainty. Settling on the one right blank to fill in eliminates the possibility of messy and equivocal answers. The tests, with their promise of objectivity and mathematical precision, suggest that our knowledge exists "out there" in the space where cultural bias and social assumptions don't affect the accuracy of what we know. We have, in short, constructed a pedagogy or learning process in our schools that is killing the spirit of critical human inquiry among our children. The passion to develop awareness and conscience is submerged by the drive to get the best score or the highest grade. Interest, curiosity, creativity, and the willingness to challenge the apparent truth are submerged by the accountability advocates and experts who wish to run schools with factory-like predictability. Report after report amplifies this same sorry abandonment of any commitment we might have to the making of a critical democracy. Perhaps, as some educational historians have argued, the spirit of democracy was never the major force that impelled public education in America.[13] Its goals were always much more about conformity, obedience, and docility toward those who held economic, cultural, and political power. However convincing this point of view is (and, I for one, believe it explains much about our education system), we cannot, as citizens, allow it to resign us to a predestined future. To work for change is to be realistically cognizant of the circumstances of our work, but never to the point of hopeless fatalism.

It is not simply standardized testing that acts to dampen the questioning spirit of our children. Even that would be far too simple an explanation. The problem goes much deeper. The very presentation of knowledge in our classrooms suggests to students the certainty and fixity of what is known. Every semester I enjoy asking my students the apparently simple questions as to the origin of human knowledge, and whether the curriculum they are exposed to in school should be thought of as consisting of true knowledge. Among those recently out of high school, these are questions that very few have encountered before. (One might think that this is somewhat paradoxical, given that the transmission of knowledge is the principle purpose of schools). Among many students there is a touching faith in the veracity and reliability of the knowledge that they receive. I suggest to them that, contrary to this view, nothing they encounter in their books, hear in their lectures, or can find in the university library should be thought of as certain knowledge. All knowledge, I continue, needs to be thought of as provisional or temporary, subject to change, development, modification, and rejection. Truly objective knowledge does not exist anywhere. What is known, I suggest, can never be fully separated from the "knower." The dancer, as Nietzsche once said, cannot be separated from the dance. "Truth" is always the irreducible product of human beings who attempt to give some coherent meaning to what they see, hear, or feel (or believe they see, hear, or touch). It is what is created when human beings attempt to make sense of their world. This is true whether we are concerned with the physical or natural world, or with the sphere of human relationships and behavior. There is, in other words, no knowing that represents a pure and objective reflection of the "reality" that is out there. Of course, I also point out that this does not reduce knowledge to simply a matter of capricious or arbitrary opinion. (For some students this is an appealing idea that seems to suggest that any and all thoughts, however simplistic or crude, need to be given the same degree of credence and value.) We need, I suggest, to see the "production" of knowledge as a difficult and serious process that involves enormous human commitment and effort. Today this involves almost always a shared community of inquiry among those concerned with a particular field of knowledge. Truth, we may say, involves a degree of consensus among this community as to what is thought to be happening, or what interpretation seems most compelling or coherent. It is also important to recognize that the agreement is rarely unanimous, because there are invariably some within the field who argue that there are quite different ways of making sense of what is being considered. This is especially apparent in the social sciences, where there have always been fundamentally different starting points and different basic assumptions in how we construct our explanations of the social world. There, nothing even resembling the "truth" is ever agreed on! But our grasp of the physical world is no less determinate. Since the advent of quantum physics and Heisenberg's uncertainty principle, it has been clear that experimental evidence is always and unalterably affected by the presence of the human observer.

Of course, all of this is very far from my students' encounters with knowledge. What they have received in their schooling is a distorted sense about knowledge that reifies what we present to them in the curriculum. In other words, the way we teach typically fixes and freezes knowledge, so that the human art of interpretation and meaning-making that creates and constructs everything we "know" disappears from view. Students have little sense that what they are learning is not the truth, but a selection from the possible ways of seeing, and making sense, of reality. Indeed, what students are learning in all the areas of the curriculum represents the product of human imagination and thoughtfulness, but may also contain the distortions and limitations set by social interests, prejudice, unquestioned assumptions, and what conforms to the culturally and ideologically acceptable (at least to the majority) conventions of the time. Even scientific knowledge is subject to the shaping influence of intellectual paradigms that provide templates for how scientists account for their empirical data. And these paradigms undergo their own changes and transformations, reshaping how we make sense of the evidence before us. Contrary to what we may think watching how detectives are supposed to solve their crimes, the facts do not speak for themselves. The human mind can and does rearrange what we experience before us so that it can tell very different stories!

A recent brilliant investigation of this is found in the book *Lies My Teacher Told Me* by James Loewen.[14] In this book Loewen sets out to show that the way we teach history in our high schools gives our students a badly distorted and limited sense of our nation's past—one that is silent about, or misrepresents, many of the injustices that permeate our history. He considers, for example, that social class is an almost nonexistent phenomenon in our textbooks, and that we give only the most limited and sanitized consideration to the genocide of the native peoples that followed the European settlement of North America. He looks at how the enduring exploitation of Asian migrant workers is virtually absent from our accounts of history, and how we avoid much of the real horror of slavery and the brutal consequences of racism. Works like this invite students into the recognition that history is never written by some omniscient "all-knowing" hand. History must always be questioned for what is included and what is not; for who the publisher does not want to offend; for what cultural bias or assumptions are brought by the authors, unconsciously or otherwise, into their writing. Walter Benjamin, the great 20th century scholar of culture, famously noted that "history is the story told by the winners."[15] It is precisely this kind of suspicion that our students need to have—a suspicion that leads them to view any text, or knowledge, not as revealed truth brought down from Sinai, but as a piece of human invention that must be reflected on, and continually questioned, for what it says, as well as what it doesn't say.

There is, I believe, a direct link between the ability of young people to see real learning as involving the constant challenge to think critically about truth and knowledge, and their capacity to become citizens who do not approach the present reality with passive, acquiescent, or fatalistic attitudes. Both depend on the ability to see things in their incompleteness, as something unfinished that demands the human responsibility for going beyond what is given. I do want to emphasize, however, that our suspicious attitude here points us not to cynicism or nihilism about the limited value of what we know, It is, instead, born of our concern that what we know may have ignored or overlooked voices, viewpoints, and human experiences that we must include if our knowledge of things is to be as full and as complete as it possibly can be. And it constantly alerts us to the way that power, privilege, and convention may work to distort or shape how we come to know our world.

AUTHENTIC LEARNING AND A DEMOCRACY OF EXPRESSION

It has been said, with humor, that children come to school as a question mark and leave as a period. There is much that is true about this simple statement. Children do generally come to school brimming with curiosity and questions about the world. And the sad truth is that for most kids, schooling is a process that gradually closes down the spirit of questioning and intellectual curiosity. Even more, it is a process that also disinvites students from challenging or interrogating the supposed truths that are set before them. The spirit of questioning and of critical thoughtfulness is not something that can be taught in a lesson once a week, or even once a day. It requires a process of learning that permeates the ambience of the classroom. Much has been written about this, and I can in no way do justice to it here. Many observers have pointed out the way that the passive learning so often found in our classrooms turns knowledge into chunks of material that is swallowed whole by students without being assimilated by them, in any meaningful way, into their intellectual or emotional being. In this sense, school comes to resemble a factory-like institution where the concern is to transmit a standardized "package" of knowledge to all students without regard for whether what is being learned resonates with the interests, prior understanding, or concerns of each individual. It is no wonder that, for many students, learning is a thoroughly alienating experience in which the knowledge they are expected to absorb is more or less completely disconnected from their lives and their experiences in the world. Students are treated, as the great Brazilian educator Paolo Freire famously noted, as empty containers who must be filled with the bits and pieces of a lifeless, inanimate knowledge. As we all know so well, it is precisely how each student does in parroting back this same material that we foolishly use to make our judgments as to the efficacy of our education.

In contrast to this, an education that takes seriously developing students' ability to become truly thoughtful and reflective human beings must attend to the question of the meaningfulness that is found in the educational experience itself. Authentic learning cannot be a series of hoops to be jumped through, or reduced to material that must be memorized and regurgitated back. This is quite simply the fake education that we see day after day in the great majority of our classrooms. Contrary to this, authentic learning is the process in which a student seeks answers to his or her concerns, and struggles to give meaning to his or her own experience. The search for meaning can be never separated from real and compelling learning. As I know from seeing it happen, such learning is always filled with human energy, passion, and the flow of our creative juices. It is also usually accompanied by the noise of dynamic human interaction and dialogue. Let us be clear. The unauthentic process of learning that is present in most our classrooms can only do great injury to the project of a society in which we want each individual to become actively engaged in producing, not passively accepting, meaning and understanding. A vibrant democracy ultimately depends on human beings who have been educated in ways that emphasize their capacity for being creative and thoughtful citizens. Such individuals learn to see that our world can be reinvented and changed, not simply received as something we must adapt or conform to. Reality, we have learned in our democratic education, is not a fixed object, but something we human beings help make through the inventiveness of our minds, our creativity and imagination, and, not least, according to the choices we make as morally aware individuals.

Stuart Ewen,[16] a researcher who studied the effects of advertising on our consciousness, made a distinction between what he called a "democracy of expression" and a "democracy of consumption." We have, he argued, increasingly fallen into the latter state in the United States—one in which democracy has become more and more a spectacle in which consumers choose between prepackaged goods, whether these goods happen to be cornflakes or politicians. In contrast to this, Ewen says, a democracy of expression is one in which the members of society actively engage in the process of determining what we believe, want, and need as a society. The contrast here between being consumers or citizens is a crucial one. The latter implies individuals whose participation in society is mainly through the marketplace. Individuals shop among the goods that are available to satisfy some private want. As citizens, on the other hand, we engage with others to determine and shape the kind of community we, together, wish to live in. It should be no surprise that we increasingly refer to participants in our society as consumers rather than citizens.[17] It is the credit card, not voter registration identification, that increasingly signifies our legitimate participation in society. Our mode of being is increasingly one of private "takers" of goods, rather than "makers" of society.

In this light we can perhaps see schooling either as a preparation for the kind of world where individuals enhance their ability to be successful consumers, or as a place that cultivates their identities as citizens. The former evokes the familiar purposes of schooling: Work hard and do well so that one can acquire the credentials, the jobs, and the income that will allow one to participate fully and actively in the marketplace. When viewed through the lens of citizenship, education looks quite different. The classroom and the school become a place that is concerned, first of all, with individuals who are thoughtful about their world and their place in it; who have learned to see reality not as fixed and unchangeable, but as a human construction that can be questioned and is open to change; and who take seriously their shared responsibility to make a difference in the world so that it is more just, compassionate, and humane. The classroom and the school are, in addition, places that are concerned with encouraging all students to value their own ideas, experiences, and perspectives, while also ensuring that all voices are heard and listened to. Democracy, in this sense, is the voice of the whole community seeking purpose, meaning, and the possibility of change and betterment. Sadly, it has often been observed that schoolrooms in the United States are rarely alive with the engaged voices of students interacting with one another, exchanging ideas, listening and absorbing different perspectives, and seeking to reach understanding. Indeed, one of the most dispiriting dimensions in my own teaching of undergraduates has been the difficulty of undoing the years of slavish or sullen silence in the classroom. The notion that students should see either themselves or others as having voices and opinions that are worth listening to is, for many students, a foreign experience. It is quite contrary to the years in which they have been expected not to disturb the one-way transmission of information in the classroom, or the belief that good students do not question or challenge the ideas presented to them. One of the saddest aspects of this process has been the way it destroys the very sense of the valuing one's own "voice"—the contribution that one might make to the flow of ideas and understandings in the classroom. This is a phenomenon that hits particularly hard at young women, who may learn to give little value to the potential intellectual or personal contributions they might make to the community's deliberations. Paradoxically, this might be the very reason that girls now seem to be doing better academically than boys in our schools. Girls are likely, given the way they are socialized, to be less outwardly resistant to the increasingly alienating kind of learning that is demanded in our test-driven educational system. Before we celebrate girls' success as a victory for feminism, we need, I believe, to ask what the price is of this academic success. It is easy to see how this stunting of the female voice has resulted in the gross underrepresentation of women's voices at all levels of public leadership. For the teacher who is concerned with ensuring that all voices are heard and attended to, the classroom must be a place that offers the assurance of respect, safety, and dignity for all those who speak. Honest articulation of views and ideas does not absolve participants from the fundamental rules that guide civil discourse. In a culture, and especially in many high schools, where racist, sexist, and homophobic views are quite pervasive and are widely used as points of humor or one-upmanship, there can be no safety of expression unless such views are honestly confronted for their demeaning and even terrorizing effect on other students.

But respect for others' points of view does not mean an absence of spirited debate and discussion. Of course, as someone who has taught for more than two decades at a southern university, I often reflect on the contrast with my own Jewish upbringing, in which disputatious children are often savored (perhaps as a future Alan Dershowitz!), and heated argument is a part of the culture, even our recreation. Among many of my students there is a distinct discomfort with the forceful expression of disagreement with others. I am compelled to say that this is, I believe, a disabling condition for students. A democracy of expression demands that we learn to articulate our views, and to defend them, in discussion with others. The "truth" that democracy arrives at is precisely through this forceful exchange of ideas, in which we seek to persuade others as to the adequacy or inadequacy of one another's point of view. My students have often pointed out to me that in their upbringing, "respect" has usually implied the absence of any public expression of disagreement. In my view, this form of respect fails to distinguish between the affirmation of the dignity unconditionally due to each person, and taking seriously the views of an individual that might, indeed, justify serious debate. As a teacher, I attempt to convey to these students that honoring others may really mean, at times, that we share our honest reaction to what they have said, even if this involves significant disagreement. They readily admit how little, in their years of experience, the classroom has provided a space where there might be an honest sharing of views around, even such important and contentious issues as racism or homophobia.

Of course, the absence of open discussion about such issues reflects the avoidance by teachers and administrators of anything that might produce an emotional reaction. The classroom becomes one more space in our society where we might, ostrich-like, bury our heads in the sand and avoid addressing the serious issues that divide us. A democracy of expression represents the belief that empowering human beings is not a solitary process. We become freer, and achieve lives of greater dignity, not through the pursuit of private ends and interests (the kind of freedom that a consumer society so avidly promotes), but through the shared struggle to improve our world so that it is more just, caring, and inclusive.[18] Educators who encourage this kind of expression believe that the good society is one where more people have the opportunity and the encouragement to speak about their concerns, their hopes, and the things that hurt or harm them. We do this in an environment where we are also encouraged to listen to others do the same, and where we may envisage a world that seeks to make life better and more fulfilling for us all.

DEMOCRACY AS LIVED EXPERIENCE

Of course, in the end, democracy is not simply about words, else it would be an empty verbalism that allows us to vent our frustration or our dreams, and not much more. Democracy is ultimately about action. It is about changing the conditions that dehumanize and limit us as human beings, and expanding the conditions for living our lives as fully and as richly as possible. This means that learning to understand and give meaning to our lives, and to articulate our needs and hopes, must be connected to gaining the power to make change. The classroom and the school need to be places where the experiences of making decisions and sharing in the exercise of power are part and parcel of daily life. School should be a place that provides students real opportunities to make significant decisions about what happens there. There is a rich history of schools that have aspired to be democratic communities in which power is not held and exercised in the usual top-down manner.[19] Our experience is always that institutions that attempt to share power among all of the stakeholders tend to be places with a much greater sense of communal responsibility and individual involvement. In this context, the words that were spoken by the People of Israel at the giving of the Ten Commandments are similarly applicable: *we shall do and then we shall hear*. This strange formulation reverses what may seem most logical—first we hear something and then we do what is required. Yet the wisdom of the biblical text is in the realization that people are often required to actually live something before its full meaning becomes apparent to them. This makes good sense in the context of educating students in what it means to live and act democratically. All of our textbook readings or lectures on the Articles of the Constitution, or the Bill of Rights, do not add up to real lessons on citizenship in a democratic community. They remain for most students dry, abstract husks of information divorced from the authentic meaning and experience of democratic life. Only the lived experience of democracy can teach us its full significance: the need to approach decision making in an informed way, the struggle to make one's case amid differing points of view, and the give and take of public debate; the importance of rule-governed discourse; the examination of the ethical and social consequences of our actions; the difficult but necessary importance of reaching compromise among diverse constituencies. All these only become truly meaningful as we live them.

There is some hope in the move toward "site-based" management of schools, which is intended to give teachers and local administrators more power to affect change in their schools. Unfortunately, as Tom Popkewitz noted, this has often meant giving teachers more power over fewer things.[20] In other words, most of the really important matters about the curriculum, assessment, and so on are excluded from the purview of people at the local level—the ones who are most effected by them. What is left tend to be issues of minor concern in setting the agenda for a school. Educational scholar Michael Apple coined the phrase "teacher proof curriculum" to describe the manner in which curriculum materials are selected and assembled in ways that deny the creative input and intellectual involvement of teachers.[21] Teachers instead are turned into clerks who are expected to teach by robotically following rote instructions. It is no wonder that talk about needing to treat teachers with greater professional respect turns to ashes as teaching is turned into another version of McJob. Its results are plain to see in the increasing difficulty of keeping teachers in the profession. Those new and bright recruits are especially prone to abandoning teaching after a few short years. The hierarchical and authoritarian way in which they are treated and the lack of opportunities for any real input into their work environments are often cited as reasons for leaving teaching. Students, it should be added, are rarely seen as even nominally a part of the decision-making process in schools. Student governance could really mean that young people are trusted to be an important part of the decision-making process. That is rarely the case. Such exclusion simply adds to the general sense of alienation and cynicism found in high school. For many young people, schools, far from a place to learn the meaning of democracy, are the very embodiment of arbitrary decision making and unaccountable authority.

WHAT SHOULD WE TEACH?

The classroom, too, needs to be a place that defines how and what we learn in a much more collaborative way. The facts are quite simple here. Learning that is "top down," in which students are expected to passively absorb the knowledge that is handed to them by the teacher, usually represents a lesson in alienation. Student interest and energy in their learning increase as the level of their active participation in their education increases. It is sad that in many classrooms the traditional kind of "chalk and talk" teaching continues, and with it the typical manifestations of boredom and disinterest among students. Much that we refer to as problems of classroom management stems from this reality. But to take seriously the notion of student participation and responsibility in their own learning requires some far-reaching rethinking in what and how we teach. There must be a shift in the authority structure of the classroom so that the students' own knowledge, interests, and experience are valued and taken far more seriously in both the process of learning, and even in the choice of what is worth learning. Obviously, this is a very difficult and complex issue. This does not mean that teachers do not continue to have special responsibility for the moral and social regulation of the classroom, as well as the facilitation of learning. We certainly cannot discount the need for schools to transmit skills and information that all citizens must have to function in a complex, technically advanced society such as ours. But it does mean moving away from the "teacher knows everything and the student knows nothing" philosophy of learning, so that education is not a process of stuffing disconnected facts and information into the heads of students, as is so often the case. The classroom must offer much more opportunity for individuals to reflect on their own lives—their moral and existential significance. This requires deepening students' awareness as to how the ideas, assumptions, and beliefs that shape identity are formed within the society to which they belong. And we need to help young people see themselves as *co-creators* of the world through our human capacity to give meaning and moral significance to our lives.

This does not offer an argument—pro or con—about whether we need more or less math, or history, or science, or English in school. What is certainly the case is that we fetishize these subject areas, and imbue them with almost magical qualities. It as if something of value must automatically happen if a student endures a year of rote learning in a history class, or has remembered a sonnet of Shakespeare, or has memorized a geometrical proof. Perhaps, instead, we need to think of subjects not as nouns that we can collect as items on a shopping list but as verbs that promise to do something for or within us. To carry this metaphor forward, such fetishizing suggests there is something valuable, in and of itself, if we come home from shopping with our bag containing all the items on our list. Of course, the real value of the food is not that we can inspect it for its presence in our pantries, but that it can be cooked and made into something of nutritious value to our bodies and satisfaction to our senses. We spend too much time thinking about how many semesters or years a student needs to "take" this or that part of the curriculum, or drawing up lists of what needs to be "covered" in the various subject areas. More and more, this is done without really considering whether this will have any implication for the life of the individual—whether as result of learning something, the person will become more thoughtful, sensitive, compassionate, socially responsible, or, dare we say it, joyful. The decision as to how and what we teach should not be on the basis of habit, or the claim to some time-tested value ("everyone must read Hamlet," or know how to solve quadratic equations). The catastrophic experience of the 20th century, and the short but bloody first years of the 21st century, should bring home to us that so much more is at stake in the education of our younger generation. It is time to confront the relevance of what we teach, in the light of what our world truly needs, in these times of great danger as well as extraordinary possibility. To avoid the "banality of evil" that is produced by a submissive, obedient, and thoughtless consciousness, we must demand an education that is guided by the concern to empower human beings so that we might live lives that are critically aware, and always concerned for the widest possible good. Let us start from that, and figure out what kind of knowledge or experience we need to provide young people so that they might draw closer to this moral, existential, and social vision.

CORPORATE POWER AND THE CRISIS OF DEMOCRACY

The dream of democracy has always meant the dream of a society where all human beings have the power and opportunity to determine the shape of their world. We face, today, a world where this dream is being cruelly undermined by powerful forces that are reducing the great majority of us to the hapless victims of unresponsive elites. It is easy to see this in the United States, where there is more than ample evidence to demonstrate just how much our political system has been corrupted by special interests who have largely bought off the public leadership of this society.[22] To an extent perhaps unprecedented in our history, the politicians who lead this nation are beholden to the monied interests that hold economic power. The "revolving door" that connects corporate interests and policy makers in Washington, DC, makes it harder and harder to effect change that might benefit the majority of working- and middle-class people, and impossible to truly help those who are poor. More than this, however, is the fact that globalization has meant that economic power is no longer confined by national borders. The transformation that has integrated financial, manufacturing, and capital markets has removed the locus of power to places beyond the reach of our national polity, or of any system of democratic accountability. This means that decisions that affect taxes, budgets, the environment, and jobs occur more and more occur in places that are outside the influence of our own democracy.[23] The quality of our lives, our security, the conditions in which we work and exist, are increasingly shaped by nameless and faceless people who have little concern for the public or global good. In short, this is a time of profound crisis for democracy. Although people might have only a rudimentary grasp of the changes that are occurring, they sense that our political system is increasingly unresponsive to all but the privileged insiders, and that the globalization of the economy means that transnational corporate interests have unprecedented power to shape the world according to their own very limited concerns. One result of all this is an increasing disconnection, by many people, from the democratic process; a decline in electoral participation; a withdrawal from civic life and political parties; disinterest and ignorance about public and social policy, and global affairs; and a turn toward private concerns such as the home, the body, and private consumption, where people can exercise choice and have some sense of control over their lives. The things that shape the quality of our lives and determine our opportunities and choices are increasingly made in far away places by people who are unaccountable to the majority of us.[24] Decisions and policies that might make a real difference in the quality of our lives, such as universal health insurance, a viable minimum wage, adequate and affordable child care, significant availability of funds to offset the costs of college, or paid family leave in the case of illness, the birth of a child, or other significant events, seem stymied by economic interests that resist anything that might encroach on the ability to maximize their profits. The erosion of democracy in the United States is by now very well documented, leading some to suggest that we will need a third revolution in our nation's history to reestablish democratic control and accountability.

However change comes, there can be little doubt as to the importance of education to democracy and to the making of a citizenry that has the human attributes that a democracy depends on. As parents, and as concerned citizens, we must now demand that our schools attend to their responsibility of ensuring that those whom they teach develop the courage, thoughtfulness, and conscience to help bring about a more responsive world that is accountable to the needs of all people, not just of a privileged minority. The belief in democracy is, despite all of the threats to it, still deeply rooted in this country. It is surely education's responsibility to see that these roots are well tended so as to ensure not just democracy's survival in these dangerous times, but its full and active flourishing. This means that educators must become catalysts for young people's capacity to question and challenge the world that they are inheriting. More than this, it means encouraging their sense of possibility and agency: that it is indeed possible for them to help shape a world that is more just, loving, and generous.

NOTES

1. Hannah Arendt. (1963). *Eichmann in Jerusalem*. New York: Viking Press.
2. Zygmunt Bauman. (1989). *Modernity and the Holocaust*. Ithaca, NY: Cornell University Press.
3. These are numerous books and studies that document this. The list may include: John Taylor Gatto. (2002). *Dumbing us down*. Gabriola Island, BC: New Society Publishers. Alfie Kohn. (1999). *The schools our children deserve*. Boston: Houghton Mifflin. Jean Anyon. (1997). *Ghetto schooling*. New York: Teachers College Press. Peter McLaren. (2003). *Life in schools*. Boston: Allyn and Bacon. Neil Postman. (1995). *The end of education*. New York: Knopf.
4. Benjamin Barber. (1992). *An aristocracy of everyone*. New York: Ballantine. Michael Apple. (2001). *Educating the right way*. New York: Routledge Falmer.
5. Douglas Kellner. (2003). *Media spectacle*. New York: Routledge. Also Neal Gabler. (2000). *Life: The movie*. New York: Vintage Books.
6. Herbert Marcuse. (1966). *One dimensional man*. Boston: Beacon.

7. Maxine Green. (1988). *Dialectic of freedom*. New York: Teachers College Press.
8. Jean Kilbourne. (1999). *Deadly persuasion*. New York: Free Press. Also Mary Pipher. (1994). *Reviving Ophelia*. New York: Putman.
9. James Garbarino. (1999). *Lost boys*. New York: Free Press.
10. Mark Poster (ed.). (1988). *Jean Baudrillard: Selected writings*. Stanford, CA: Stanford University Press.
11. Douglas Kellner. (1990). *Television and the crisis of democracy*. Boulder, CO: Westview. Also Matthew Kerbel. (2000). *If it bleeds, it leads: An anatomy of television news*. Boulder, CO: Westview.
12. Philip Slater. (1991). *A dream deferred*. Boston: Beacon.
13. Joel Spring. (2004). *American education*. New York: McGraw Hill.
14. James Loewen. (1995). *Lies my teacher told me*. New York: Norton.
15. Walter Benjamin. (1998). *Illuminations*. New York: Harcourt, Brace and World.
16. Stuart Ewen. (1992). *Channels of desire*. Minneapolis: University of Minnesota.
17. Zygmunt Bauman. (1995). *In search of politics*. Stanford, CA: Stanford University Press.
18. Greene, op. cit.
19. Joseph Featherstone. (2003). *Dear Josie: Witnessing the hopes and failures of democratic education*. New York: Teachers College Press. George H. Wood. (1993). *Schools that work*. New York: Penguin Putnam.
20. Thomas P. Popkewitz. (1991). *A political sociology of educational reform*. New York: Teachers College Press.
21. Michael Apple. (1996). *Cultural politics and education*. New York: Teachers College Press.
22. See for example Charles Lewis. (2004). *The buying of the President*. New York: Harper Collins. Also Charles Derber. (2000). *Corporation nation*. New York: St. Martin Press.
23. Joseph E. Stiglitz. (2003). *Globalization and is discontents*. New York: Norton.
24. David C. Korten. (2001). *When corporations rule the world*. San Francisco: Berrett-Koehler. David Held and Anthony McGrew. (2002). *Globalization/anti-globalization*. Cambridge, UK: Polity Press.

6

∨∨∨∨∨∨

For You Were Strangers in Egypt

Looking upon myself from the perspective of society, I am an average person. Facing myself intimately, immediately, I regard myself as unique, as exceedingly precious, not to be exchanged for anything else.

No one will live my life for me; no one will think my thoughts for me or dream my dreams.

In the eyes of the world, I am an average man. But to my heart I am not an average man. To my heart I am of great moment. The challenge I face is how to actualize the quiet eminence of my being. ...

It is through the awareness that I am not only an everybody that I evolve as a ... somebody, as a person, as something that cannot be repeated, for which there is no duplicate, no substitute.

It is in the awareness of my being somebody that freedom comes to pass. ...

Turning from the discourses of the great metaphysicians to the orations of the prophets, one may feel as if he were going down from the realm of the sublime to an area of trivialities. Instead of dealing with the timeless issues of being and becoming, of matter and form, of definitions and demonstrations, one is thrown into orations about widows and orphans, about the corruption of judges and affairs of the market place. The prophets make so much ado about paltry things, employing the most excessive language in speaking about flimsy subjects. So what if somewhere in ancient Palestine poor people have not been treated properly by the rich ... Why such immoderate excitement? Why such intense indignation?

Their breathless impatience with injustice may strike us as hysteria. We ourselves witness continually acts of injustice, manifestations of hypocrisy, false-
hood, outrage, misery but we rarely get indignant or overly excited. To the
prophets a minor, commonplace sort of injustice assumes almost cosmic pro-
portions. (from Abraham Joshua Heschel, *I Asked for Wonder* p. 47, 79–80)

As I sit down to begin writing this chapter, I am mindful that it is only a week
away from the beginning of the Passover festival. This is a holiday loaded with
pleasurable memories for me: of being with family, eating the delicious foods that
are prepared only during the week of Passover in accord with the special dietary
rules of that time; of the craziness that went along with the effort to spring-clean our
home in anticipation of the holiday. Such memories evoke the never-to-be
recaptured wonder of childhood as the everyday routine is disrupted, and an aura of
the mysterious and the mystical seem to descend on one's world. But wrapped
inside that joyous time was the yearly recital of the events that Passover was
intended to commemorate. The holiday was the time when we "remembered" the
great formative historical experience of the Jewish people, the Exodus and
liberation from Egyptian slavery. In the rendering of this story at the ritual meal of
the Seder, Jews are enjoined not just to recall and recite the events leading up to the
exodus. They are expected to re-experience the oppression of slavery as if it is we,
today, who are living out these events. The biblical text makes this imperative
clear: You shall not wrong a stranger or oppress him, for you were strangers in the
land of Egypt (Exodus 22:20–24). This was no dry lesson in the history of a
long-gone event (in the way history lessons are typically experienced in school). It
was instead an admonition to see, and feel oneself, as a slave; to know for oneself
the pain and suffering of being treated in this dehumanized way, and to know and
feel the extraordinary blessing of freedom as we emerge from this state of
oppression. In this sense the Seder meal with its storytelling and rituals—eating
bitter foods; leaning rather than merely sitting in our chairs; breaking and sharing
the flat matzo, the so-called "bread of oppression"; singing songs of liberation;
opening the door to the presence of the stranger—is something more than a
pleasurable celebration. It is, above all, a pedagogic experience: a yearly
educational exercise in which we are to remind ourselves, both children and adults,
through all of our senses, that we should not abide oppression, whether our own, of
those near to us, or that of anyone who shares our world.

It is, I believe, a lesson I learned well. Of course, I am no longer a child, but I do
continue to share the Passover experience each year. In recent years, to make its
central ethical message clear to ourselves and to our children, we will sometimes, at
the Seder I attend, ask participants at the meal to reflect on the more recent forms of
enslavement and oppression. What, we ask, are our present "Egypts"? There are,
unfortunately, no shortage of examples. The ways in which human beings hurt and
oppress others are numerous, and as we move around the table eliciting examples,
the list grows rapidly: racism, sweatshop labor, poverty, the inability to afford

health care, homophobia, sexism, ethnic cleansing, sex-trade slavery. These are just some of the modern "Egypts" we name (I should add, both children and adults participate in this process). There is a wonderful small ritual at the Seder table that involves tipping some of the wine in our sacramental cups out onto a saucer. So, although we are enjoined to experience the evening as one of celebration, we are also reminded in this way that our joy must always be tempered by the recognition that others, including our erstwhile oppressors, are not as fortunate as we. Indeed, we are reminded that the price for Jewish freedom was a high one for the Egyptians who perished as they pursued the fleeing slaves. Even our oppressors have their humanity—we need to feel compassion for their losses and suffering. There can be little that is harder than this lesson of compassion even towards those who have caused you so much pain. Yet history has made clear that failure in this regard means yesterday's slaves become tomorrow's oppressors. Millions have suffered, and died, as those who were previously at the bottom are now able to wreak their vengeance on their erstwhile tormentors. As we have seen too often, the wheel of suffering and revenge, oppression and vengeful cruelty, takes another spin of its brutal circle. Yet there is hope that this lesson is finally being learned as we see remarkable counterexamples (most notably the Truth and Reconciliation Commission of South Africa), where a society seeks to ensure that healing rather revenge shapes the newly freed majority.

LOVE WITH JUSTICE

My own faith taught me, at an early age, to see a concern with unnecessary human suffering as central to a life of meaning and purpose. And, of course, the call to pursue social justice is inseparable from this concern with suffering. In the course of my work with teacher preparation I meet many who wish to enter teaching because they "have a love for kids." Of course, to feel this is not a bad thing. Few of us who are parents would not want a teacher for our children who does not have this strong positive attitude toward the young lives placed before him or her. For most of my students, love here is envisaged as a strong, affirming personal bond between the student and the pupil. When I ask these students about the connection between love and social justice, however, they are mostly stumped. (I should add that this is not generally the case among my African American students.) Few of them have learned from their education (or anywhere else, such as their religious traditions) that personal kindness and care for the individuals before them, as fine as it is, cannot address the deeply embedded and systemic way that lives in our world are stunted and diminished. A concern for justice in our world means that we become aware, and challenge, the way that institutions and social practices have "encoded" into them processes that maintain and regenerate harmful, oppressive relationships that damage and destroy human lives. Love without social justice, I tell them, is sentimentality; it is the Hallmark card that offers sweet words but leaves human lives and relationships pretty much the way they were before the card was delivered. It could well have been the case that in ancient Egyptian society there were those slave owners who were relatively benevolent in their attitudes (just as there were such individuals in the antebellum South in the United States). Yet such "kindness" in no way changed the deep, underlying inequities that created so much suffering and degradation. Although, of course, I want teachers to treat others with respect and kindness (indeed, I want this to be the case in all of our dealings with one another), this alone is not enough. Quite simply, a meaningful education can be that only if it is seized with the passionate impulse to help repair the hateful, callous, and dehumanizing ways that societies on our planet so often structure human relationships. With misery, hunger, poverty, and diminished lives so prevalent all around us, we need what Michael Lerner has called a new bottom line[1] in our educational goals—one that will be concerned not with the usual emphasis on individual achievement and personal success but with the great challenge of the 21st century, the ending of a world that excludes so many from the possibility of decent and secure lives, free from the debilitating oppression of material want.

The wisdom that speaks to the need for social justice is found, of course, not just in the ethical teachings of my own Jewish faith. It is recognized, again and again, in all of the great faiths and wisdom traditions. No society, they make clear, can be considered truly ethical unless it ensures that the least within it are ensured of respect and of adequate care for their physical and material needs. It is also spiritually indefensible to allow some to grow rich while others are unable to take care of their basic human needs. The coexistence of huge privilege and great deprivation is, these faiths agree, a moral offense to the spiritual order. Such divisions create a fragmented and divided universe and deny the fundamental oneness of being. This is, of course, inseparable from our modern statements of democratic belief and our universal declarations of human rights. Each asserts the fundamental entitlement of all human beings to those things that ensure a decent and secure existence: respect and full inclusion in the civic and political culture, and the expectation that society exists for the benefit of all citizens, not just for the increasing aggrandizement of elites.

A WORLD OF INJUSTICE

Tragically, our world denies and offends all of these expectations. We live in a world increasingly torn apart by the sheer horror of social and economic inequality. Preventable diseases such as tuberculosis (TB) and malaria run rampant in the Third World. Thirty thousand children die needlessly each day from malnutrition and treatable illnesses. The 2004 annual report of UNICEF noted that more than half the world's children (640 million) are suffering extreme effects of poverty, seriously deprived of basic goods and services such as food, health care, and adequate shelter. A poor country like Ethiopia has 7000 doctors for 67 million people.[2] Estimates of the cost of providing basic health care for all those presently deprived of it amount to $13 billion a year, much less than is currently spent in the affluent world on pet food.[3] David Held and Anthony McGrew noted that "the 900 million people lucky enough to reside in the Western zone of affluence are responsible for 86 percent of world consumption expenditures, 79 percent of world income, 58 percent of world energy consumption. … By comparison, the poorest 1.2 billion of the world's population have to share only 1.3 percent of world consumption, 4 percent of world energy consumption, 5 percent of world fish and meat consumption."[4] Michael Lerner noted that although our planet experiences unprecedented economic growth there is also a "staggering polarization of wealth." In 1960, he noted, the richest 20% of the world's population owned 70% of the world's wealth; today they own 86% of the wealth. And, in 1960 the poorest 20% of the world's population owned just 2.3% of the wealth of the world, but today this has shrunk to less than 1%. Clearly, said Lerner, globalization—the integration of world markets, which has promised to "lift all boats," both rich and poor—has not succeeded in producing a just global order.[5] To convey the sheer scale of social inequity, we might look at a recent report of the United Nations. It noted that to ensure that the global population received all of its basic needs (food, water, health care, and elementary education) would require deducting less than 4% of the 225 largest fortunes in the world.[6]

Behind these numbers are the brutal hardship of lives lived without adequate food, the discomfort of poor or nonexistent housing, the lack of availability of even primary education for children, the emptiness of a jobless existence, and the pain and early death from untreated diseases. The growing divide between the haves and have-nots has left huge and increasing numbers in the Third World in dire poverty and living on less than a dollar a day. Although there have been repeated promises to reduce poverty, the actual number of people living in poverty has increased by almost 100 million. This, as the economist Joseph E. Stiglitz noted, has occurred at a time that total world income increased by an average of 2.5% annually.[7]

Of course, we do not have to leave our shores to encounter the terrible social inequities that are the source of unnecessary human suffering and that represent a continuing denial of our desire for a compassionate, caring, and fair society. After Hurricane Katrina we surely can have little doubt about this. A new report by the National Urban League[8] indicated that Black Americans are less likely than White Americans to own a home, to earn as much, to do as well in school, or to live as long. Blacks are denied mortgages or home improvement loans at twice the rate of Whites. The average prison sentence received by a Black person is 6 months longer than for Whites. Black students continue to graduate from high school at rates significantly lower than among White students. And, on average, Blacks are twice as likely as Whites to die from disease, accident, and homicide. The life expectancy for Blacks is 6 years less than for Whites. The United States has the highest percentage of people in jail of any developed country—75% of these are Black or Brown. Henry Louis Gates has noted that although it is true that since 1968 the Black middle class has tripled in size, the percentage of Black children living at or below the poverty line is almost 35%, just about what it was on the day Dr. King was killed.[9]

Of course, the problem of poverty and life expectancy, although falling disproportionately on minority groups in the United States, is broader than this. At the time of writing 34.6 million people, one in eight of the population, falls below the poverty line. Of these, 13 million are children. Nearly 35 million Americans (including 13 million children) are considered "food insecure" (i.e., they do not know where there next meal was coming from).[10] Over 9 million were categorized by the U.S. Department of Agriculture as experiencing real hunger. And more than 40% of people standing in the food lines at churches or civic organizations are the working poor. More Americans now live in poverty than there were in 1965. Julian Borger noted that the United States has the highest child poverty rate (currently around 21% of the population) and the lowest life expectancy of all the world's industrialized countries.[11] In addition, he said, although poverty rates have been rising in the past few years, the number of Americans on welfare has been steadily declining. This is one effect of the 1996 welfare reform that meant the unemployed were required to take jobs at the minimum wage (at the time of writing, $5.15 per hour) without benefits, such as paid holidays or health insurance.

To understand the real offense of these statistics on poverty and life chances, we really need to see them in the context of a society where there has been an extraordinary increase in the polarization of wealth. In a remarkable piece,[12] the economist and political columnist Paul Krugman wrote that we are now living in a new Gilded Age—one, he says, that is as extravagant and as grotesque as the original one in the 1920s. Krugman noted that "Over the past 30 years most people have seen only modest salary increases: the average annual salary in America (adjusted for inflation) rose from $32,522 in 1970 to 35,864 in 1999. That's about a 10 percent increase over 29 years—progress but not much. Over the same period, however, according to Fortune magazine, the average compensation of the top 100 C.E.O.'s went from $1.3 million—39 times the pay of an average worker—to $37.5 million, more than 1,000 times the pay of ordinary workers."

This explosion in the pay of top executives, continued Krugman, is part of the broader story of the reconcentration of income and wealth in the United States. Over the past 30 years most of the big gains in income went to the very, very rich—to the top 0.01%. Almost half of the gains in income, he said, went to a mere 13,000 taxpayers who had an income of at least $3.6 million and an average income of $17 million. These 13,000 richest families, said Krugman, had almost as much income as the poorest 20 million households. They had incomes 300 times that of average families. How, we must ask, has this extraordinary increase in the wealth of the richest members of our society occurred? The simple answer, said Krugman, is that like the character Gordon Gekko in the Hollywood movie *Wall Street*, who asserted that "greed is good; greed works," moral strictures that limited avarice and social responsibility to the company and its employees evaporated in the post-Reagan world. In its place emerged managers whose only concern was to raise short-term profits as high as possible, at whatever costs to others. The repercussions of this outlook are not hard to see: the dismantling of whole industries to serve financial speculation, the plundering of pension funds, laying off of huge numbers of workers and rehiring at substantially less pay, union busting, outsourcing jobs to Third World economies, corporate malfeasance that produced windfall profits for a few and economic disaster for employees. All of this was supported and augmented by a political process that was controlled, and paid for, to an unparalleled extent, by corporate interests who demanded more tax breaks for the few, and a relaxation of the laws that made firms at least somewhat accountable for their products, the treatment of their employees, their effects on the environment, and their obligations to the community.

To see the impact of this greed on ordinary workers, we might look at what has happened to the incomes of ordinary workers. Andrew Hacker noted that today most American jobs do not pay enough to support a full household.[13] He says that in 2001 (the most recent year for earnings figures), of the roughly 100 million men and women with full-time employment, over half made less than $35,000. The days of a "family wage" that could support a household are gone. More and more Americans work in industries that maintain their profit margins by paying their workers at, or near, minimum wage (telephone call centers, temporary services, etc.). It is telling that between 1981 and 2003 General Motors shed more than half its workers, going from 746,000 to 350,000, while employment at Wal-Mart went from 27,000 in 1981 to 1.3 million people in this same period. The typical new job at Wal-Mart, he said, pays about one-third of the wage for many of the jobs that no longer exist. This downgrading of incomes falls particularly hard on women. The median paycheck for wives who worked in 2001 was under $18,000. For women who head households on their own, says Hacker, the median income was $18,472, (meaning, he adds, that half of them made less than that). "Three quarters of single mothers now work, mostly at bottom tier jobs, often because their welfare stipends have been cut off. ... Currently, 22.4 percent of US children are being raised under these straitened conditions." In this environment it is not hard to understand why there is support among many employers for relaxation of immigration controls. Migrant workers are willing to accept low-pay jobs—in hospitals, hotels, agriculture, construction, and so on. Since 1970 the Hispanic population has increased by a factor of five. And more and more workers are threatened by the loss of jobs to countries where cheap (and often submissive or cowed) labor is available. We need to add to this litany the fact that 47% of the private employees in this country—about 86 million workers now get no paid sick leave. Almost a third of all American families, according to the Economic Policy Institute, make less than what is needed to meet basic needs. It is telling that if the minimum wage had risen at the same level pace as executive pay since 1990, it would be $25.50 an hour, not $5.15.

STRUGGLING FOR TRANSFORMATION

We have here only provided the barest outlines of trends that reflect the growing disparities in life experiences and opportunities among human beings in today's world. But it is probably enough to make clear the way that the crisis in social justice is growing in our own country as well as throughout our world. "Justice, justice, you shall seek!" cried the ancient prophets. Today we too are in desperate need of a moral and spiritual transformation that will make the grotesque and terrible social inequities that blight our world intolerable to us, and politically and culturally unsupportable. Such social injustices are an offense to our deepest impulses as human beings to care for others. They are also an alarm bell to what awaits us if we continue to allow such suffering and deprivation to exist, in the face of the extraordinary surfeit, greed, and waste that are present in our world. Violence, terrorism, social breakdown, and increasing divisions among human beings are bound to continue and escalate. It is morally incomprehensible, and socially catastrophic, to imagine that we can continue in a "two-thirds world"—that is, a world in which two-thirds of the global population starve, or eke out a bare existence, while the remaining minority live in affluence. (Of course, this social structure more and more exists not just between the countries of the affluent and developing worlds, but within the rich countries themselves.) We cannot, for long, allow some in our world to continue living in unsurpassed and extraordinary luxury, while so many struggle to achieve the basics of a decent existence—adequate income, a job, health care, education, a home, and security in sickness, disability, unemployment, and old age. There is no more important moral task that faces us today—to transform the dysfunctional and debilitating inequities that confront us as citizens of our country, and as members of the global community. We must, quite simply, work to establish an alternative social and economic order that can make available to all of us the extraordinary benefits of human intelligence and ingenuity. This world, which systematically diminishes and stunts so many lives, has no inevitability to it. Billions of human beings are not necessarily fated to become part of what Richard Rubenstein[14] has called "surplus populations"—those who are treated as if they are unneeded human beings, and are discarded like our garbage or waste materials.

How can such change occur? I have no simple formula. Those who in the 20th century promised a direct and clear line to social improvement have usually provided false prophecy. But the suffering is too great, nonetheless, for us to abandon our efforts because of human failures. We may also note some of the extraordinary achievements in human betterment that have, indeed, come about: systems that provide pensions for those who are retired, unemployment insurance, medical insurance, free elementary and secondary education, legal protections for women, minorities, consumers, and workers, low-income housing, benefits for children, the disabled, and the mentally ill, food stamps, legislation to protect the environment, and much more. However flawed and poorly financed these public interventions often are (and, in the United States, frequently stigmatized), they nonetheless tell us that the possibility of a more secure and compassionate society is much more than the pipe dream of utopians. More than the institutions themselves, we may take heart from the enormous generosity, concern, and activism that exist today concerning the need for a more equitable and compassionate world. There is, now a worldwide civic culture that merges spiritual and ethical faith with political commitment, focused on the need for a transformation in our global order, toward a more just, caring, generous, sustainable, and environmentally sane world. On all sides the system of unfairness, social injustice, greed, and waste is under attack, and demands for radical change are voiced with greater urgency and clarity. Of course, this takes place within a political context that supports trends toward a more competitive and insecure environment for most people where jobs, health and disability insurance, pensions, unemployment assistance, financial aid for college, and other forms of social and economic support are eroded or removed. One wit noted that the conservative promise of an ownership society seems more like an "on your own" society!

This, then, is a time of extraordinary possibility. Amid the wars, violence, waste, and pain of human suffering there is also an unparalleled human awakening, and mobilization, for the healing and transformation of society. Beneath the usual news headlines is another story of change—one that involves a broad range of individuals and groups who increasingly recognize the inhumane, callous, and wasteful world we now inhabit, and the need to challenge and transform it. Inseparable from this concern for change and transformation is education. Such an education is, of course, quite different from the usual kind of schooling with its focus on individual conformity, competitiveness and personal advantage. This is an education whose goals are much more like the Passover Seder; its concerns are to develop, among children and adolescents, sensitivity to the suffering of so many, both in our nation and in our world, and the compassionate concern to use their life energies to change the sources of this suffering. Such an education will aim to awaken young people to the extent, forms, and causes of the terrible inequities and injustices in the world. It aims to encourage young people to see things in the world not as fixed and unchangeable, but as something that can and should be challenged. And it aims to develop within young people the sense of possibility that can enable them to reimagine our world as one based on care, compassion, and justice for all.

The greatest challenge facing the human race is, I believe, the creation of a just and caring planet. Given the extent and urgency of this task, it is impossible to imagine a purposeful life that does not see itself, in some way, concerned with this task. To live meaningfully today demands that we connect our lives to this struggle for a fairer society and world. To restore meaning to education is to connect it to instilling a sense of the importance of this task in our children. Commitment to the importance of this work calls for a transformation of both the mind and the heart. An education that serves the goal of making our world more socially just is an education of the intellect (i.e., an intellect that helps us to think more critically), but it is also concerned with our moral and spiritual lives. In the Passover Seder we are asked to not simply remember the dry facts of things that happened a long ago time, but to feel within our bodies the meaning of injustice; to reflect on the part of ourselves that wishes to turn back and stay within the familiar—even when the familiar is not, necessarily, in our best interest; and to experience the sense of possibility that comes as we emerge from oppression. It also requires us to find the understanding and compassion we need to deal with those who have, till now, treated us in unkind and demeaning ways. Finally, it encourages us to reflect on the extraordinary capacity we, as human beings, have to transcend our lives and to recreate who we are, both internally and in our relationships with others. An education for social justice calls on us in all of the wonderful complexity, even mystery, of our being.

SCHOOLING AND INEQUALITY

Of course, we know just how far school is from the pedagogy of the Seder. Indeed, in many ways school is an important component of the engine of inequality in our society. No facile talk about "Leave no child behind," or equalizing opportunities, can deny the role that education plays in maintaining and legitimating the inequalities found in our society. Indeed, as we noted earlier in this book, school is the great "sorting machine" that perpetuates the hierarchies of race, gender, income, status, and opportunity in the United States. It "teaches" the lessons of inequality through the everyday experience that young people have in school, which makes the way we divide and rank people part of our common sense understanding of the world. Social scientists like to talk about the school as a "transmitter of ideology"—the institution of schooling, in other words, conveys to students a set of powerful beliefs and assumptions about the world that seems to make the sorting and ranking of human beings plausible, predictable, and necessary. Ideology is not merely a term that refers to the ideas and beliefs that hold sway in society (the material consequences of which accrue disproportionately to the most privileged groups or elites in that society). It also implies ways of making sense of our world that are not just intellectually persuasive but also seem to conform to what seems like common sense. In other words, the particular way we come to know and give meaning to our world is felt, in our marrow, to make good sense. The great English scholar Raymond Williams once suggested that we should not assume that ideology is like an onion—that we need only peel off the top layers to get beyond the dominant beliefs of a society. If it were, he suggested, people's ideas about what is true or sensible could be undone and changed relatively easily. In fact, what we believe about the world can continue to be believed in the face of strong contrary evidence. We are emotionally invested in the meanings we give to things. We feel that what is at stake, when we question or challenge some of the basic assumptions we have about reality, is a threat to who we are. Such challenges may be felt to go to the very heart of our identity. Thus, even those who are obviously disadvantaged by social inequalities may continue to resist the possibility that their legitimacy and justification are questionable.

All of this means that releasing us from the grip of the thinking that supports and gives legitimacy to our present social order, with all of its unfair and harmful human consequences, is not something easily achieved. Yet we must also remind ourselves that the very purpose of ideology to justify, and give credence, to what we do and how we behave in the world is made necessary because we also have available to us some very different beliefs and convictions about what it means to be human. Such beliefs remind us that all human beings have inestimable worth, deserve equal respect, have lives that are precious, and are entitled to the possibility of a good, secure and full existence. Whether the support for these counterbeliefs comes from our religious faith (we are all made in *B'tselem Elohim*—the image of God), or whether it reflects our democratic values that assert that all people deserve to be treated as "ends" not "means," we cannot doubt the powerful and contrary view of how human beings should be treated that this provides. In the next pages we look at some of the ways that young people learn the ideology of social injustice, and we will contrast the harmful and damaging effects of this ideology with counternarratives that offer to young people a very different vision of how human beings might interact with one another, so that instead of recreating relationship based on hierarchy, division, and unequal recognition of worth, we might instead work to establish connections of loving community, mutual support, and equal regard for one another.

JUSTIFYING INEQUALITY

1. Education as a Race or as Community

From the first day when children step into the typical school they become immersed in a process of sorting and hierarchy. If we sincerely want our children to be disembedded from the consciousness of ranking and inequality, we have to confront the fact that school has been made into the great racetrack that instills in students the need to compete with others for roles that make them superior or inferior to others. School has become the primary means for teaching to our young that these kinds of human relationships are the inevitable and necessary way in which we relate to one another. It is strange indeed to talk of "leaving no child behind" when the ethos of finding winners and losers utterly pervades our classrooms and schools. In many ways the language of President Bush's federal law No Child Left Behind tragically confuses what our classrooms actually do, day in and day out. If one thinks about our kids' lives, the obvious truth of this becomes apparent. From the first day in school, teachers begin to sort and separate children—through reading or math groups that have clearly different levels of classroom status; through the awarding of gold stars or smiley faces to those they regard as doing best; and through grades that become the litmus test of children's success and failure, their worth or worthlessness. For most of us, the long years of our schooling are marked by the endless process of being judged, graded, sorted, and ranked; finding ourselves in "dumb" classes or "smart" ones; being channeled into tracks that promise further educational distinction, or the dead end of poor or mediocre standing; ascending the stage at the end of the school year to receive awards and recognition, or waiting below till the humiliation ends. There is almost no aspect of young people's daily lives that are not transformed into an opportunity to privilege some while downgrading others. School provides a relentless propaganda of division and inequality; it confronts kids with the constant reality of a world where everything is about finding winners and losers, and everything is about competing for the distinction of success and avoiding the ignominy of failure. For teachers, this capacity to judge and rank offers a powerful source of control over young people's behavior (badly needed because much of what goes in classrooms is a source of mindless boredom and alienation for most students). For young people, the badges of merit and recognition that schools dispense are, at least for the successful ones, a way to have their worth affirmed and their identity respected—something of extraordinary importance for children and adolescents. For parents, the process is, from the beginning, freighted with the concern for the security and welfare of their offspring. For good reasons, our increasingly insecure and competitive world means that almost all parents are concerned, from the very beginning (and sometimes before!) with their children's education, with their capacity to "make it" in the world. The anxiety-filled quest to "gain an edge" for one's own child is the driving force behind much of what parents focus on in regard to matters of education—what school or kindergarten their children will attend, which teachers or classes they will get, and so on. Of course, the well-off understand especially well how all this works, and decisions about where to live, or about which school or even kindergarten to have their children attend, are most certainly weighted with concern about eventually attending the right college, and having the social and economic opportunities that school success brings. The concerns of less well-off parents are not much different, except that economic survival, and gaining some material security, becomes more salient as one moves down the social ladder.

We looked in earlier chapters at some of the sad consequences of making school so much about sorting kids and erecting hierarchies of worth, rather than being concerned with more meaningful and humanly enriching concerns: the increasingly narrow focus on tests and test scores; the reduction of education to only those things that can be turned into quantifiable data; and the narrowing of the curriculum down to a more and more limited set of concerns (excluding areas like the arts). In addition, the increasingly test-driven, so-called more "rigorous" education, drives out the sense of play and pleasure from education, replacing it with an experience that is more stressful and anxiety filled. School then is, quite simply, the major vehicle for giving legitimacy to our grossly unequal social structure. It is the place, above all others, that begins the social sorting that will later end up by giving those who do well the imprimatur of justification for their disproportionate wealth, greater opportunities, better health care, and probably longer life. Conversely, those who will have few of these things are, indeed, shown to be unworthy of them—because they lacked the ability and/or the commitment to work hard enough at school to be successful. Once this becomes clear, the idea that school, as it is presently ordered, could work to leave no child behind becomes pure obfuscation—a bald-faced deception that asks us to ignore what we know about the relentlessly competitive nature of schooling, which is nothing if it is not about doing exactly the opposite of this. We might simply ask, what would happen if tomorrow all those who had been doing poorly in school started, miraculously, to demonstrate great improvement—would it mean that now there were no longer children falling behind? Would it mean, not just that they had better results on their standardized tests, but they could look forward to attending the more prestigious colleges that are the route to jobs that offer a life of relative wealth, security, and respect? No, it would mean no such thing! Those who are now economically and culturally advantaged are unlikely to concede the advantages they, and their children, now have. The bar can, and would, be raised as to what constitutes a good or successful performance in school. But more to the point, the criteria as to which students are considered desirable and worthy by the "best" colleges are always about a lot more than a few extra points on a test. Knowing this, and how it can be manipulated to one's advantage, is the "dirty little secret" of social class.

School, then, is a racetrack that teaches our children that there is nothing more natural or desirable than a world where people constantly need to compete for their relative standing on a "ladder" of success. Such experience prepares them well for the seeming inevitability of our socially unequal and divided world. It also subjects them, and us, to the deception of a race where each young life starts at the same point and thus has an equal degree of opportunity to succeed. The promise of "equal opportunity" has been subjected to a great degree of scrutiny, and its shortcomings are well demonstrated although usually ignored by legislators and others who control educational policy. In the United States there is no equal starting point for our children. The race is unfair from the start. Race, ethnicity, gender, and social class constantly mediate school achievement. Students come to school carrying their social and economic advantages and disadvantages. The advantaged (disproportionately White and upper middle class) bring with them the cultural and linguistic "capital" that enables them to immediately "decode" what is required of them in order to be judged successful. They also bring the knowledge and experience of their parents' own successful schooling (comfort and ease with the written word, familiarity with the "abstract" kinds of speech patterns used in the classroom and so on, a vocabulary that marks one as more intelligent), and the expectation that they can, and will, succeed in their own education. For the children of the upper classes, school is a vehicle that promises achievement, recognition, and success. It helps that for the children of those who are in the economically and socially more privileged groups, choice of school is in itself a factor of enormous importance. Choosing a private school, or a public school in the right city or suburban neighborhood, means more experienced teachers and the expectation of higher achievement, materially better equipped classrooms, smaller classes, and more curricular choices. There is also the reality that students in the higher achieving schools, or classes, are taught differently; they learn in ways that encourage their capacity to use more reasoning and creativity in their work, to have somewhat more autonomy, and to have the opportunity to think in more open-ended or "divergent" ways. Against this, among kids in the lower achieving schools or classrooms, instruction is generally more by rote, teaching is more rigid and didactic, and opportunities to think expansively or creatively are much more limited.[15] Of course, sociologists have pointed out that these differences are not accidental; they actually point kids in the directions of their future work lives—the bottom layers toward jobs that require very little in the way of independent thinking or creative judgment, and depend for their success mainly on knowing how to follow the rules set down by those in authority (of course, this does not mean that this necessarily happens—students in these classes can, and frequently do, contest the authority that seems to make classroom life such a drudgery, remote from anything that might seem interesting or useful to their lives). By contrast, the upper levels are directed toward colleges, and then work, that will expect higher levels of creative thought and more autonomous decision making. But more than this, the divergence in classroom experiences actually reflects and repeats the experience of many parents who themselves, in all probability, had the same kind of schooling as their children. This is what social theorists call the "reproductive" role of schooling. Of course, the United States is not a caste society. Children do not inevitably end up in the same social or economic strata level as their parents. Still, we cannot underestimate the extent that one's future success is influenced or determined by one's parents' relative social and economic standing. The main corporate source of testing in the United States, the Educational Testing Service, estimates that for each $10,000 increase in family income, students can expect to receive an additional 30 points on their SAT!

As I have found when presenting this information to my students (often first-generation college students), such evidence is uncomfortable for many brought up on the myth of equality in American society. Although there is, of course, a good deal of opportunity for social mobility in American society we should not imagine that the race for success is anything resembling a fair one. The race is most certainly a rigged one. The late Louis Althusser,[16] a famous French philosopher, suggested that the real "trick" of a dominant ideology is that it manages to find a way to paper over the contradictions between what we say and what we do—to make it seem as if there is no conflict in the way things actually operate in a society. What we have seen here is a good example of what Althussser had in mind: To talk about equal educational opportunities in a society where there are such great social and economic inequalities is, if we think about it, an obvious impossibility. Those parents who have material, social, and cultural advantages will, we can be sure, find ways to pass on those advantages to their children—through the schools they choose, the tutoring they can hire, the wonderful trips and experience they can offer their children, their offspring's exposure from an early age to literacy, their college resumé, and their ability to meet the costs of the most prestigious schools.

Is there an alternative to the deeply embedded way we prepare our children to accept the inevitability of inequality, ranking, hierarchy, and the competitive struggle for superior status? Of course there is. We could educate our children in environments where we make the process of testing students a small part of their lives (and then only used to help teachers make a diagnosis of whether a child has mastered a particular skill); we could eliminate from our education grading that diverts attention from the interest and joy of understanding and meaning-making, to the constant concern with comparing oneself to others; and we could end the pernicious process of tracking kids, which depresses the interest, motivation, and sense of competence of many students, as well as reinforcing the "ladder" of success and failure. Beyond this, we could attempt to make school a place that encourages a loving community of individuals—where each person's different strengths, interests, talents, and personality are valued, in and of themselves, not immediately placed on a scale of comparative worth, and students are encouraged to support and encourage each other regardless of their differing abilities. Such a school would celebrate the variation and differences among young people, not use these as opportunities to create new forms of ranking and division. Of course, there is no greater obfuscation in our ideology than to believe that changing the culture of school will somehow bring some immediate change to our larger social world. School is, after all, only a small part of our social system, not the engine that powers it. Still, our classrooms could certainly be places in which our children are encouraged to question the reality of a world where there is so much injustice, and where so many look forward to only the most blighted of lives. And they could certainly be encouraged to imagine the alternatives to a world in which we are always and everywhere expected to compete with others in the race for a decent life.

2. Education for Scarcity or Abundance

Beneath the surface of the compulsion to turn so many of our human relationships into competitive ones is, I believe, the phenomenon of fear. Seared into our sense of how the world operates is the belief that there is not enough of what we need for everyone. Recognition of our worth by others, love and affection, and money and material satisfaction are, we have been convinced, in short supply. Not everyone, we have been taught, will be able to acquire those things that seem to guarantee a good and fulfilling life. The world, ideology has persuaded us, offers only a limited amount of all these things, and this means that we will have to jostle and fight for our place in the sun. This idea of scarcity has very deep cultural roots—some argue that it is encoded in the parts of the human brain that are, in the process of our evolution, the most primitive. One can certainly understand its origins in terms of the limited means of sustenance available to early human societies. Of course, in all class-structured societies, although ruling groups or elites had available to them a surfeit of riches, the mass of people were compelled to fight it out for the leavings. Indeed, this scarcity of what was needed provided elites with a powerful tool to divide people against one another, as those at the bottom were encouraged to fight among themselves for the little that was left after the powerful had taken their share. "Divide and rule" has been a principle policy of powerful elites throughout the ages. Today we face a different kind of world, yet one that is filled with the fear and suspicion that continues to be bred by the mentality of scarcity. In an earlier chapter I described the significance and centrality of the "bell curve" in the process of schooling. It is in many ways a key dimension of the "hidden curriculum"—that set of attitudes, beliefs, and values that school teaches us through the ways that students learn to see themselves, as well as how they are taught to relate to others. Scarcity is encoded into the very idea of the bell curve, the concept of which is "taught" to all children in our culture from the moment they set foot in the schoolhouse. Quite simply, kids learn that success in the classroom is a limited commodity, and is not available to everyone. The "law" of the bell curve makes it necessary that only some children can be outstanding, whereas others will not succeed. The rest will be of average or mediocre achievement. Scarcity of success is, in other words, built into the very structure of our classroom culture. However much we may want or hope that all children are successful in school, the scarcity mentality, built into the bell curve, excludes that possibility. Here is another example of our friend Althusser's argument that ideology functions so as to paper over, or obscure, the way that cultures have contradictions built into their modus operandi. So although politicians or policymakers might talk about leaving no child behind, or teachers may work hard to ensure success for all of their charges, and every parent prays that their child might do well, the socially constructed reality of school necessitates that we sort out the purported chaff from the wheat. The ideology that governs schooling is one that means children must be constantly evaluated and judged so as to sort and select them—to ascertain winners and losers. Our culture has built the very idea of educational legitimacy around the notion that schools, can and should pick out and reward the best and the brightest from the rest of the population. Indeed, the more "rigorous" this process of sorting, the more seriously we regard the intent of the school. The very idea of "raising the bar" of academic achievement means little if it does not imply that success and achievement are made harder to get—school is required to become increasingly discriminating. So where "too many" children get good grades, or passing test scores, there is a panic that our standards are too low. Maintaining educational standards means ensuring that there are an adequate number of failures!

Of course, more is at stake here than a letter on a report card or a number on a test result. These indicators of assessment are in fact the gateways to social affirmation and recognition by the official institutional world. They are also the path for many kids to attain parental approval, praise, even love. Later they translate into opportunities for or barriers to attending a college, and acquiring the means to economic well-being and social respect. In all of these respects the mentality of scarcity underpins the belief that only some can be considered smart, successful, well recognized, and economically secure. This is a very powerful means through which to legitimize our class divisions. The concept of scarcity instructs people that there is not enough of the "good stuff" to go around, and only some may expect to be treated with the respect that will guarantee them good, fulfilling, and decent lives. When we go to school we are taught, from early on, that anyone may be successful (if they are smart, talented, and/or work hard), but—and here is the kicker—not everyone can. The social reality we have built has within it a consciousness that allows only for some of us to be rewarded, whereas others must pay the penalty for their lack of success! When we are urged to work hard in school so that we can "get ahead," we rarely stop and wonder—"ahead of who?" How does it come to be that my success requires somebody else to fall behind? It is a strange moral economy indeed that we have created!

I have earlier alluded to some of the consequences of this scarcity mentality. The "culture of separated desks" means that the ethos of the classroom is one of competition among students, as each individual must vie for the praise, or recognition, of the teacher. It produces suspicion and distrust as each individual views the knowledge, skills, and competencies of his or her neighbor as something that provides the other person with a potential advantage. Even among the graduate students I teach, the mentality of scarcity, sadly, often shapes classroom interactions as students view with some suspicion, even hostility, the knowledge that some of their peers seem to possess.

Of course, in the wider culture, the consciousness shaped by scarcity invades our thinking and feeling. The constant reiteration of sales in which only a few of what we want remain, or are available, sends us into a shopping panic. The sense that there are not enough jobs available instills in us a sense of insecurity and vulnerability, as well as potential hostility to others who are our competitors (this easily becomes transformed into racist or antimigrant feelings). We are told that soon there will not be enough money to guarantee a decent retirement pension for all older Americans, or medical care will have to be rationed. On the geopolitical level the belief that there is not enough oil to go around propels us into wars to "protect" our supplies of energy from those who might wish to take it from us. Or we come to believe that famine and hunger exist because there is not enough food to go around. The mentality of scarcity is a powerful vehicle that generates fear, distrust, and hostility. Yet so much of it is based on false premises. The sales frenzies are created by retailers to stimulate sales. The lack of jobs is a result of "man-made" causes—a choice to "export" work to other countries, the decision to make more profit by replacing people with machines, the desire by Wall Street to keep an "excess" pool of labor to weaken workers bargaining power, or our inability to consider transforming the work culture—to shorten the hours and days of labor—so as to share the employment needed. The projected shortage of funds in Social Security, and the rationing of medical care, are the results of political decisions to reduce taxes, mostly for the wealthy, and to protect the privileged power of the medical lobby. Shortages of fuel have everything to do with our scandalously wasteful and irresponsible culture of transportation. Famine, it has been well established, has much more to do with the politics and economics of food distribution than with a shortage of available food—one only has to consider the fact that although two-thirds of the world's population is seriously undernourished, the other third has to worry about the growing problems of obesity![17]

The goal of challenging and uprooting the consciousness of scarcity in us and our children will be a difficult one. Although it produces a culture of endless competition, insecurity, distrust, and fear, we are, nonetheless, "hooked" on it. Obviously, changing our school culture so that it no longer reflects this mentality will not undo its effects everywhere else in our society, but it would at least be a start. Our school can heal some of the harmful effects of scarcity thinking by creating a culture in which we encourage the sense of mutual support and the sharing of what we have—our knowledge, experience, skills. None of these things should henceforth be viewed as the means to gain an advantage over someone else. The school culture can become one in which all children are honored and respected, not just those who are "awarded" respect through being better at something than someone else. Obviously, this means that we need to eradicate the incessant forms of judgment used to divide students, and the forms of evaluation that reinforce the bell curve of success and failure. We will need to teach that there is an alternative to the "zero-sum" kind of world in which my gain means your loss—a way of living that makes us suspicious and aggressive toward others who may become a threat to who we are, and what we have. In place of this, we want to encourage relationships in which the most joyful experience comes not from hoarding what we have, but sharing these things with others. This means, too, that we need to help our children understand that our culture mistakenly encourages us to believe that having privileges of possessions, position, power, or celebrity that few others have makes you a happier or a better person. Much more likely is the result that having access to scarce resources actually stimulates jealously, rivalry, and hostility toward you. We can also teach our students a critical skepticism toward the claim that there is a scarcity in the resources needed to feed, clothe, house, educate, and care medically for everyone in our world. Finally, we need to teach a different kind of wisdom in which we understand that there is a potentially endless abundance among human beings of loving relationships, generous hearts, creative ingenuity, thoughtful intelligence, beauty, and the sense of wonder and appreciation for the extraordinary nature of life.

3. Teaching Us/Them, or Educating the Whole

There is an unmistakable link between scarcity and racism. The consciousness of scarcity brings with it, as I have noted, a pervasive sense of insecurity and anxiety. Human beings have to deal with the constant nagging fear of others taking away, or threatening to take away, the gains and advantages that have been won in the struggle for the limited material or social rewards that are available. However well one is doing, the society organized around the principle of scarcity is one in which others threaten to take from you the things you now possess, or the status you have acquired. Put simply, you are only as successful as your last success. Tomorrow represents a whole new day in which the battle for one's advantage, or security, must begin again. A society that functions in this way is one in which there is, not surprisingly, an enormous amount of free-floating anxiety that emanates from one's sense of a continuing vulnerability to the predatory behavior of others. Such anxiety easily, and frequently, shifts into suspicion and hostility, and into a demonizing of others in the society, who become one's real or imagined competitors. There is always the danger that this hostility might fall on those elite groups who have gained most advantage in the society and who live lives relatively immune from the insecurity that affects the daily existence of ordinary people. This would, of course, threaten to expose the socially unjust way in which society is organized, and the manner in which the scarcity game is loaded in favor of those at the top of society—a game that keeps most people constantly scrambling to make ends meet, and to ensure their survival, and that of their family. In this kind of social system, racism (anti-Semitism more often in Europe), has played a crucial role in diverting resentment and fear in directions that are much less threatening to elites. The fear of others that is the unavoidable product of competitive social environments becomes focused on a particular social group on which can be projected much of the insecurity, frustration, and anger that are the product of this environment. So, in the United States, Blacks have long been identified as the preeminent group that collectively threatens the well-being (albeit insecure) of White people. Of course, defining African-Americans in this way is ludicrous given their real position in society, one in which they have almost always been on the bottom rung in terms of power, wealth, and opportunity. Despite this, whether in jobs, housing, education, crime, or taxes, African-Americans have been depicted in ways that position them as threats to the security and well-being of working- and middle-class White Americans. The destructive, racist narrative holds that it is Black competition for jobs that drives the economic insecurity of White workers; or that insecurity in our homes or streets is because of the dangers posed by Black males; or that our taxes are inflated by the need to support irresponsible Black females; or that school standards are endangered by the presence of too many Black students.

Of course, it goes without saying that the mendacious and simplistic narrative of racism in America has a long history that reaches back into slavery and segregation. Although the story has gone through shifts and turns, it remains, at its core, one that constitutes a group of human beings as possessing traits, behaviors, and characteristics that continuously marks them as dangerously different, and threatening, to the majority population. When teaching about racism in my undergraduate classes, I pry from my (White) students the list of racist markers that they have grown up with, whether in their homes or in their wider communities: "shiftless" "threatening," "lazy," "dependent," and "lacking intelligence" are the kinds of things most often articulated. It should be said that most of these students are aware that these adjectives are damaging distortions that carry hurtful consequences. Many of them struggle to free themselves from the presence of these stereotypes in their thinking. Yet it is also true that this is a difficult process made harder by the continual reinforcement they receive in the racist stories that are transmitted through our culture—whether on the news (where Black males are relentlessly presented as thugs and dangerous criminals); in movies, where Blacks are constantly associated with violence and drugs, or as clowning buffoons; in political discourse, with its constant association between welfare abuse and African-Americans: on or in the distorted representation of Blacks in public life and popular culture (as preeminently athletes or entertainers or gang members). Still we must also confront the grain of truth in these representations. Where young people grow up in environments that provide few opportunities for economic and social advancement and where there is a sense of hopelessness or realistic possibility of change, at least through legitimate means, in one's life possibilities, rage and nihilism are likely to become endemic. Cornel West, among others, made the point that where life-giving meaning and purpose cannot find ground to adequately root, the market morality which saturates our culture will shape behavior and attitudes; desensitized and exploitative relationships fill the space of human interaction, and dreams of money, celebrity, and power become the focus of one's life energies. Attached to our culture's pervasive masculine images of physical power, sexual conquest, and domination, the combination produces the grotesquely violent, misogynist, and self-destructive gang culture so prevalent in the minority neighborhoods of our cities.

Still, America has made some remarkable progress in confronting its racism and dismantling some of its effects. The claim that we can be a democratic society that simultaneously relegates a whole group within that society to second-class status has been exposed as a contradiction that gives the lie to any such claims. And the struggle for liberation from the terrible consequences of slavery, segregation, and racism has been one of history's great and noble stories. It is a story that remains, nonetheless, unfinished. There is still a chasm of understanding that divides Blacks and Whites in America as to the salience of racism in contemporary life in this country. Blacks perceive a society that still makes judgments about others that is dependent on skin color—this holds true whether it relates to the experience within the criminal justice system, where there are glaring differences in the likelihood of arrest and in the kinds of sentencing that is meted out to felons; or the access that is available for decent jobs, bank loans, or mortgages; or the availability of property—whether for rent or purchase; or in the kind of educational opportunities that are offered; or in the availability of quality health care. And the list goes on.

Whatever the progress, we are still a society of enormous denial in regard to the problems of race. The solutions that are posed in many ways avoid or obfuscate the real issues that confront us in regard to the legacy of inequality in our treatment of racial and ethnic difference in this society. Of course, nothing makes this clearer than in the pseudo-solutions posed in regard to the failures of education, where there is willful refusal to place this problem in its proper social context. We seem unable to come to terms with the reality that educational issues are really reflections of enduring forms of social, economic, and cultural injustice. When over 30% of Black and Latino children live in poverty, and the federal government has neglected to meet the social, economic, and health needs of most children, it is preposterous to believe that educational reforms such as No Child Left Behind will make much difference to the likelihood of these children's success in school.[18] Our schools continue to mirror a divided society that relegates the majority of Black and Brown children to what amounts to a segregated system of education. Fifty years after the passage of the famous Supreme Court ruling that ended legal separation of schools, minority children still disproportionately attend schools that offer a wretchedly inferior environment for education. Gary Orfield, a respected scholar of our nation's racially divided system of education, wrote, "Black students are the most likely racial group to attend what researchers call 'apartheid schools,' schools that are virtually all non-white and where poverty, limited resources, social strife and health problems abound. One-sixth of America's Black students attend these schools."[19] It is important to add that Blacks are not the only group to suffer the injustice of racism in America. Orfield noted that Latino students, are even more heavily segregated, by language, race, and poverty. Educational failure cannot be separated from the deep social and economic divisions in our society. Racial segregation in schools, he observed, is strongly linked to segregation by class: "Nearly 90 percent of intensely segregated black and Latino schools are also schools where at least half of the student body is economically disadvantaged. ... Today's segregated schools are still unequal. Segregated schools have higher concentrations of poverty, much lower test scores, less experienced teachers and fewer advanced placement courses."[20] We might add that today only 14% of White students attend multiracial schools—schools where three or more racial groups are present.

All of this underlines the fact that any real concern our society has with educational failure cannot be separated from the continuing, and broader, racial and class divisions in America. Alfie Kohn, the educational critic, has questioned, for example, how many of the schools that have been identified as "struggling" have actually received the financial resources they need to meet their palpable deficiencies.[21] The promise that students not being served well in their present schools could opt to move to other, more successful, ones makes little sense. How, we have to ask, could the millions of poorly educated minority students in this country move to other schools, whether private or public, without overwhelming these schools? This is a phony solution to a massive social and educational disaster. The constant attempt to subject such schools to high-stakes testing, Kohn argued, has brought no positive results ("unless you count higher test scores on these same tests"), other than humiliating and hurting schools that were already identified as struggling with difficult problems. He continued: "More low-income and minority students are dropping out, more teachers (often the best ones) are leaving the profession, and more mind-numbing test preparation is displacing genuine instruction."[22]

Racism is one form of that virulent disease that seeks to divide human beings into categories, one or more of which is stigmatized as having inferior status or worth. Such stigmatization is based on a fiction that is used to create, maintain, and justify societies where human beings receive vastly different, and unequal, kinds of treatment, whether in employment, in the justice system, in education, in the mass media, in health care, or in other social provisions. Categorizing human beings in this binary, or "us/them," manner gives those in the privileged group a sense of their superior worth, justifies their advantages, and gives legitimacy (at least to those who gain from the system) to the oppressive and exploitative treatment meted out to those at the bottom. Racism not only produces deep social, political, and economic inequalities; it also warps human relationships by undermining the reciprocity and mutual respect that such relationships depend on. The effects of all this are found not just in the external world but also in the disfigured, and distorted, way that the injured groups sometimes come to see themselves—as less able, less attractive, and less worthy. In educating our children about this, we need to convey the all-too common human tendency to create "us/them" societies. Racism is but one example of this. Anti-Semitism, ethnic cleansing, tribal massacres, hostility toward immigrant groups, homophobia, communal-religious intolerance, xenophobic nationalism, can all be found aplenty in today's global society. It is a paradox of the contemporary world that as the world becomes smaller and more integrated, there is an upsurge in the virulent demonizing of others. The need to teach our children about the terrible effects of racism, ethnocentrism. and all other forms of intolerance grows ever more urgent.

It is a sad reality of schooling that, either out of fear to address emotionally difficult issues, or because of political resistance to dealing with such concerns, racism, cultural difference, or intolerance is rarely made an active focus of the curriculum. This is one more example of the refusal of schools to address with their students the real issues that confront human beings today. And it is the way that schools remain places without meaningful opportunities for the young to deal with the urgent challenges of the real world. Despite this, there is an extraordinary abundance of curriculum materials that address every dimension of racism and intolerance—whether viewed historically, sociologically, psychologically, through literature and personal narrative, or through the expressive arts. Although multicultural education is often dealt with in a watered-down and trivialized form, there are certainly available serious and penetrating materials that enable students to critically explore the intersections of political and economic power, culture and identity in the making and maintaining of racism. Education, I believe, must deal with intolerance and racism, both through the lenses that are provided by critical scholars that enable us to understand its social function in the past and in the contemporary world, and through the more immediate and intimate process of dialogue and interaction with others. The latter should enable young people to personally confront and hear the pain and hurt that are the human consequences of racism and other forms of negative categorization.

Nor can we be shy of offering an alternative vision to the terrible social injustices and human suffering that are the consequences of the damaging fictions that allow us to oppress and humiliate others. Sometimes such constructions work through their invisibility, making it possible for some of us not to see the suffering and deprivation of others in the world. This is perhaps especially so with the exploitation of workers in the developing world (these are often children or adolescent girls), who provide the cheap goods that our affluent Western culture depends on. If they can be regarded as somehow fundamentally different from, or "other" than, the way you and I are ("these people are happy to work for a dollar a day"), then we are able to ignore their dreadful work conditions and life prospects. Or if they are Africans suffering the scourge of AIDS, we might view their plight with an indifference that comes from our learned inability to view these people with the same sense of empathy we have for other human beings. All forms of racism imply a desensitization to the human reality of others' lives, a deadening of our feelings of compassion for the other. We need, finally, to offer our children a different vision of our humanness—one that sees ourselves, not in endless categories that mark our differences from others, but with understanding that we all are part an undivided unity, or oneness, where there are no limits or borders to our responsibility to care for, and ensure the dignity of, others in our world.

4. Blaming the Victim or Challenging Injustice

One of the most powerful forms of support for racism, and other kinds of social injustice, is through the process that the sociologist William Ryan termed "blaming the victim."[23] Ryan developed the term to refer to the way in which we learn, in America, to blame the plight of poverty on those who are poor, rather than attributing it to the social and economic system and the way that it creates and maintains a stratum of impoverished individuals. Sometimes, in trying to get this idea across, I draw an analogy to the way courts and judges will suggest that women who have been raped or sexually assaulted have invited such violence by their demeanor or personal behavior. Of course, this is a phenomenon that continues in our courtrooms, although progress has been made in making a woman's prior sexual history inadmissible in court. In turning rape into the consequence of an individual woman's personal behavior, the society can ignore the pervasiveness of violence toward women in this culture. Such violence is then regarded as a matter of the individual actions of its victim, having little to do with the systemic way our culture defines masculinity as a matter of the power that men can exercise over women. In an analogous way, poverty is seen as the result of inadequate or improper socialization that makes poor people lazy, irresponsible, and dependent on others. So much of the debate on welfare reform in the 1980s and 1990s (leading up to the overhaul of welfare under President Clinton) was cast in these terms. Welfare was widely seen as a vehicle by which some people could abuse and exploit a system that fed their socially irresponsible attitudes and behavior. Of course, such accusations, although having some truth, ignored the great majority of clients, for whom welfare was a badly needed (albeit minimal) safety net for them and their children. The crusade against the poor—usually misrepresented in the media, and by right-wing politicians, as primarily Black and unmarried, with large numbers of children—raged on despite all the evidence that showed just how misguided these media-fed stereotypes were. In reality, people on welfare typically stayed on it for only short periods, and had families that were about of average size.[24] Contrary to the idea that those on welfare sought to stay on it indefinitely, most recipients very much looked forward to holding a regular job (although this was made complicated by the lack of affordable day care where young children could be safely left during the work day, the need for transportation to get people to jobs, and worries about health insurance for kids). Indeed, research made clear that, contrary to the stereotypes, most poor people in the United States were White and usually already working in low-income jobs.[25] A sad postscript to the debate is that although the welfare reform led to large numbers of women losing their eligibility for welfare and being required to take any jobs that were available, this had no effect on the extent of poverty in the United States. Today we have a larger number of women working in poorly paid jobs, without the benefit of health insurance or adequate day care for their children. The United States has a disgracefully large number of women and children living in poverty (a greater percentage than any other comparably wealthy nation), which has little or nothing to do with the existence of welfare benefits.[26]

It is easier for many to turn society's problems into ones that are about individual behavior rather than a flawed social system. The welfare debate showed that there was a deep wellspring of poisonous thinking in this country that did not wish to face up to the systemic nature of poverty in America, and that had little to do with an individual's personal values and behavior. The facts that 45 million people are without health insurance, and that around 20% of children live at or below the poverty line, and that 70% of single women with children live at or below the poverty line should make it clear that the issues are wider and deeper than can be explained by the action of individuals. This does, however, have a great deal to do with the lack of social justice and compassion in a society that has failed to enact social policies to ensure that all citizens are well taken care of, able to live with a minimally decent standard of living. Instead, it is easier to simply blame the victims.

Education has always been a powerful vehicle for reinforcing this individualistic ideology of success and failure. School has always tried to present itself as an institution where achievement is the result of personal effort, commitment, and native "smarts." In this sense, schooling promises to judge children based only on the capabilities that each individual child might bring with him or her to the classroom. This ideology is reinforced by the "positivist" or scientific claims of educational testers and psychologists who represent their methods of assessing children's abilities, or intelligence, as objective and precise.

In this way, the resulting hierarchy of success and failure in schools—the meritocracy—can be regarded a as a fair and accurate reflection of students' natural aptitudes and intellectual abilities. Such a claim is, however, nothing short of preposterous. From its very beginnings, intelligence testing has always been marked by its racism, ethnocentricity, and gender bias. Although it has always resisted owning up to the truth, such tests have a long, well-documented record of racial, ethnic, and class bias. In a wonderful and important book, *The Mismeasure of Intelligence*,[27] author Stephen Jay Gould showed how intelligence and aptitude tests have a strange habit of demonstrating the intellectual superiority of those groups who have a dominant social, cultural, and economic role in society.

We have already shown that, far from being a meritocracy, success in schools is highly influenced by where one is able to go to school—a choice usually determined by one's residence. The location of one's school determines the quality of teachers, resources, materials, courses, and other opportunities available to students. Who one goes to school with is enormously important in shaping the expectations one might have for further studies, jobs, and so on. Within schools, far from an objective process of picking "winners" and "losers," classrooms are notorious for the unequal way that teachers respond to, and treat, students. Educational researchers have made very clear just how differently teachers respond to, and judge, students, based on their race, gender, and income, and how these differences then become "invisible" labels that shape and limit how individual students view their own abilities, competence, and expectations of success. In the well-documented idea of the "self-fulfilling prophecy," the particular, and usually prejudicial, judgments made about students' abilities and competence become a "reality" as individuals internalize and accept the "truth" of these judgments (in much the same way as individuals given the title of "professor" eventually come to see themselves as all-knowing and wise!).

The very idea of aptitude or natural ability must be viewed with suspicion. With the right preparation, students can learn to become successful at SATs (we have already noted that success on the SAT is heavily related to the income level of one's parents). African-American students who have done well on standardized tests in trial situations have been shown to crumple when placed in the stress-inducing conditions of the actual exam.[28] Intelligence tests that have been redesigned so that they speak to the cultural knowledge and experience of minority groups show very different, and vastly improved, results. It is important to remember that intelligence itself is a socially constructed phenomenon. No one actually walks around with a numerical value stuck to their brain like a manufacturer's label. IQ is a statistical artifact that supposedly reflects abilities on a combination of tasks. As researchers like Howard Gardner have made clear, human ability and intelligence exist in a wide variety of forms, and it makes no sense whatsoever to compress these into a single numerical index (about as much sense as suggesting that a man who has one foot in a pail of boiling water and the other in a pail of ice can be said to have a temperature that reads 50°Celsius!). The real purpose in constructing a single numerical value like this is transparent—to find a way to quickly rank and compare people. This process is made a lot easier if we can believe that an individual's intelligence can be reduced to a single number. Beyond this, we know from anthropology that intelligence is situational—it has everything to do with the things that are valued and emphasized in a culture, with the kinds of intellectual, linguistic, and social competencies that have the most currency in that society, or in a subculture of that society. The skills, knowledge, and "smarts" valued among kids living and surviving in the barrios of Los Angeles, are likely to be very different from those of young people growing up in the Detroit suburb of Bloomfield Hills, a community of great wealth, where the expectation is to attend one of the nation's elite universities or colleges. In our increasingly pluralistic society, the demand of social justice requires that we recognize that there is no one standard for indicating intellectual or creative ability. We have to work to move from the "one-size-fits-all" standard of culture and education, to a far more complex view of human ability, talent, creativity, knowledge, and reason.

The tendency to transform the extraordinarily fluid and adaptive nature of human intelligence into something fixed and permanent is a characteristic dimension of schooling. It is necessary if we are to convince ourselves that there is legitimacy to the way we assess, divide up, and rank students, place them in ability groups, or assign them to different curricular tracks. The reification—the process of giving something humanly created a stone-like facticity—of ability allows us to believe that the system of inequality we produce in school follows some natural order. In this way, differences, such as who belongs in a special education class, or who is to be placed in an honors class or college preparation track, seem to naturally and permanently inhere in individuals, and are not the result of a socially biased process of sorting people out on the basis of spurious qualities. Ultimately, this is a process that enables those in society who benefit most from the way things function to feel no real responsibility, indignation, or empathy for what happens to those who are end up among the schools', or society's, failed members. Rather than understanding that poverty, joblessness, lack of health insurance, and school failure are the consequence of a system that actually creates winners and losers, the fortunate can choose to regard it as the result of things—poor choices, lack of effort, or differences in ability—that are neither their fault nor their responsibility. Perhaps it tells us something about our time that there has been renewed talk about the unequal distribution of intelligence among different racial groups as a way of "explaining" school failure among minority groups. The phenomenon of "blaming the victim" is a recipe for social indifference to the fate of our fellow citizens; it is a license to callousness and irresponsibility. For our young people to grow up with a developed sense of social justice, empathy, and concern for others in our world, we must help them understand the way that "blaming the victim" works, including how it hurts

women, poor people, minority students, immigrants, and others. It is important
that our young people grasp the fact that we live in a social system in which
suffering and hard consequences befall people not mainly because of the
inadequate choices they might have made, or some God-given deficiency they
may have, but much more because of the system's built-in tendency to treat
people in differential and unequal ways.

Of course, this in no way is meant to suggest that individuals do not carry some
responsibility for their lives. Acting in the world with a sense of responsibility and
concern for the decisions we make is certainly a part of the process of becoming
mature and developed human beings and citizens. Although this must be
emphasized in our education, we also want young people to feel a strong sense of
compassion, and responsibility for those whom the system fails. Individual
responsibility for one's life and the need to care for those who are in need of support
are not mutually exclusive aspects of a good society. We need to encourage young
people toward a sense of responsibility in their own lives, as well as a readiness to
challenge the injustices that they see limiting the possibilities of others' lives. Our
education must ensure that they do not take the easy or smug path of believing that
others' hardships or pain are simply their fault, or their burden alone. For as, the
sage Rabbi Hillel once asked, "If I am not for myself, who am I, but if I am for
myself alone, what am I?"

5. Democracy Versus. Capitalism

We must return one last time to Louis Althusser's belief that ideology works
through hiding or obscuring the conflicting or contradictory tendencies in our
belief system. There is no more important area for understanding this conflict than
in the relationship between democracy and free markets. One of the things that we,
in America, are continually reminded of in our news commentaries, textbooks,
political speeches, and so on is the idea that democracy and the market place are
bosom buddies; that the values and practices that govern each of these parts of our
public life reinforce each other in a harmonious fashion. The fall of the Soviet
empire did, indeed, seem to suggest that capitalism and democracy are two sides of
the same coin—that the emergence of democracy meant also the simultaneous
emergence of the free market. On the surface, it has certainly looked that way. Yet a
closer reading of our history in this country, as well as the experience of other
countries in what we usually refer to as the free world, suggests a much more
complex relationship between the two. Far from representing things that merge
seamlessly into one another, my own belief is that this picture is very far from
describing the way this works. The actual social and political history of countries
with both market economies and democratic political systems is one of constant
tension and conflict between these parts of the society. In fact, I believe that to
understand something about this conflict is to unlock a crucial secret of the social
system. Let me explain why this is so. The answer is to be found in the very

different, often opposing, values that are embodied within democracy and within the market system.

At the core of capitalism is the belief in the unfettered freedom of individuals, or corporate businesses that are treated as if they are individuals, to use their skills, knowledge, and entrepreneurial acumen to gain as much profit as they possibly can. This is done within the freewheeling and competitive environment of the marketplace, where one's capacity to outsmart ones competitors is the supreme goal of those within the system. To outsmart refers here to a host of possible behaviors and decisions—the creative ingenuity that produces new products and ideas; the capacity to reduce the costs of what one produces so as to corner a greater part of the market (that includes lowering the cost of what one pays employees to the maximum extent possible); the ability to convince the buying public (through advertising) that one's product is both desirable or necessary, and the best of its type available. While playing within the rules of the game (obviously something we know may well not be the case), the simple goal is to out-hustle competitors so as amass the greatest amount of money that is possible and provide the greatest return on stock that can be achieved. The name of the game within the capitalist world is competition, and the accumulation of whatever power is needed to increase one's wealth. It is a world that is obviously about winning or losing, making money or being driven from the market. All of one's intelligence and efforts must go toward besting those one competes with. The fruits can be an enormous expansion of wealth; the creation of a myriad range of new products, services, and technologies; and economic growth that provides large numbers of jobs. But the market also produces economic cycles of booms and busts that make life for workers an insecure one. As companies constantly search for new ways to lower their costs, they are driven to "export" jobs to countries where they can pay workers less money and where there is less need to be concerned with their general well-being, and also to shape the rules of international trade to benefit those that have rather than those that don't. Far from being a truly "free market," the market also leads to a concentration of economic power as the big "fish" swallow the small ones; such concentration leads to the very undemocratic capacity to influence the political process so as to get the kind of laws and policies that enable powerful economic interests to prosper. And (as we showed earlier in this book) capitalism depends on "educating" people to want the ever-changing and expanding array of commodities that businesses can produce—our desires must be constantly aroused and stimulated through the mechanism of the advertising industry, which reaches into every corner of our emotional lives. This emphasis on the ever-increasing production of new material wants places a tremendous, even ultimately catastrophic, strain on the earth's ecosystem in terms of the exploitation of the earth for primary resources, the pollution of the planet's life systems, and the volume of waste that must be daily discarded.

Although the marketplace is about the interests of particular individuals or groups seeking their own increased money, power, and control, democracy speaks to the needs of the whole community (remember here that the reality of democracy has been a deeply flawed version of the ideal). The first declarations of democratic rights and freedom in 1766 applied to a small coterie of privileged White males that excluded most of the population in the United States, whereas the democratic "imaginary," as it has been called, has been a powerful catalyst to including more and more people as entitled to the rights of citizenship. Sometimes this expansion has proceeded through gradual change, but at other times it has meant fierce struggles against those who wish to exclude other people from full citizenship. It is a proud dimension of our public life in the United States that almost of those groups that were once excluded are now a part of our democratic political and legal system (although groups such as gays and lesbians are still denied their full civil rights). The civil rights struggle of Black America, as well the struggles of women, labor, and the poor, native people, other ethnic groups, disabled groups, and today gay and lesbian men and women all provide inspiring and extraordinary examples of the courage, commitment, and determination of people to achieve their democratic rights. Democracy, in its essence, asserts the equal rights of human beings—regardless of their wealth, status, gender, religion, race or ethnicity, linguistic community, sexuality, or disability. But the struggle to achieve equal civil and political rights in America is not the only form of democratic struggle. There is also the demand that citizenship means ensuring that all members of society are provided with those things that guarantee a decent life—the right to an education, and to adequate food, to housing, health care, insurance against unemployment, security in one's old age or infirmity, and so on. We can refer to these as our social and economic rights within a democracy. In the United States the struggle for the expansion of these rights is part of what we mean by liberalism, although, in other places, such as Western Europe, it is usually referred to as social democracy.

It is probably apparent at this point that there is serious conflict between Right and Left over the extent that our democracy ought to be a social and economic democracy. At its core is the question of whether it is the market or the state that should be the arbiter of how our social and economic needs are provided for. Those who believe it should be left to the market argue that the quality of one's life should be primarily a matter of how smart, hardworking, or entrepreneurial one is. Of course, determined in this way, things like health care become subject to the spin of the roulette wheel of a person's life. Following this, some will find themselves living lives of plenty and comfort, whereas others will find themselves lacking the rudimentary resources to provide a decent existence for themselves and their children. For social democrats, citizenship that offers civil and political freedom without the capacity to feed, house, and protect oneself from sickness, disability, and joblessness are meaningless. The market, for all of its creativity and energy, has not, and cannot, meet all of the public needs of a society. It is a dangerously misguided idea to believe it can. The private sphere, left to itself, only ensures that those who are better positioned in the society are fully taken care of. The much-touted freedom of the market often becomes the freedom of some to get ahead, and to take advantage of their economic or cultural privileges, whereas for others it means a "freedom" to fall further behind without seeing any improvement in their lives. The freedom of the market becomes a banner through which to eliminate all those hard-won gains of working-class and middle-class people that guarantee at least some protection from the vicissitudes of the market and the insecurities of life. This is a freedom for private interests, untroubled by the belief that a good society is measured by a sense of social justice and broad public concern that ensures that all of society's members are looked out for.

There are currently many battlegrounds where the conflict between private freedom and public responsibility is being played out; today these include health care, social security, taxes, to name a few. Education, too, is a particularly important focus for this struggle. It is important to emphasize two things about public institutions in the United States: They are our primary vehicle for ensuring that this country is a fairer, more socially responsible, and more compassionate society; at the same time they are usually inadequately funded, excessively bureaucratic, and constantly under the gun of those who would like to see an America in which almost all services are privatized and are part of the marketplace. Indeed, unlike for our cousins in Western Europe, there has always been a high level of hostility to the state, and the public sector, that enables right-wing politicians to be elected and to set the agenda of the society. The right wing promotes the argument that freedom (not social justice) is the moral priority of this society, and private interests are the best way to ensure that everyone's needs are met. This promotion of private interests often turns out to be much more a self-serving recipe for economic gain than a genuine proposal to ensure the widest availability of the good.

As I am writing this book, the effects of No Child Left Behind in this regard are plain to see. Proposed by a very right-wing government as a way to improve public education, it appears to be more a Trojan horse for privatizing education. The reform's proliferation of standardized tests fuels the belief in the widespread failure of public education (of course, most of the failure, not too surprisingly, is found in those schools that serve low-income and minority populations). This evidence supports the agenda of those wishing to move students and financial support towards religious and private schools whether through the system of vouchers, or through supporting a rapidly developing network of for-profit schools (such as former Secretary of Education William Bennett's company, K12). The Bush Administration's Department of Education has (at the time of writing) funneled more than $75 million taxpayer funds to pro-voucher groups, and to various for-profit educational concerns. In addition, No Child Left Behind has proved a windfall to the companies that design and score standardized tests, as well as private tutoring services like Sylvan and Kaplan that provide tutoring services. As the *Wall Street Journal* noted in a story about it, "Teachers, parents, and principals may have their doubts ... But business loves it."[29]

PUBLIC SCHOOLS AND PUBLIC RESPONSIBILITIES

Of course, there can be little doubt that reforms like No Child Left Behind really do speak to the way that public education has failed many kids, even in providing the most minimal forms of schooling. It's calls for excellence and equity certainly resonate with many parents' frustration at their children's experience. There is more than one world of public education. These are deeply differentiated in terms of the money that is spent on students, the adequacy and safety of school facilities and the resources that are available, and the experience and qualifications of teachers, among other things. Like so many things public, in this nation, behind the promise of universal responsibility are so often the divisions of race and income that betray this intent. Public institutions frequently exhibit within them the same inequities that scar the rest of our society. A few hours spent at a local social service agency can leave one in no doubt of that. Yet to believe that the answer to this sorry situation is to abandon the whole ethic of public responsibility, leaving it to market forces and private interests alone to serve our human needs, is to define all these needs as purely egoistical and selfish. However well or badly it might be honored, to speak of a public institution is to connect the work of this institution to our nation's cherished democratic values. It means that our concern is not about whether this individual or that will succeed in advancing his or her interests. Instead, democracy's concern is with the well-being and progress of the whole community. Although the ethic of the market place is about advancing individual interests and personal gain, democracy speaks to our needs as a whole society. Thus, in purely material terms (as President Franklin Roosevelt famously noted), the richness of a society is measured not in terms of the wealth of the most affluent but by how the poorest are treated. Making private gain and individual interests the guiding star of our society will certainly produce a world that is fractured by growing inequalities. It will also be a society that is disfigured by greed, selfishness, and a lack of concern for our fellow citizens. Commenting on the push to privatize social security, Benjamin Barber noted:

> Privatization—whether of education, housing or social security—makes us less of a public. It diminishes the republic—the res-publica, or public things that define our commonweal. It turns the common "we" into a collection of private "me's." It opts for market Darwinism, in which smart investors prosper but others lose, rather than social justice as its organizing principle. It demeans the 'us' by turning "us" into "it"—the big, bad, faceless government bureaucracy. And it privileges the private and individual by appealing to market liberty, as if people could really be free one by one or as consumers.[30]

Can public schools more fully live up to their public responsibilities? Of course they can. But that will require a transformation in our attitudes so that school is less dominated by the competitive sorting and ranking of individuals. Instead, education would offer young people the opportunity to examine the needs and challenges that face us as a community, and to join that with engaging in considering how society can be changed so as to meet these challenges. To repeat something I have already said several times in this book, genuine education is a quest for meaning—and meaning is found not in some private oasis, but in the midst of our shared human lives. Nothing is more central to a life of meaning than the making of a world that is more socially just—a world where fewer human beings suffer lives that stunt, diminish, or deprive them of worth, dignity, and possibility. In this chapter I hope I have made it clear that both our nation and our global community, are faced with the extraordinary moral, spiritual, and political challenge of growing injustice and deprivation in the midst of plenty. Sometimes this injustice, with its resulting suffering, is simply not visible to others; sometimes the lack of knowledge of others' plight is willful ignorance—it's easier not to know; and at other times there are elaborate mental constructions that make the moral and social offenses of our world palatable or acceptable to us. Our job as teachers, parents, and citizens is to ensure that the young are aware of the great challenges facing human beings in the 21st century. We must help them, also, to think in a critical way (as we have done here) about some of the mechanisms that allow us to accept or adapt to so much injustice, and to see how far are our promises regarding democracy and equality from society's reality. Finally, and perhaps most crucially, we must work to ensure that our children possess the sensitivity, concern, and, yes, outrage toward so much suffering and human indignity. Without this depth of feeling, no change is likely. Unlike our Passover education, this task cannot be a once-a-year affair, but must, instead, be a part of educators' everyday concern. Only in this way can education play a role in the moral and spiritual transformation so urgently needed in the human community.

NOTES

1. Michael Lerner. (1997). *The politics of meaning*. Philadelphia: Perseus Books.
2. Guardian (online). (2004, February 16). *A new deal for the world's poor*.
3. David Held and Anthony McGrew. (2002). *Globalization/anti-globalization* (p. 77). Cambridge, UK: Polity Press.
4. Ibid. (p. 77).
5. Michael Lerner. (2004, March/April). Passover supplement. *Tikkun Magazine*.
6. Marie France Collard. (2000). *Working women of the world*. [film]. Brooklyn, NY: First Run/Icarus.
7. Joseph E. Stiglitz. (2003). *Globalization and its discontents* (p. 5). New York: Norton.
8. News and Observer (Raleigh NC) (2004, March 24). *Blacks face wealth gap, report says*, p. 3.
9. Henry Louis Gates. (2004). *Behind the color line*. New York: Warner Books.
10. David Oliver Relin. (2004, April 4). How we can help end childhood hunger. *Parade*, p. 6–9.

11. Julian Borger. (2003, November 3). Long queue at drive-in soup kitchen. *Guardian* (online).
12. Paul Krugman. (2002). For richer. *New York Times Magazine*, p. 62–77.
13. Andrew Hacker. (2004, February 12). The underworld of work. *New York Review*, p. 38–40.
14. Richard Rubenstein. (1987). *The cunning of history.* New York: Harper Collins.
15. Jean Anyon. (1997). *Ghetto schools.* New York: Teachers College Press.
16. Warren Montag. (2002). *Louis Althusser.* London: Palgrave MacMillan.
17. Eric Schlosser. (2002). *Fast food nation.* New York: Harper Collins.
18. Arlene Holpp Scala. (2002). No Child Left Behind. *NWSAction, 15*(2). p. 20–21, 33.
19. Gary Orfield and Erica Frankenberg. (2004, Spring). Where are we now? *Teaching Tolerance*, p. 57–59.
20. Ibid. (p. 59).
21. Alfie Kohn. (2004, April). Test today, privatize tomorrow. *Phi Delta Kappan*, p. 568–577.
22. Ibid. (p. 573).
23. William Ryan. (1976). *Blaming the victim.* New York: Knopf.
24. Alvin Schorr and Herbert Gans. (2001). *Welfare reform.* Westport, CT: Greenwood.
25. Sharon Hays. (2003). *Flat broke with children.* Oxford University Press.
26. Barbara Ehrenreich. (2002). *Nickel and dimed.* New York: Henry Holt.
27. Stephen Jay Gould. (1996). *The mismeasure of man.* New York: W. W. Norton. See also Kincheloe, Steinberg, and Gresson. (1996). *The bell curve examined.* New York: St. Martin's Press.
28. Theresa Perry, Asa G. Hilliard, and Claud Steele. (2004). Young, gifted and Black. Boston: Beacon Press.
29. Alfie Kohn, op. cit. (p. 573).
30. Benjamin R. Barber. (2005, January 27). Privatizing social security: 'Me' over 'we.' *Los Angeles Times,* latimes.com.

7

vvvvvv

Educating For Peace

Reality may be read through an infinity of lenses. Each refraction carries its own unique bias. Children speak of true and false; adults know better. This is not to say we have given up on truth, only that we now understand how elusive it is. Nor is it to suggest that truth is relative. Indeed we now suspect there is an absolute truth and that it is mysteriously connected to what some people call "God." God is not truth but standing in God's presence may be. How matters appear to God, that is true.

We choose our truth by the scope of our vision. To see beyond the present and beyond the end of our allotted days is to understand why we have been created. As our priorities are rearranged, meaning is revealed, truth glistens. To see our place in creation, in other words, is an act of faith. To comprehend our intended task is our only shot at glimpsing what is enduring and absolutely true. Without the long range lens, nothing is false, but nothing is true either. We are adrift.

And what can be told of what we finally see? Only that All Being at its core is One. Everything else may be false. This may be the meaning of Moses strange death and inability to enter the Promised Land. Denied entrance, he was given something better: The ability to see it all from a high mountain, a vision of truth.

A fact is always the same. Once you learn it, you have it forever. But truth is different. Once you understand it, you are forever changed and the truth disappears. And because you are now someone else, you must learn it all over again. (from Lawrence Kushner, *The Book of Words*, Jewish Lights Publishing, 1993, p. 115)

Six years ago, at the turn of the new millennium, there was anticipation that the world was about to enter a truly new age. Alongside those who awaited the event with anxiety, expecting catastrophe, there were many others who felt that the 21st century might truly augur a time when we might look to the end of a human history of war, needless suffering, and torment. Of course, one might argue that there was nothing especially rational about either expectation. The level of human suffering changes with the transforming of the conditions that produce pain, not the movement of a calendar. Still, it was hard not to feel that something was stirring. For me the most memorable aspect of this event was simply how it created a sense of common connection across so many of the world's peoples. The innovations of communication technology made it possible for us to follow on live television the inauguration of the new century from time zone to time zone, and from continent to continent. We could watch, and share, with people all across our planet this common event. There was something wonderful, I felt, about this celebration that was inclusive of people all across our world, focusing on our common human destiny rather than on the differences that separated us. Through the immediacy of television we could witness, and share, in our living rooms the joyful celebrations of human beings in the rich diversity of their physical appearance, and in the extraordinary multiplicity of their cultural and spiritual expressions. Yet unlike most shared global events today, such as the Olympic Games or the World Soccer Cup, we rejoiced not in our victories over one another as individuals and nations, but in the pleasure of a shared renewal of time, and with it the sense of new possibility.

The events of six years past now seem a very long time ago. The hard-headed realists were right that all of this celebration would mean little in hindsight, because not much had really changed in the human condition. Poverty, malnutrition, disease, unemployment, war, greed, racism, ethnic hatred, environmental despoliation, and so on were still with us even after the advent of the new millennium. These things cannot be denied, so what did we expect? But perhaps, some of us can be forgiven if, for a moment, it was as if the heavens had opened and we were given a glimpse of a world that shared a common sense of joy and hope, in which we experienced a feeling of our common humanity, while relishing the multiple and diverse ways that this humanity manifested itself. For a moment we could be forgiven if we imagined a world that had seen beyond those often lethal markers of difference—race, ethnicity, nationality, religion—and could recognize the value and wonder of our shared humanness.

THE DREAM OF PEACE AND THE CULTURE OF VIOLENCE

This idea of peace, which does not deny our differences, but allows us to engage with one another in dignity, respect, and mutual reciprocity, is a very old idea. All the great monotheistic faiths do, indeed, recognize and elevate the value of peace above all other goals (although our religions, it need hardly be added, have often become primary vehicles for inciting hatred and violence against unbelievers). Perhaps the ancient prayer to bless the peacemakers has become joined, in the modern age, to awareness about the insanity and wastefulness of war, violence, and killing. Globalization, for all its social and economic injustices, also makes our world a much smaller place, in which human connectedness becomes a more palpable reality. Telecommunication now compresses space and facilitates hitherto unimagined forms of relationship and intercourse among peoples. Images from space reinforce our growing knowledge about the fragility and preciousness of our small life-support system called planet earth. Flows of population from one continent to another bring even the remotest hamlets into contact with those who are culturally and physically different, but still share common human desires for physical well-being, economic security, and improved lives for their children. Of course, all of these phenomena also produce effects that are anything but peaceful—increasing competition for jobs, fears about cultural or religious assimilation, awareness as to how unfairly distributed are material resources and wealth. Few of us were aware in 2000 that less than 2 years from the start of the new millennium this country would find itself confronting a rage that would unleash unprecedented terror on thousands of innocent people in its greatest city. Few anticipated that the world would be plunged into a new spiral of violence and war. This new war pointed to the complex, even intractable, dimensions of violence in the world. In particular, it made horribly evident the fear and hatred that are spawned by political arrogance, economic power, and cultural domination. In the face of this, ancient religious faiths turn rabid, intolerant, and violent as they absorb, and become a vehicle to mediate, humiliation, insecurity, powerlessness, and social injustice. On all sides, people become convinced that right, even God, is on their side, and the enemy comprises not flesh and blood human beings, but a demonic force that must be swiftly annihilated.

And so we were awakened from our tantalizing dream of peace, and the possibility of a world without the bloody death, maiming, and physical suffering that encroaches on so many lives. Today, it seems, violence names our lives. Wars continue to rage all over the world; countries threaten one another with nuclear annihilation; brutality and violence, especially against women, know no borders; terrorists treat their own bodies and those of their hapless victims with a horrifying indifference; racism, ethnocentricity, and homophobia provide reasons to inflict emotional and physical pain on one's neighbors; tribalism gives license to mutilate and annihilate parents and children. Across the globe, recent surveys by the United Nations have shown the appalling number of children (estimated at over 2 million) now actively mobilized as combatants in wars. And there is the structural violence that is less immediately visible as a form of violence but builds human suffering into the very means by which a social system operates. Included here are the millions who are deprived of necessary AIDS medicine because the pharmaceutical giants do not want to reduce their profit margins; the hunger that results when the sustainable farming of indigenous peoples is destroyed by agribusinesses and extractive industries that forcibly appropriate the land for their own greedy needs; the huge arms industries in the Unites States, Britain, France, Israel, and elsewhere that supply weapons to buyers around the world without concern for their use; the inequities in global trading that ensure continued debt and poverty for the world's underdeveloped countries; military conquest and domination as the means to ensure continued cheap oil for the fossil-fuel addicted Western economies, especially the United States. All of these bring incalculable physical suffering, starvation, sickness, and death.

Nor can we ignore the culture of violence that so influences everyday life in this country. The number of firearms in circulation in the United States is estimated to be at over 190 million. It sometimes produces the horrifying outbursts of school violence that, from time to time, focus a nation's shocked attention. But less visible are the thousands of other victims of violence. Homicide is now the third leading cause of death among children 5 to 14 years old and the second leading cause of death among youth and young adults.[1] The dangers faced by women both in their homes and on the streets are well documented. Violence and terror directed at gay people and migrant workers, or out of racist and anti-Semitic motivation, continue. And there are the everyday forms of violent intimidation, such as bullying in schools, and abuse of children by adults, which may not produce permanent physical consequences but scar the soul in ways that can be equally long term in their effects. Behind this is a culture that endlessly celebrates war, guns, violence, and aggressive behavior. Although it is far too simple to blame Hollywood, with its ceaseless outpouring of movies that graphically portray killings, torture, and murders, we may assume this contributes to our culture's addiction to violence. Hollywood has always celebrated the gun; now it provides, for our viewing pleasure, a vivid exposure to a whole new range of murderous technologies. Can we doubt that young people's constant exposure to such images produces what Zygmunt Bauman has termed the disease-like state of adiaphorization—desensitization to the reality of human pain and loss.[2] Movies that graphically depict mutilation, rape, and torture are meant to evoke a cool detachment among young people. The latter are invited to enjoy the terror as entertainment and release. Elsewhere, gangland brutality and rap music exist in a symbiotic relationship, each goading the other toward greater excesses of aggressive posturing, misogyny, and ultimately violence. Heroic depictions of the Mafia underworld have jumped from the screen versions of Italian-American culture to the real world of poor urban Blacks and Latinos.

Of course, the violence we are talking about here belongs overwhelmingly to the world of boys and men. It is sometimes easy to forget that the vast preponderance of violent acts are committed by males. Violent crimes committed by women are an insignificant proportion of the total. Shootings, bombings, and mayhem are the focus of many, if not most, of the popular video games (almost always played at by males), with their ever more realistic simulations of violent and life-threatening behavior. War games and the glorification of military culture are a pervasive influence on the male psyche. And we should not forget here the role of professional sport in constituting a popular culture that so much emphasizes and celebrates testosterone-driven aggression. Hockey, football, basketball, baseball, and wrestling, provide only the most visible vehicles for a culture of intimidation, threats and physical attacks. The value of the aggressive will to win at all costs is something that is relentlessly glorified in our culture, and permeates now not just the highest levels of professional sport, but increasingly college athletics, and even athletic leagues for adolescents and children.

COUNTERING VIOLENCE:
THE EDUCATIONAL CHALLENGE

The shocked horror that accompanied the Columbine shootings has given way to more muted reactions to subsequent school murders. The demands for action have been tempered by an increasing sense of inevitability and even paralysis. School violence has been assimilated into a broader sense of fatalism and passivity about the perpetuation of violence in our nation and in our world. The deeper questions about why such things happen give way to the pragmatics of detecting early warning signs, setting in place emergency response procedures, and providing grief counseling to the survivors. Instead of being understood as a symptom of, or response to, a toxic social environment, killing is seen as the outburst of deranged or psychologically abnormal individuals. Yet as we enter the 21st century, it is surely time to question the inevitability of violence in our world. Can it really be true that human brutality, war, indiscriminate terrorism, and torture are the inevitable fate of humankind—the unavoidable products of human frustration or conflict? Must we regard violence as an unalterable dimension of human—especially male—behavior? Whatever kinds of progress we have made as a species, the world continues to be awash in violence and bloodshed. And the new millennium that began with so much hope already looks very much like the old one—although our capacity to inflict harm on others grows dangerously with our technological sophistication.

The answer to all these question can, and should, be no. Despite all the awful events that seem to surround us, it is also possible to see an emerging consciousness that points to the possibility of transcending such behavior: international courts that hold torturers and war criminals accountable; global treaties that renounce genocide, or the use of inhuman means of combat; an increasing cognizance of the terrible emotional and physical consequences on children of adult violence; and public resistance and denunciation of the brutality and coercion directed at women. All these suggest a growing counterconsciousness to the usual human behavior. Despite continuing wars, there is good reason to believe that there is increasing public revulsion to the use of violence in dealing with human difference and conflict. We can look at unprecedented worldwide mass protests at the use of military means to resolve the crisis in Iraq. But, in the broadest sense, our greatest human challenge—to end the violent nature of our existence—is an educational one. The growth of a counterconsciousness to the acceptance of violence needs to be the result of a deliberate human effort to develop an understanding of, and sensitivity toward, its destructive and futile consequences. Educating for a more peaceful world must, I believe, be placed at the center of our educational vision. Of course, this educational challenge is quite unlike the ones that our politicians and their bureaucratic henchmen now insist are central to the current agenda for education. Peace education is certainly very far removed from the compulsive quest for higher test scores, or the concern for technical competencies that has emptied educational experience of meaningful intellectual, emotional, or spiritual purpose. Despite what our political and corporate leaders would like us to believe, the quality of life in this new millennium will depend much more on the capacity of human beings to find ways to resist the draw of victimizing and brutalizing their fellows and the seduction of joining those who build their sense of identity and value on the indignity or pain of others. Rather than increasing competitive pressures and stressing individual differences, as our current education does, peace education aims to transform our culture and our consciousness. Peace educators make the point that ending violence is ultimately not a pragmatic matter of containing, or enacting laws against violence but a matter of creating a culture of peace—one rooted in respect for life, social justice, humility toward one's own truth, empathy for the other, and a commitment to addressing differences and conflict among us through democratic processes of dialogue and reciprocal understanding.

The events of recent times have brought home to us the horrifying and painful consequences of human hatred as this is mobilized around ethnic, religious and national divisions. To these we can add the hurt and suffering that result from differences of race, social class, language, gender and sexuality, and migrant status. Hopes that the pain unleashed by these social divisions is somehow the smoldering embers of ancient, human behaviors—aggression, intolerance, irrational discrimination against "outsiders"—seem to find little support in the ever-present, human propensity to hate and destroy those in some way different to oneself. These seem not to be simply the residues of an earlier, more violent and intolerant world, but an apparently much more intractable dimension of the human condition. Still, this does not mean that behind the irrational demonizing and stereotypical fantasies about others are not real grievances. There is certainly validity to the claim that before there can be peace there must be justice. And human history, with all of its miseries, suffering, exploitation, genocide, and the brutalizing of one group of people by another, ensures that stored up injustice, with its accompanying pain and anger, is abundant. The demand for justice, if not for vengeance, is not easily satisfied. It is because of this that the process of peacemaking—the bargaining between aggrieved parties—is often a glacial process, full of heartbreaking misunderstandings, difficulties, and failures. (Anyone who has even been through a divorce will know what I am talking about!) Yet ultimately, breaking the cycle of violence, hatred, and injustice must depend on some kind of process of negotiation and reconciliation. We can see more clearly than ever that peaceful understanding and coexistence between human beings depend on something more than deal-making or grudging toleration of the other. They require a transformative process more deeply rooted: a profound change in our cultural attitudes, beliefs, and behavior, as well as a change in the psychological dispositions that shape how human beings react and relate to those others who share our world. Political agreements and treaties are necessary but not sufficient dimensions in the making of a world where difference is respected and valued, and violence gives way to an appreciation by all of life's incalculable preciousness. The latter can only be achieved through an educational process that seeks to influence the way our children think about, and treat, others who share this earth with them. I believe we can learn from the terrible barbarism, callousness, and insensitivity of human experience, so as to begin to construct an education for our children that might lead them away from our culture's endemic violence, dangerous stereotypes, and conformity to intolerant behavior.

The overriding challenge to education for our new millennium is surely to be found in this struggle to educate our children for a culture that truly values peace rather than war, compassion instead of hate, and respect rather than intolerance. In the remainder of this chapter I want to sketch out some of the ingredients that I believe are needed to teach our young people about the meaning and importance of peace and peacemaking. I suggest six elements that together may comprise a vision and a practice of peace education. Let me reiterate that educating our children for peace should not be seen as an add-on to the more important educational tasks of schools. In a world that is filled with ever more menacing threats to life and the continued existence of the planet itself, peace education needs to be seen as something that is, more than ever, essential to all of our individual physical, social, and spiritual survival.

DIMENSIONS OF PEACE EDUCATION

1. Where You Stand Depends on Where You Sit

For most of my life I have had a passionate involvement in Zionism and in Israel. As a young Jew growing up in England, I was always acutely concerned with the fate of Israel. However secure and comfortable life in England was for me, and other Jews there, I always felt the shadow of Jewish history around me. I carried the suspicion that Jews were never really secure even in a land that seemed peaceful and democratic. German Jews, too, had believed that "it couldn't happen here"—that a country that had made such great contributions to human knowledge and culture could not possibly become a vast "killing field" for Jews. History, I believed, made it quite clear that wherever Jews lived and settled, they were always under some threat to their lives and their freedom. Sometimes this threat went underground, but sooner or later it was bound to reappear, bringing with it torment, fear, and pain. Although my parents were born in England, this never freed them from the sense of being "strangers in the land." The children of immigrants, they could never quite see the land of their birth as a place where they truly felt at home. This sense of being alien was, to some degree, passed onto their children. At each Passover Seder—the ritual meal that celebrated the ancient escape from Egyptian slavery—we would speak the words, "Next year in Jerusalem." Whether or not we really intended to leave for Jerusalem in the coming year, the words signified our sense that we really belonged to another place, and that place was Israel. Although we, like most Jewish families, did not feel the immediate demand to pack our things and move to this new country, Israel represented for us, and for most Jews, a place that offered security from the threats, and potential threats, of a dangerous world. Only a few years after the end of the Holocaust that had destroyed a third of the Jewish people, Israel's establishment, in 1948, seemed like a miracle of redemption that offered hope and opportunity to the thousands of displaced Jews. More than this, the new country with its legendary vitality and pioneering spirit gave all Jews a renewed sense of pride and courage. The defenseless and vulnerable wandering Jew that, over the millennia, had silently endured humiliation and terrible oppression had now, we thought, given way to the strong and assured Israeli who would protect Jewish lives with the power and vigor of our new state. It was not too long before I made my first trip to this country and, like every other Jewish visitor, felt awed by the extraordinary sense of being in a place where Jews were the masters of their fate, not the passive recipients of an unwelcoming, prejudiced Gentile world.

During these years our excitement and pride as well as deep concern for Israel, swimming, as we saw it, in a sea of Arab antagonism, precluded the possibility of my having any understanding of why this hostility existed. The Arabs, conforming to the worst European-inspired stereotypes, seemed filled with an irrational hate for the Jewish state. Their intellectual inferiority and organizational incompetence, as we learned to see it, meant that although we feared for Israel, we also believed that the Arabs could be no match for our smart and courageous soldiers. This seemed to be borne out in the Six-Day War of 1967, when the armies of five Arab states were rapidly destroyed by the Israeli army and air force. Like many young Jews, I came to Israel soon after the end of the battles to volunteer my help. It was a time of elation about what was thought to be the end of the Arab threat to the Jewish state. Yet in the months following this event my understanding of the conflict between Arabs and Jews was about to be transformed. I began to read about the history of the region, and for the first time befriended Arabs at the university I was attending in London. Although my belief in the need for a Jewish state that could offer Jews safety and sanctuary in a hostile world never wavered, I also heard a very different saga of suffering and humiliation. I learned that there was a people who, as a result of the establishment of the Jewish state, had lost their homes and land. I also learned that, from the Arab viewpoint, the establishment of Israel was no miracle, but a disaster that evoked shame and humiliation. Jews, from this standpoint, were not seen as returning to a land that had been part of their prayers and hopes for two millennia, but as the latest wave of European settlers come to dispossess Arabs of their land and inheritance. I learned that far from the land being empty when Jews came to farm and establish their settlements, there was already a Palestinian people living and working there, a people dispossessed by the settlers The creation of the State of Israel made thousands of these Palestinians second-class citizens in their own land. And following the Six-Day War, several million Palestinians found themselves living under military occupation. This occupation would continue for the next four decades, creating an endless circle of hate and enmity as Palestinians resisted the occupation that deprived them of political, civil, and economic rights and freedom. The occupation made everyday living a nightmare of land expropriations and loss of property, military invasions, and roadblocks that made travel to schools, work, and hospitals difficult, even impossible. This transformation in my thinking, it is important to say, was a difficult process, requiring me to have my original beliefs and understanding challenged and tested. Most of all, it required me to step out from my own secure point of view and attempt to see the world from a very different—indeed opposite—vantage point.

Of course, the conflicting viewpoints on what is happening in this small but troubled area of the world turn every event and dimension of the situation there into to a struggle over which version to believe.[3] There is the basic issue of who is the victim in this struggle: Palestinians who are deprived of the elementary rights to national self-determination, or Jews who want nothing more than a safe and secure homeland. For Jews, the wars and battles that have been fought against Arabs represent the struggle for survival in a region that for a long time refused even to recognize their legitimate presence. For Palestinians, there has been a parallel process of denying their presence, their losses, and claims to land and property. For each side, the actions of the other represent a brutal and insensitive demonstration of human behavior. On each side there are parallel forces that claim that God, or national right, is on their side, promising them sole ownership of the territory. These forces have taken on an apocalyptic character in which each views itself, as Robert Jay Lifton noted,[4] "as on a sacred mission of murder in order to renew the world." Although, he continued, "these apocalyptic groups are not in the majority, they can manage to dominate events by acting more or less in concert, responding to each other's acts with murderous passion, stimulating one another to set a tone of continuous confrontation and killing. In this vicious circle, feelings of grief and vengeful rage, which sooner or later take hold in ordinary people not otherwise committed either to holy war or biblical politics." The peace negotiations that have gone on over the last decade or so have been marred by the constant sense of bad faith on one side or the other, as each sees the other's compromises as falling well short of what would satisfy the fundamental needs of the other. Each sees the other as not serious about wanting peace, so the "dance of violence and death" continues.

I have taken this brief excursion through this seemingly endless, and often deadly, dispute between these two long-suffering peoples because it illustrates well what makes human conflict so difficult to resolve. In the many talks and discussions I have been involved in over the years that have to do with this conflict, I am struck, again and again, by how angry and frustrated people become that others cannot see the world as they do. "Why can't you stop and listen to what I have to say—and you will see that I am right and you are wrong!" In teaching about peace, we have to start by recognizing that in most disputes each party is convinced that their position is the one and only one that makes sense and is morally justified. However difficult is the process, peace starts through a process that must affirm the right of each side to be heard, and its thoughts, feelings, and arguments to be treated with attention and respect. More than this, however absurd or even heinous the other side's position seems to be, peace education requires us to listen to it with an attitude of humility. One must believe that there is something important to be learned here about the anguish and frustration, hopes and dreams of other human beings who may inhabit a world, and a history, quite different from one's own. One must start by acknowledging that one's own perspective is a story that might occlude, distort, or silence the experience of the other. There is wisdom to the notion that your enemy may often be someone whose story you have not yet truly heard. Peace education means that one must learn what it means to listen to the other's story even when it contradicts our most cherished beliefs.

A culture of peace does not mean a world without differences. On the contrary, to educate for peace means to take very seriously the way that our different social positions in the world—who we are, how we live, who we identify with, what has been our experience—produce very different understandings of reality. It is an extraordinary consequence of what we sometimes refer to as "post positivist" philosophy that we can now recognize that reality is much more about the way people perceive things, rather than being about something that exists in an objective state, something that can be ascertained by human beings through means that are unsullied by passions, prejudices, and preconceived assumptions. The truth of our situation cannot easily be separated from the way that people make sense of it. People's capacity to discern what is going on is always shaped and limited by the place from which they view the world, and this place is likely to be one where they have important emotional, ideological, or material interests at stake. With this in mind, it becomes very difficult to talk about eliciting "just the facts," as if the facts can be extricated from the passionate investments that we have in seeing and making sense of our experience in a particular way. To teach peace means, in the first place, educating our students to recognize the need to hear the stories or narratives that each side tells about what this conflict is, in its eyes, truly about. We must learn to view the "truths" that emerge as not mutually exclusive, but as an additive process in which the conflicting views deepen our understanding, and widen our perspective, on the whole reality.

I have said elsewhere in this book that contrary to what we are often taught, the facts do not speak for themselves. It is people that speak, and the facts are selected, shaped, and massaged so that they say what we want them to say. Much as it seems to defy our notions of justice, anybody who has attended a trial knows that decisions in a courtroom have much more to do with the persuasiveness of lawyers than they do with a mere presentation of the facts of the case. In this sense, finding understanding is not a simple matter of rational argument. People's identification with a particular point of view is, first, a matter of our emotional connections to it. That is why it is hardly a surprise to me when I engage in discussions about the Palestine–Israel conflict people become very agitated and highly emotional, not infrequently ending up screaming at each other (by the way, this is as often likely to happen among Jews themselves arguing about how they see the policies of the Israeli government). When we ask students in a classroom to deal with matters of significance to them—racism, homosexuality, religion, capital punishment, war and matters of politics, even gang or clique loyalties, as well as the more personal things that divide people—we must expect that the arguments are not really about the facts, but about how people make sense of things in their world, and the emotional investments that they have in defining issues in a particular way. In a certain sense we could say that their lives depend on how things are defined or given meaning. That is why it is always easier for teachers to stay away from the contentious issues (usually anything that has to do with politics, religion, or sex—the things that usually interest us most!). Sadly, when, as educators, we do this, we not only make education a bland, uninteresting business, we also deprive young people of the opportunity of learning the difficult art of listening, and the crucially important capacity to search for understanding among diverse points of view.

It should be clear from what I have said that even the willingness to listen to the other's story is insufficient. To really hear the other side's frustration and suffering requires us not merely to take to mind what is being said, but to take it to heart. We must develop the capacity for compassionate attentiveness to the words of the other. We have to teach what it means to really listen to the words of others without the immediate intervention of our own beliefs and assumptions. These often only serve to defend us from having to seriously engage the experience of the other, and block our ability to "walk in the shoes" of someone else. Such a process means developing those human characteristics of empathy and sensitivity toward the other. Among boys, in particular, a great deal of recent research has shown just how contrary these characteristics are to so much that currently shapes masculine identity.[5] A virulent masculinity has insinuated itself into some of the most influential areas of popular culture—professional wrestling, rap music, video games, radio talk shows, and the kind of political and social commentary typically found on cable TV. All of these spread an outlook of belligerent masculinity that reinforces misogynist and aggressively homophobic attitudes, bullying, even gangsterism, to say nothing of how detrimental it all is to even the needs of everyday intimate relationships. Not unimportantly, it is also a way of being that is seriously damaging to the health and psychological well-being of men. The cumulative effect is a culture that emphasizes a "cool insensitivity" to the feelings of others. Almost certainly a reaction to the gains of feminine-centered values of recent years—concern with relationships and connections, nurturance and care of others—this hypermasculinity emphasizes emotional invulnerability and an aggressive individualism. The latter also feeds a go-it-alone, warrior kind of mentality (manifested in a swaggering, chauvinistic, kind of politics) that is the very opposite of the kind of emotional sensitivity and empathic openness that antiviolence education demands. Such education requires the space and support for developing identities in which emotional expression and compassion for the feelings of others are neither suppressed nor reviled. This is not easily achieved in the current climate of many of our schools—at least beyond the elementary level. Indeed, it requires a fundamental shift in the culture of the institution in ways that I have already described in this book. These would include less emphasis on the competitive dimensions of schooling—whether in academics or in athletics. These certainly contribute to the development of hostile and aggressive attitudes and highly individualistic dispositions. There needs, instead, to be greater emphasis on cooperative and helping relationships and service-related activities. In the classroom there need to be greater opportunities for experiences that accentuate the relational and the expressive—shared projects, dialogue between students, much more opportunity for reflection and disclosure about students' lives. It is also valuable to have a curriculum that provides much more time for the arts and all those activities that encourage self-expression and self-awareness and promote personal synthesis and meaning-making. We have also previously referred to the importance of a critical media literacy that would encourage an exploration of the impact of current imagery in popular culture and the way this imagery promotes an insular, emotionally constricted masculinity. Of course, schools are only a small part of the culture. They can, nonetheless, offer young people a space to practice the difficult art of attentive listening to the perspective and story of the other. However limited, it would be a useful antidote to a culture that, on the one hand, falls too often into a smug complacency about its own correctness, and, as we see night after night on TV, turns complex disagreements about how to view issues and events into the material for simplistic and belligerent shouting matches.

2. First Justice, Then Peace

Violent conflict, wars, riots, and insurgencies, even terrorism, are almost always, in some way, related to the imposition of injustice on individuals or collectivities. To teach peace as something more than sentimental kitsch is to help students see how inseparable is the dream of peace from constructing a more just world. Social injustice, which means the systematic devaluing of human worth and the restriction of the opportunities for living full and free lives among a particular group of people, inevitably brings frustration, resentment, and anger. It is the almost certain catalyst for rage and violent reaction. Without clearly recognizing the consequences of creating a society and a world that devalue and thwart the opportunities for so many human beings, our students cannot begin to unravel the reasons for much of the violence that surrounds us. Obviously, this is especially important given the threat of terrorism that we all now face. Clearly those who perpetrate terrorist acts must be brought to justice for their crimes against humanity. However, we must also consider the difficult question of what are the sources of this terrorism—why there is so much anger in the world that can be harnessed by those preaching hate, violence, and destruction. For students this question should be of crucial importance as they are educated into becoming citizens who can engage some of the most critical questions of our time. Our students surely need to analyze the global conditions that spawn the rage that has become terrorism. This will certainly mean that they confront the reality of the wretched circumstances in which so many human beings presently live. They will need to recognize the terrible inequalities that pervade our world, and to understand how those of us living in generally privileged societies benefit from the labor of those who work in the underdeveloped countries that supply so many of the things that maintain our high standard of living. As a matter of both morality and social awareness, it is important that young people know that half of the world's people now live on less than $2 per day, and that 1.3 billion people must get by on less than $1 per day, or that 4 billion people do not have enough food to eat, and 40,000 children die each day from the inability to purchase basic medications or to have access to clean water.[6] We must find ways to ensure that our students acquire some sense of the hopelessness, deprivation, and misery in which so many people live today. A critically aware citizenship makes it vital that our children know something of the scale of social injustice in the world. They need to understand that where so many grow up without hope or real possibility for living decent lives, we must expect a growing fury directed at those who have, in comparison, so much. Our students need to understand that such injustice begets anger, which in turn can become terror or some other violent manifestation.

Perhaps the most difficult issue that we must confront with our students is the fact that, for many people around the world, there exists a new kind of empire—one that dominates through economic, cultural, and sometimes military power—that is centered here in the United States.[7] This empire is viewed as one that exploits and manipulates the poorest, most vulnerable countries on earth, an empire whose primary beneficiaries are powerful corporations whose prerogatives and investments are protected by the government through the use of its political and military power. If we are to understand the roots of anger in the world, especially that directed at our own country, we will, as teachers, have to honestly explore the way in which we relate to people and countries in other parts of the world. We will, for example, need to examine the extent to which our government (regardless of which political party was in power) has supported undemocratic or repressive regimes to protect what gets referred to as our national interests, without concern for the human consequences of their activities.[8] We will need to question the ways our national security state undermines democracy, with secrecy and lack of public accountability. There is also the extraordinary extent to which our human, intellectual, and material resources are diverted to military uses—far out of proportion to any other country in the world—as well as the presence of U.S. military bases in so many countries, with their imperial presence that is so sure to create local hostility and resentment. In his recent book *Democracy Matters*, Cornel West noted that the U.S. military budget accounts for over 40% of the world's military spending. We possess 9,000 nuclear warheads and have more than 650 military bases in 132 countries on every continent except Antarctica. In addition, there is the widely held perception that the United States feels itself able to act unilaterally, outside of an international community unready to accommodate its interests to the larger global interests (such as in the U.S. refusal to abide by the Kyoto Protocol on carbon dioxide emissions, or its unwillingness to support an International Criminal Court). We will have to address, too, the way that powerful corporations, with the support of U.S.-dominated institutions like the World Trade Organization (WTO) and the International Monetary Fund (IMF), operate so as to maintain and exacerbate the gross inequities of wealth and living standards in the world; how the "religion" of free trade has left millions of people without an adequate means of livelihood, and countries without the means to educate or ensure the health of their young people.[9] There is now, fortunately, an extraordinary amount of information available on these issues, as well as a proliferation of groups and activities that are focused on issues like human and labor rights, fair trade, the indebtedness of poor countries, the conditions that face workers in developing countries engaged in making things like sneakers, clothing, and other consumer goods, the destruction of indigenous and sustainable cultures, and the "export" of toxic wastes to these societies. At the same time, I know from conversations with teachers that raising such issues, with their critical social and political implications, can often put one's career on the line. These are not easy time to help students think in ways that challenge the politics and economics of privilege, the harmful uses of power, and their relationship to war, terrorism, and violence.

Of course, in teaching about the meaning and effects of injustice one does not have to look far from where many students now sit. Schools themselves, we have already seen, are potent sites of unequal treatment and oppressive hierarchies of privilege and disadvantage. Schools typically mirror the larger inequities of race, gender, ethnicity, and social class in our society: in dilapidated inner city schools versus comfortable, well-resourced suburban schools; in the tracking of students into more or less advantageous academic classes; or in the use of standardized tests that reinforce the disadvantages of poverty and race. The violent explosions of rage among boys in our schools are almost always connected to the hierarchies of recognition and exclusion in those institutions. The kind of moral ambience that teaches the worth, value, and dignity of all children is in serious conflict with a school climate that is constantly emphasizing the achievements and capabilities of some individuals over others. The relentless attention to grades, test scores, honor rolls, Academically Gifted (AG) and Advanced Placement (AP) classes, and acceptance to prestigious universities, mocks at our intention to create the affirming, loving environments all youngsters crave. Of course, in an environment that places so much stress on winning and being successful, those who are the losers can experience only shame and embarrassment. And if the losers are disproportionately poor and from minority groups, as indeed they are, then shame is easily transformed into resentment and anger. In 1993 a panel convened by the National Research Council published a detailed analysis of the factors connected with youth violence. It confirmed that the most powerful and consistent predictors of violence were economic hardship and deprivation. Such hardship shows up both in the conditions that children face as they grow up—the lack of resources that make healthy physical and social development possible, the impossibility, for academic and financial reasons, of going on to higher education—and the unlikelihood of living decent and secure lives in their adult years. It is well to remember that although we have more recently focused on the violence committed by White children, it is the violence perpetrated by Black males that still represents a disproportionate share of these acts. A recent report of the Children's Defense Fund noted that although there has been an escalation in the rates of violence among all adolescents, the rate among Black youth is still about 11 times higher than among White teens. The report notes that guns take their highest toll among African-American males (in the 1990s, 60% of the deaths among this group between the years 15 and 19 were from firearm injuries). In our inner cities, lack of work that is more than casual or for minimum wage continues to leave minority youths without any real sense of hope for their futures. The nearly jobless economic recovery of 2001–2004 has done little to brighten this picture. Continuing rage toward "official" institutions such as schools, which are seen and experienced as part of this oppressive reality, finds its outlet in the physical violence of the streets, as well as in the symbolic violence of rap music, belligerent language, and other forms of aggressive popular expression. No meaningful discussion of youth violence can ignore its powerful connection to issues of poverty, racism, joblessness, and a culture that places so much emphasis on success and materialism, and simultaneously excludes so many young adults from access to this culture of consumption.

The contradiction between the ever-present carrot of material prosperity and indulgence, and the reality of impoverishment and hopelessness, hangs over more and more people in our world. Whether in the streets of Detroit, the *favelas* of Rio de Janeiro, or Palestinian refugee camps, people are exposed as never before, through the popular media, to the stark injustices of the world they inhabit. We cannot expect that the reaction to this injustice will for long remain quiescent. Our choice is between a world that treats fairly and decently all its members, or one where those who have more will need to erect higher walls and develop stronger armies to protect what they have. At the very least, our children need to understand the moral choices that confront them.

3. Somebodies and Nobodies

The tragic events at Columbine High School forced us to change, if only for a few moments, the usual discourse of educational concerns in this country. Suddenly we found ourselves attending to issues that were not about academic skills and test scores, accountability of teachers, and the measurement of our state's, or our country's, educational performance. What burst to the surface was an ugly and disturbing brew of issues and concerns that most of the time remain buried under the all-consuming focus on kids' and schools' academic achievement scores. We were instead compelled to confront issues of alienation, competition, social isolation, and rage.

The question of school community loomed large in this and other similar school tragedies. Talk to any group of high school students and the issue of social groups and social relationships in their school emerges as a central concern for them. Yet for most others who are concerned with what schools do—legislators, policymakers, media commentators—the social milieu within which our kids live out their school lives seems like trivial stuff having little real bearing on matters of serious educational importance. How surprising then to find that the social relationships in school are the locus of so much emotion—and, for some, so much anger, bitterness, and pain. From the Columbine and Santee high schools we learned that school cliques are places of privilege and power, inclusion and isolation. We learned that behind the veneer of the well-organized, efficient suburban school is a social context in which young people routinely deal with one another in ways that demean the other, and where differences of appearance or orientation become the vehicle for insults, "putdowns," and threats. In the undergraduate class I taught a few days after the shootings, many of my students, themselves not long out of high school, easily recognized the environment of hostility and intolerance among social groups. It was not hard for them to identify with the anger over privileged athletes and cheerleading favorites. For many, these invidious comparisons are the day-to-day stuff of social relations in high school. They readily recognized, too, the way such divisiveness can become degrading or dehumanizing when the other student comes from a racial minority, is gay or lesbian, or appears, acts, or talks in ways that are outside of the cultural mainstream. Although they certainly did not endorse the destructiveness and killing, they could understand how the competitiveness and intolerance of the high school environment produced intense frustration, and even rage. These students also found it relatively simple to see how the ever-increasing focus on success and achievement in our schools left less and less room for a meaningful focus on community and respect for others. Our national preoccupation (obsession) with increased test scores, higher academic competencies, and the like leaves little serious space for developing relationships of care and concern among young people. Getting ahead and doing well are the preeminent agenda of high schools, not learning how we might create loving communities in which differences are respected and cherished.

It has been said that schools are mirrors of our society. Certainly the salience of social divisions, invidious distinctions, and cruel and insensitive behavior is the inevitable price paid for a culture where so much attention is paid to hierarchy and comparing human worth. Indeed, the moral economies of schools surely cannot be separated from the obsessive emphasis, in the wider culture, on winning and losing, becoming someone by distinguishing oneself from those who are left behind as nobodies. The typical insecurities of adolescent identity are now appropriated and exploited to an unprecedented degree by the market, which powerfully and continually sells to young people not just products but the importance of fitting in and achieving acceptance. The booming adolescent market (now the largest segment of the consumer market) is nothing if not a series of markers for what it takes to be "in" and to be "cool." By design, it is a place where such status is always insecurely held; the market ensures that what it takes to be accepted is a moving target—today's fashion, style, and so on change rapidly into what is, tomorrow, an outmoded and embarrassing mode of appearance. The powerful emotional needs of adolescents to find a sense of belonging among peers comprise a process made difficult for many by the competitive and judgmental ethos of youth culture and its excessive preoccupation with the right looks and behavior. Failure to meet these standards of judgment can indeed produce a damaging sense of alienation from one's fellows. The consequences of this can be a hostility that is turned inward to produce depression or suicide, or outward as anger and resentment toward classmates.

In popular books like *Awakening Ophelia*, authors have described well the destructive effects of the increasingly competitive climate among teens on the emotional stability and well-being of young people. What is at work here is a psychological process shaped and directed by the marketplace, which, with ever-intensifying effect, manipulates the wants of young people and sets the standard for appearance and success. The so-called post-Fordist economy with its endless and dizzying proliferation of niche stores and styles has aimed, with extraordinary effect, at young people whom it organizes into consumers desperate to measure up to what passes for acceptable or "cool" in the eyes of their peers. The power of the marketplace to seduce the young into the most self-destructive behaviors has become all too nauseatingly evident in the campaigns run by the tobacco industry. We should also remember the kids killed on the street by other kids desperate to get their hands on a pair of Nike sneakers. These are, of course, only the more glaring examples of the relentless efforts of corporations to stimulate buying on the part of children and young adolescents through advertising campaigns that emphasize the link between products and peer acceptability. If you are still unconvinced of this, pick up a copy of *Teen Magazine*, *Seventeen*, or one of the other magazines designed for young people. You will be left with little doubt of the extent to which corporate America organizes and influences the emotional life of the young. There can also be little doubt about how much this influence is about promoting norms of appearance and social acceptability. These shameless efforts to market clothes, cosmetics, junk or fast food, alcohol, and so on require selves that are fragile and dependent on fitting in by buying the "right" stuff. Not surprisingly, their effects are to exacerbate the self-consciousness and anxieties of the young—to promote an ever more intense scrutiny of themselves in relationship to their peers. One should hardly be surprised that in the resulting climate of anxiety, the indices of child and teenage suicide and depression have reached epidemic levels, drugs and alcohol abuse are widespread, female bodies are often mutilated, starved, and available for unbounded sexual promiscuity, and vengeful and angry behaviors explode out of seemingly placid teens. Quite simply, we have created a culture that terrorizes the young into the fear of losing ground or being out of place. The inevitable awkwardness and fears of youth become the fodder for a market that shamelessly exploits these anxieties, turning huge profits by instilling an obsessive concern for how individuals measure up in comparison with their peers, reinforcing the importance of conformity and fitting in among young people.

Of course, critical social commentators have made clear that young people are not mere shills for the culture industry, passively and unquestioningly being manipulated by the style makers or others who set social norms and expectations.[10] Indeed, youngsters perennially rebel against the dictates of society and social institutions. The so-called "trench-coat mafia" at Columbine was but one more in a long series of examples of kids contesting who gets to be honored, have privileges conferred on them, or receive a modicum of power from the institution. Every high school has them—those students who feel themselves alienated from the official norms of success and recognition: kids who reject, and turn on its head, the sanctioned and legitimized value system of the school hierarchy. Such students resist the behaviors, attitudes, and appearance of the student mainstream. They create, through their own dress, language, and rituals, a subculture of style that violates the institutional norms. They express, sometimes aggressively, their anger and frustrations at how power and privilege are distributed in the school. At Littleton and elsewhere we know this culture produced not just the more typical forms of nonconformity and deviance, but an explosion of rage and destruction. Yet this too could be predicted. What has come together in recent high school violence is an outlook born of intense hostility toward the pecking order of status and worth at the school, the high emotionality surrounding issues of identity and recognition typical of the adolescent years, and the easy accessibility of dangerous weaponry that now characterizes American society. Of course, the insanity of the ready availability of guns—handguns, semi-automatic weapons, assault weapons, and so on—is apparent to more and more of us, although this produces little change in the form of legislation that would seriously reduce their availability.

4. The Threatened Self

The quest for more compassionate or empathic relationships should not be confused with believing that one can know everything there is to know about another. Differences among human beings are a permanent dimension of being human and cannot be smoothed away. We live in a world that confronts the paradox of being at once smaller and more connected and, at the same time, having social, cultural, sexual, religious, and political differences confront us more starkly than ever in our daily lives. The issue of differences, and how we learn to live with them, is one of the most important, and vexing questions, of our time. To learn to live in a less violent world we will need to confront the deep fears and anxieties that the differences among us stirs. In his brilliant essays on difference, Zygmunt Bauman described some of the contradictory ways we approach this phenomenon.[11] On the one hand, at least for the more economically privileged, there are the cultural differences that lend spice and variety to life—exotic lands to visit, interesting culinary experiences to sample, strange spiritual traditions to try out, and so on. But for the more hard-pressed, difference comes in the form of what Bauman called sliminess: the feeling of being invaded by others who threaten one's language, job, the value of a house, the quality of a school, and so on. Although the rich are tourists who can easily and safely return home from their trips, the poorer classes cannot leave behind the changing neighborhood or workplace. Acceptance of difference is certainly related to economic well-being and security, and in their absence, hate, racism, and ethnocentrism flourish.

There is, however, more to our anxieties about difference than this. The example of homophobia comes quickly to mind, with all of its complex psychological fears and concerns about what it means to assume a "normal" human identity. Education today, in its broadest sense, has the difficult task of ensuring the formation of a self in which identity is securely grounded and reasonably stable. At the same time, our postmodern world opens the door to identities that are fluid and flexible. It is a world in which we have the unprecedented possibility of choosing and transforming who we are and how we wish to live, our religious faith, the form of our family life, our sexuality, even our physical appearance. As the sociologist Anthony Giddens[12] has argued, this "reflexivity" about the self is one of the extraordinary, liberating possibilities of contemporary life. All of this means that in educating our children we must help them develop what it means to be human in ways that are neither emotionally rigid nor dogmatic. Surely when we learn to see our own identities as something that we both choose and make, we are better able to see others without the fear that they threaten some eternal and fixed way of being human. At their best (i.e., when they are not reduced to the triviality of "ethnic festivals" and the like), multicultural curricula offer students the possibility of gaining insight into how our identities are anything but permanent and immutable—who we are is what we are in relationship to others, and that is always changing. Robert Jay Lifton talked about this as the "protean self"—a self that is many-sided, flexible, and capable of change and transformation.[13] This protean self, he said,

> stands in direct contrast to the fundamentalist or apocalyptic self. Indeed, the closed fundamentalist self and its apocalyptic impulses can be understood as a reaction to protean tendencies, which are widely abroad in our world as a response to the complexities of recent history. Any contemporary claim to absolute certainty, then, is compensatory, an artificial plunge into totalism that seeks an escape from the ambiguity that so pervades our historical legacy.

Sadly, the pervasive influence of the marketplace in organizing our world fragments and privatizes our lives. It stunts our growth into the confident and autonomous, as well as connected, individuals that must be the goal of a culture that properly nourishes our emotional and spiritual lives. The market's emphasis on competitive individualism ensures a culture in which self-interest and personal reward are far more significant than the sense of interdependence and connection between human beings. The experience of a world in which each of us finds meaning and purpose through our collective ties and responsibilities to one another gives way to separation, division, and envy. The overwhelming emphasis on the values of individual success and personal gain must encourage the sense of rivalry and antagonism between us. Connection and caring can flourish only to the extent that we see each other not as opponents or rivals, but as beings whose individual lives are enhanced by the degree to which we are mutually supportive of one another. A world whose human relationships are organized around the pole of competition, not care, is a sure breeding ground for a culture of hostility. Violence is the inevitable offspring of this environment.

More than this, however, we will need to find ways to explore with our students the destructive social and psychological effects of modernity itself on so many lives. However pitiful are the real life circumstances of so many people, almost all are constantly exposed to the "good life" as this is portrayed through the images of television, Hollywood movies, and advertising—images that drive home the huge discrepancies in how people live on this earth, and with it often the deep feelings of injustice and humiliation. Such images, with their emphasis on materialistic, sexual, and individualistic desires, are also an assault on many people's traditional identities and values. Modernity, in its present form, is hugely disruptive to the traditions and beliefs of millions of people. It produces a world that breaks down the bonds of communal support, replacing them with highly competitive and individualistic social relationships. In this new world the primary identity is a self insatiably hungry for more things, pleasures, and experience. It is a place in which mutually supportive relationships give way to a world full of jostling individuals always pushing themselves forward so as to achieve more success and more recognition. Modernity means, for many, an increasingly transient and precarious world in which the traditional anchors of people's lives are disrupted and dislocated by rapid economic and cultural change. In these conditions, livelihoods are unpredictable, and frequently mean that families are uprooted or divided by the need for parents or children to move far away from their loved ones to provide an income for those remaining. Many migrants find themselves in new and alien environments where they feel excluded and marginalized, and sometimes humiliated. Anyone who studies the life of Mohammed Ata and the others who hijacked the planes on that September day in 2001 will recognize in them the stories of marginality and humiliation that life in a disorienting, if seductive, new culture can produce. More than almost anything else we know, it is the sense of humiliation that sets off in human beings a raging anger and a thirst for vengeance. Violence, as Robert Lifton told us, promises to eliminate the vulnerability that is exposed by our humiliation. However, the violence perpetrated on others only succeeds in feeding the others' fears of vulnerability and maintaining the endless spiral of pain and anger. It is this endless circle of humiliation, violence, and counterviolence that we can witness in conflict after conflict.

As difficult to grasp as all this might be, we will have to ask our students to explore this complex world in ways that seek to understand how it can produce what we can no longer ignore—the dangerous flows of alienation, exclusion, and humiliation. And we need to remember that human beings are, in all places, a meaning-hungry species. Chris Hedges, in his book on war,[14] made us aware that war offers people a powerful way to fill what are often empty and bored lives. Even with all its destruction and carnage, he said, it gives us what we all long for in life—purpose, meaning, and a reason for living. In a world where meaningful lives are, for millions of people, in short supply, it cannot be surprising that human beings are easily susceptible to the propaganda that might turn neighbors into despised enemies, workingclass youth into warrior heroes, and the cause of war, a struggle that pits good against evil. All of this demands that our education compel our young people to think beyond the simplistic slogans that justify any current march to war with its demonization of an enemy, and the need to inflict destruction and death on untold numbers of innocent lives. Such binary thinking—we versus them, good versus evil—knows no borders. It is the way of war and violence throughout human cultures.

But beyond this we may want to examine with them the meaning and possibilities of a more humane and socially just kind of modernity. Such an examination is more than critique; it also demands from our students an affirmation of those dimensions of modernity that they hold precious, even where they seem to disrupt communal values. These might include democratic rights and equality, including the rights of women and minorities. Or perhaps it may embrace the scientific spirit—free and uncontrolled inquiry, skepticism, and a pragmatic attitude toward truth. However we approach these complex questions, what we must make clear to our students is that their lives, as well as our fate as a nation, are inseparably connected to what is happening even in apparently far away places. Over the past few years our culture has become increasingly self-absorbed and focused on distractions, sensations, and sleaze. Talk shows and news programs have shown pathetically little concern with the seismic social, economic, and cultural changes that are affecting the lives of so many millions of people around the world, and with it the emergence of terrible anger, frustration, and violence. Yet whether for moral reasons or simply self-interest, we cannot afford to bring up a generation of young people whose education has not helped them begin to grapple with the most critical questions of the 21st century—our interdependence as individuals and as nations, and the consequences of profound social change with all of its turmoil, disruption, and rage.

5. *B'Tselem Elohim*—The Infinite Value of Each Individual

There can be no education against violence that does not affirm the infinite and unconditional worth of each human life. In trying to answer my own students' questions about making sense of September 11 and its aftermath, I suggested to them a number of lessons, among which was the way the terrible attacks reminded us of the extraordinary value of human life. The human slaughter with its incalculable consequences in personal loss, pain, and suffering confronts us with the irreplaceable preciousness of each individual life. The senseless and horrifying murders underlined for us the sacred or infinite worth that belongs to each person. Such an assertion may seem banal until we remember that the firemen who raced up the stairs of the World Trade Center to save lives didn't stop to find out who they were trying to save—whether they were Black or White, Latino or foreign born, U.S. citizen or migrant. Nor did they check on people's religion, sexual orientation, or how wealthy or poor they were. Each life was *B'tselem Elohim*—the biblical Hebrew wording that signifies being made in the image of God. The lives were equally valuable whether they were those of wealthy stockbrokers or restaurant waiters and kitchen staff. I have pointed out that for educators there was here a powerful moral lesson: the need to help our students recognize the sacred worth of all human lives. Such a lesson, if it is to be more than sentimental cant, must, however, also confront the ways, in our personal behavior, institutions, and culture, we so often fail to embody this truth. It means attending to the ways we diminish the value and dignity of those we designate as "other" in our world. It means confronting the ways that prejudice works to misrecognize the intrinsic humanity of others. It also means learning to understand how such misrecognition functions to legitimate an unjust social order. So, for example, we can blame those who are poor for their economic failure because of what we assume is their laziness, indolence, or sheer lack of intellectual capability. And for students engaged in such ethical and critical learning, school itself becomes a good laboratory through which to explore and understand how our society is constantly engaged in making invidious human comparisons. Such comparisons inevitably diminish the worth of some individuals while elevating the worth of others. They legitimate the hierarchies of student recognition and honor that are the moral axis of contemporary schooling. Difficult as it might be, our lessons on the value of human life require us to look critically at the way school functions as a "sorting machine"—one that celebrates and affirms some students while at the same time devaluing and marginalizing many others. Public education provides us with a powerful example of our society's schizophrenic view of human worth—at once a place that affirms everyone's right to dignity and opportunity, and one that simultaneously works furiously to differentiate and rank human beings. In contrast to our culture's pervasive focus on creating hierarchies of human worth—whether because of our looks, who we associate with, what we own, how we dress, our celebrity or lack of it—September 11 reminded us, if only for a brief moment, that each and every life must be regarded as of inestimable value.

The affirmation of the infinite and unconditional value of each human life implies always being concerned with the importance of respecting the sanctity of the human body. Peace education insists that violence against the human body negates a fundamental article of faith in the sacred worth of each life. It is a faith that finds its expression in Emanuel Levinas's assertion that we see in the "face" of every person a dimension of God. To see this is to recognize how each life places on us ethical demands to treat that life with infinite care and devotion. Each countenance must be seen in its incommensurable particularity—in other words, a unique beauty that cannot be replaced, substituted, or reduced to another. It is the denial of this—when this face is turned into the "other"—that makes possible the violation, exploitation, or murder of human beings. This is something we know is all too common in our world. The infinite preciousness of human life is certainly intimated in all the great religious traditions, although there is no denying religion's role in the murderous history of humankind. It is also clearly implicit in the language of human rights. Whatever influences we acknowledge, there can be no peace education that does not assert that human life is of incalculable worth, and anything that denies this contributes to a culture of violence. And our reverence for life can never be separated from our concern for how the body is cared for, treated, and protected. For teachers, this means encouraging an attitude of reverence toward life and respect for the body—something that is of particular importance given our culture's relentless exploitation and commodification of sexuality and of the female body. It also means working to bring to awareness the ways in which our culture objectifies and dehumanizes those who are, in some way, unlike us. It means helping students become aware of how racism, nationalism, sexism, homophobia, and ethnocentrism reduce others to a set of despised attitudes that define a person's identity—lives that can never be captured or characterized by so limited a range of traits. Reducing human beings to an aspect of their appearance, their sexuality, language, and so on denies the mysterious fullness—the ineffable particularity—of each human life. To teach for a culture of peace means to encourage seeing within others this sacred, uncapturable quality of each life, and our own moral responsibility to nurture and preserve it.

In the United States, there is a deep sense of unease about our public culture and the way it continues to provide images of behavior that cheapen and profane any notion of the sacredness of the human body. Indeed, the sense that this culture is permeated by a tasteless, exploitative vulgarity cuts across the usual fault lines of political identity. Often (and I believe unfortunately) identified as conservative voices, these insist that there needs to be a religious or moral critique of our popular culture.[15] There is a sense in which television and other popular media are prepared to produce and market any cultural product that can win an audience and make a buck. It matters not whether this means shows that are sleazy in their depictions of sex, crass and sophomoric in their humor, deliberately coarse in the language used and the images projected. So-called reality TV is without moral boundaries in its willingness to expose human frailty and insecurity, as well as the ruthless will to win or survive at all costs. One of my graduate students, Jessica Eads, writing about reality dating shows on TV noted the constant depiction of relationships "that showcase casual sexual encounters, interchangeable partners, and the erosion of any sense of commitment or private space between loving couples."[16] It can hardly be a surprise that sex education has emerged as an arena of intense parental concern, as depictions of sex that are severed from caring and responsible relationships fill our media.

In addition, there is the increasingly pervasive and graphic nature of violent imagery in the popular media. I referred earlier to the erosion of moral sensitivity that relentless exposure to such images is sure to produce. Of course, there is no single reason that is adequate to explain the growing callousness in our relationships. Still, it is not hard to see how electronic technology has turned violence into video games—shooting, killing, rape, and mayhem are the staples of such pastimes. The increasing sophistication of computers accentuates the sense of reality in such games, as they become ever more present in our homes and in public places. This "aesthetic" of violence permeates movies and TV, where it is made increasingly vivid with the help of special effects wizardry. The point here is not just that violence becomes dramatically more present and available in the popular culture, but that it is represented in ways that make the horrors of bloodshed and brutality the source of entertainment and pleasure. One only has to think of hugely successful films like *Pulp Fiction* or *Silence of the Lambs* and their sequels to see how much human brutality, vividly and explicitly portrayed, is played for our amusement. Moral sensitivity or abhorrence is replaced by the pleasures of the chilling experience whose adrenaline rush is the momentary antidote to the tedium of humdrum routines. There is also the way in which technology erodes the clear distinction between the reality of death and pain, and its simulation in video form. Two recent wars in Iraq provided images in which the real horror and pain of death, injury and mutilation, caused by bombs and bullets were somehow absent despite the long hours of coverage. The terror and pain among the population being attacked were replaced by the breathless excitement of a spectacle. In a culture awash in graphically constructed images of torture and killing that seem to last only as long as the picture on the screen, we might expect a continuing desensitization to the real consequences of guns and other weapons of killing. It is important to remember that the prime audience of these representations is composed of the young. Twenty-five children (the size of an average classroom) are killed by guns every two days in our nation. It is fair to assume that there is some connection here to the callous and destructive images that fill our airwaves. Certainly, if we are serious about bringing our children up to see all life as precious and of infinite value, we have much to do and change to ensure that our media "village" teaches this lesson and not its opposite. To teach *B'tselem Elohim* will require that all of us engaged in the education of our children lose no opportunity to affirm the inestimable worth of every life, indeed of all life, and have the courage and commitment to continually point out the ways our nation and our world fall short in making this moral and spiritual injunction a reality in all people's lives.

Given the brutal and despicable attack on innocent civilians, it is not surprising that September 11 and the events that have unfolded since would unleash angry emotional responses. Yet most of us have tried hard to distinguish the real perpetrators of these deeds from others who might be blamed by what appears to be association—being Muslim, coming from the Middle East, or simply having critical things to say about U.S. policy in the world. Our government has made some attempt to demonstrate that this is not a war with Islam. Still, the mixed signals have helped to engender religious and ethnic blame. There have been too many cases of individuals taking out their frustrations on innocent people who are misguidedly associated with the attacks, or acting in ways that are blindly prejudicial. For some, the threat to our communities is a license to act with racist hostility toward those who constitute religious or ethnic minorities. Of course, this is not just an American problem, as the surge in anti-Semitic and anti-Muslim behavior across Europe demonstrates. Our concern for more security—when, for example, we fly—raises the ugly prospect of ethnic profiling. And our deep concerns need to be expressed regarding the jailing without charges of so many whose only "crime" may be their religious faith. Still, as a society we seem to be far from the mentality that produced Japanese internment camps in World War II. This is to be celebrated as a growth in our moral maturity. The lessons here for young people are clear. The world presents us with many causes for insecurity, frustration, resentment, and anger. We know how easily human beings respond to these situations with a blind hatred for whole groups of people who can somehow be blamed for one's present unease and fear. Whether in our own country or elsewhere in the world, there is no lack of the ways that human concerns become transformed into a misdirected rage acted out against a convenient scapegoat. Indeed it is not hard to think of current examples where our own anxieties turn into hate-filled and vengeful acts of rage. As educators—whether as teachers or parents—we must acknowledge the entirely human capacity for apprehension and anger, while insisting that these must never be harnessed to the misdirected evil of demonizing whole groups of human beings. In a similar vein, the flags that decorated so many homes and automobiles after September 11, 2001, represented an assertion of national resolve, and an expression of solidarity with the victims of terrorist attacks, as well as with those who were asked to defend or safeguard our lives. Yet we must also need to ensure that students are taught the difference between this kind of communal solidarity and an arrogant and militaristic chauvinism in which we somehow come to believe we are superior to other people, and where we triumphantly celebrate our capacity for military or others forms of domination in the world. We are seeing again how patriotism easily turns from national pride into a witch-hunt against those who raise the necessary, if disturbing questions, about why and how we have become the enemy for so many other people. Our educational task is to educate young people to know the difference between the suspicion and hostility of a fearful nationalism, and the justifiable pride and mutual concern of a healthy national community.

To see within others the precious quality of each life means finding ways to go beyond the anger and pain of the lingering hurt that have been inflicted on us. Pain and anger distance us from the capacity to see the other's humanity. Instead, what is demanded from us is that most difficult of human capacities: forgiveness and the will to find reconciliation with our erstwhile enemies. Few events in recent times have been as moving as the extraordinary efforts in South Africa, following the fall of the apartheid regime, to bind up the wounds of so much suffering through that country's Truth and Reconciliation Commission. This commission was the product of the recognition that healing the wounds of past oppression would not be achieved through vengeance and retribution. This would only continue the circle of hatred and dehumanization. Instead, what was called for was an honest acknowledgment of past cruelty and oppression, and a willingness to transcend understandable bitterness to see the humanity of the other. The commission's work has already inspired similar ventures in other places with histories of violent brutality and suffering.

Peace Education and the Language of Hope

To educate young people for peace requires that we teach them to see the world as it is, but to see also the possibilities for change. As educators we must certainly help students face the realities that surround us honestly and critically, but we must also encourage creative and imaginative images of a transformed world. Put simply, we must encourage our young people to be grounded dreamers. Years ago the philosopher and social critic Herbert Marcuse taught us to see how a culture makes itself seemingly unchangeable by shutting down our capacity to imagine alternatives to what presently exists.[17] Social change depends on critique, but it also requires that human beings be able to envisage other ways to live than the ones that presently constitute our world. In my experience as a teacher I have found that there is often serious resistance to thinking that attempts to re-imagine our world and how we live our lives. It is often dismissed as wasteful utopian thinking, an exercise in the pursuit of pointless fantasies. Behind these accusations is the deep-seated despair of individuals who have been educated to reject anything that is not about navigating or surviving the present reality. I am also no longer surprised that few teachers, asked to list the primary values of their educational vision, include in this imagination or creativity. It is a telling comment on the hyperrationalism of our present educational world, which has little interest in encouraging among young people the capacity to seriously re-envisage the making of our social reality. It is certainly no surprise that in schools the arts and aesthetic experiences are at the bottom of the priority list of what should be expected in a student's curricular experiences. Such experiences, with their propensity to encourage students to re-imagine and re-create the narratives and metaphors that structure human lives, are not considered an important part of the current agenda for schools. Yet it is not hard to understand that to educate against violence requires that we get beyond the present violence-saturated culture to imagine that alternative ways of how human beings relate to one another are possible. The present culture, with all of its brutality, callousness, competition, and aggressiveness, does not exhaust the possibilities of human existence. Without the capacity to re-envisage our identities and lives as centered on gentleness, compassion, and loving connections, the violence in this world will be not a catalyst for our transformative dreams and efforts, but simply one more dimension of a cruel world that evokes only resignation and a despairing cynicism.

The goal of our lessons in peace, then, is certainly not to produce a sense of hopelessness. Our lessons are aimed at increasing students' awareness, concern, and sensitivity, so that as citizens of this country, and as part of the world community, they will have the knowledge and understanding that can help to bring about change. It is an extraordinary fact that, with social, political, and cultural storms blowing through the world, schools continue as if it were another calm spring day. I remember my outrage when my daughter (then a high school junior) reported to me that during the same school year when the events of September 11 occurred, there was no attempt to seriously study their meaning or consequences. It was an opportunity missed to explore the dangerous affects of injustice, humiliation, and misdirected rage. It was also a missed opportunity to reflect on the profoundly moving examples of those whose lives are defined by service to others, and by the way that so many, in a time of crisis, chose to give to others in the most selfless of ways. Instead, instruction continued to be focused on the same tired, if iconic, material that is so appallingly divorced from the critical issues that now confront us. The typical American classroom, trapped more than ever by the dead hand of "standards" and "accountability," is a world that is emotionally, intellectually, and morally disconnected from the real and pressing demands of the human condition. Filling young minds with information divorced from the contexts that give it salience substitutes for questions about meaning, purpose, and possibility in the shared spaces of our nation and our planet.

The education I am advocating here is about hope—the sense that the world can be improved and problems surmounted by concerned and thinking citizens. To teach students so that they have a greater sense of possibility means to challenge cynicism, conformity, or the sense of fatalism that many young people have about their world—the belief that not much can be really changed. Among other things, this involves teaching a different sense of history than the remote and anesthetized version that students typically receive. This anesthetized version suggests little to them about their capacity to "make history" by challenging the violence and brutality that surrounds them. Such capacity would require them to know something about how people have struggled to stop wars, to find alternatives to the violent resolution of conflicts, and to organize movements to end the brutal and inhuman treatment of others. This lesson of hope requires that we nurture not only the critical capabilities of young people, but also their sense of emotional involvement in the important issues of peace, social justice, and human dignity. Nothing stirs the sense of hope and possibility as much as an active engagement around these issues. Nowadays the internet can bring immediate connection for young people to the multitude of groups concerned with ending torture, stopping violent conflicts, and respecting human rights. In this sense, schools exist not simply to prepare young people to fit in with what presently is, but also to encourage them to be passionate and active agents of change in our world. Education needs to be understood as more than simply a mirror that reflects the existing culture; it may also represent a light that directs our way to a more hopeful future.

To educate for peace is intimately bound up with questions of social justice and human dignity. It must always, in some way, be connected to how people treat one another. Creating spaces where different voices can be heard does mean sometimes listening to words of anger, hostility, and resentment. What are needed are educational spaces where there is a commitment to the constant struggle to bridge differences, to create compassionate connections among people, in spite of the frustrations and resentments that exist. Unlike the hollow institutional integration typically practiced around race or disability or language differences, where students "co-exist'" but remain largely strangers to one another, real educational communities would make possible human encounters with significant dialogue and interaction. Such places would enable individuals to learn to face and deal with issues of anger, distrust, and intolerance. It is probable that the large, impersonal, competitively oriented high school is incapable of creating this kind of dialogic educational community. This would require learning communities that are smaller and more intimate, and where the curriculum emphasizes cooperation, mutual support, and critical reflection on the purpose and meaning of students' lives. Where schools are so much about success and "getting ahead" it is hard to imagine creating the kinds of compassionate and caring communities that make possible honest and open dialogue: places in which individuals learn to really struggle with the painful issues of difference, injustice, and humiliation, and the anger and violence that are their consequences.

Although educating for peace does seem to require continuing the effort to recognize and value our differences as human beings, I also believe that this is only half the story. Certainly justice and democracy, which are inseparable from the vision of global peace, do imply the full recognition of our living in a pluralistic world–a world of multiplicity and complex differences. Yet I believe that to educate for peace means also to teach about that which connects us across cultural borders–our shared humanity. It is this underlying connection that drives the extraordinary and ever expanding movement for granting human rights throughout the world. It nurtures, too, the sense that all human life is something sacred, a matter of incalculable value. And it brings us to the radical idea that only loving communities can truly and fully honor the infinite worth and dignity of each person. Educating for peace means, I believe, teaching students to recognize this precious or sacred quality of life, and its inseparability from the loving communities that are needed to nourish and develop it.

When talking in class about the importance of the vision of a loving community to the repair and healing of our world, I am sometimes asked if we can teach love. I confess this is a difficult question. In jest I sometimes reply that Gandhi, when asked what he thought about Western civilization, answered that he thought it would be a good idea! Perhaps there is something more than irony in his response. When wisdom cries out for change in human behavior, the arbiter of what we teach cannot be simply what is empirically most evident or predictable. The vision of loving connections between human beings not only stirs our imagination to the sense of possibility. It also forces us to confront the hateful and violent character of so much of our world. It compels us to recognize how far we are from what Daniel Landes and Sheryl Robbin called ethical mindfulness—the demand that in all of our human contacts and relationships we consider the sensitivities and imagine the pain of others. For many of those I teach, the terrible dissonance between how we are and what we might be seems to nourish a yearning for change. A pedagogy for peace does not in itself produce peace, but it does encourage what is called "immanent critique": a deeper appreciation of the contradiction between this world of so much unnecessary suffering and insensitivity, and the ageless dream of a mutually caring and just human community. If only for the short time we are together with our students, the classroom might become a place where we dream of such a world and consider, practically, what we could do to bring it closer for all of us.

NOTES

1. Children's Defense Fund Report. (2001). Washington, DC: Children's Defense Fund.
2. Zygmunt Bauman. (1997). *Postmodernity and its discontents*. Cambridge, UK: Polity Press.
3. For a wonderful account of how Palestinians and Jews view this conflict, in different ways and out of different experiences, see Michael Lerner. (2003). *Healing Israel/Palestine*. Berkeley, CA: Tikkun Books/North Atlantic Books.
4. Robert Jay Lifton. (2003). *Super power syndrome* (p. 17–18). New York: Nation Books.
5. James Garbarino. (1999). *Lost boys*. New York: Free Press.
6. Joseph E. Stiglitz. (2003). *Globalization and its discontents*. New York: W. W. Norton.
7. See, for example, Noam Chomsky. (2001). , *9–11*. Seven Stories Press. Ziauddin Sardar and Merryl Wyn Davies. (2002). *Why do people hate America*. New York: The Disinformation Company.
8. Charles Derber. (1998). *Corporation nation*. New York: St. Martin's Griffin. David C. Korten. (2001). *When corporations rule the world*. San Francisco: Berrett-Koehler.

9. Tariq Ali. (2002). *The clash of fundamentalism*. London: Verso.
10. See, for example, Henry Giroux. (2003). *The abandoned generation*. New York: Palgrave MacMillen.
11. Bauman, op. cit.
12. Anthony Giddens. (1992). *The transformation of intimacy*. Stanford California: Stanford University Press.
13. Lifton, op. cit. (p. 197).
14. Chris Hedges. (2002). *War is a force that gives us meaning*. New York: Public Affairs.
15. Michael Lerner. (2000). *Spirit matters*. Charlottesville, VA: Hampton Roads.
16. Jessica Cole Kirsch Eads. (2004). *Construction of adolescent girl's sexual identity in the age of reality television*. Unpublished PhD dissertation.
17. Herbert Marcuse. (1969). *An essay on liberation*. Boston: Beacon Press.

8
▼▼▼▼▼▼▼

Tikkun Olam

Over and above personal problems, there is an objective challenge to over-come inequity, injustice, helplessness, suffering, carelessness, oppression. Over and above the din of desires there is a calling, a demanding, a waiting, an expectation. There is a question that follows me wherever I turn. What is ex-pected of me? What is demanded of me?

What we encounter is not only flowers and stars, mountains and walls. Over and above all things is a sublime expectation, a waiting for. With every child born a new expectation enters the world.

This is the most important experience in the life of every human being: some-thing is asked of me. Every human being has had a moment in which he sensed a mysterious waiting for him. Meaning is found in responding to the demand, meaning is found in sensing the demand. (from Abraham Joshua Heschel, *I Asked For Wonder* p. 60.)

There is, today, an extraordinary disconnection between the education we offer our young people, and the needs that must be addressed to cope with the world within which they are growing up. This disconnection (chasm is probably a more appropriate term) makes much of what passes for education a strangely out of touch experience for youngsters–one that at best bores, and at worst draws contempt or cynicism. The world our children are subjected to is, as we have seen, one that relentlessly advertises the importance of money and material possessions. This is quite simply the most powerful and pervasive aspect of our young people's "education." Whatever else they might hear, be instructed in, or learn pales besides the incessant drumbeat of persuasion regarding the importance of learning to be avid consumers. No aspect of their lives is immune from the message that *I buy, therefore I am!* The young, like all of us, learn that identity is shaped and secured in the marketplace, which, more than anywhere else in our society, promises the means to achieve popularity, sexual success, pleasure, emotional release, and meaning. The very pervasiveness of the market place culture makes its full effects difficult to fully comprehend in our lives. It becomes harder to see just how much our values and norms are being constructed around what we can buy; how much of our dreams and hopes are infiltrated by images that are delivered to us by the merchants of materialism. The fact that our society spends more each year on advertising than it does on public education should give us some hint as to what is the real "educational" force in our world.

The culture of consumption contaminates the lives of our young not just because of its constant focus on money and possessions at the expense of any more enduring values, but because its materialist focus inherently denies purposes that derive from the quest for spiritual, moral and social meaning. The consumer culture is one that emphasizes appearances and impressions. Who I am is what is what I make manifest in what I own, the way I dress, how I look, my "performance" and how it affects those who see me. As the recent trend in "reality" TV shows concerned with "makeovers" demonstrates all too clearly, my psychological well-being is now attached to the clothes I put on, the contours of my body, the desiring gaze I evoke in others, and the elimination of the physical signs of aging. On other "reality" shows, young couples choose one another for marriage through a process of selection that attends to the most shallow and fleeting of human attributes, mocking deeper notions of loving commitment. The relentless emphasis on show and impressions becomes a culture that is obsessively focused on garnering attention, if only for a short while. Glamour, novelty, scandal, and sensation feed the cultural machinery whose overriding goal is to draw our attention to the latest "happening." One thing follows another as our attention is briefly drawn from each "shocking" manifestation to another. Because our attention is always on the impression each makes, nothing affects us too deeply before new images and stimulations to our senses replace the previous ones. The superficiality of "makeovers" is matched by the limitedness of our attention to whatever else happens to be "big" at the moment. Glitz and superficiality mark our public culture. And every response to the stimulations offered by the culture is measured for its potential to generate lucrative returns to those hustling a product. Every interest, fad, fashion, and taste is another opportunity to turn a profit. And nobody knows this better than those who sell to young people.

The real "curriculum" of our children's lives, then, is their subjection to the constant influence of a culture that turns every aspect of life into a commodity—something that can be bought and sold. This culture of commercialism not only reduces things to their most degraded and vulgar forms. Even news events are selected and presented to garner the largest audience as coverage accentuates the sensational and the shocking. Politics becomes a matter of hawking images, evoking fears, and finding the most simplistic formulas for constructing constituencies that might support a candidate. Everywhere we look, life is organized as a competition. The culture of money and consuming is joined at the hip to the culture of winning and losing. The latter is, in many ways, the psychological driving force of the former. One dresses "right" to be accepted into a social group. What we own is the marker of our success. Our car, house, digital equipment, physical appearance, travel opportunities, and so on tell us, and others, we have made it. Or, at the very least, we are not a loser. The force of comparison within our social reference group incites us to keep buying so that we don't feel as if we are being left behind. We are emotionally in a constant state of hyper-awareness not only of what our friends and peers have, but even of the wider circles of the rich and the famous. All of this is grist for our ever-present envy of those who seem better off than we are—for what they have, what they look like, the opportunities and experiences that are available to them, and how others look up to them or admire them. It can be hardly surprising that the world our children are growing up into is one that surrounds them with what appear to be the trappings of others' success, admiration, and good fortune. The moral axis of this world is the relentless need to vie with others for the accouterments of success. And emotional life is permeated by jealousy of others and self-doubt concerning our own apparent inadequacies or failures.

The consequence of all this is an emotional world in which meaning is sought in smaller and smaller circles of concern. Our culture of consumption encourages an obsessive focus on the self—how do I appear? What impression do I make? How secure, confident, or comfortable do I feel? How successful am I? Am I living optimally? Maximizing my opportunities? Being all I can be? This is a world that has shrunk to what Christopher Lasch once called the "culture of narcissism."[1] It is a culture that makes it hard to find purpose and meaning in the larger world because that world is now only a canvas on which you can depict your own self's psychological portrait. Others are only there as instruments through which to leverage our own emotional needs. It is no wonder that in this increasingly "privatized" world young people feel alienated and disconnected from social and political events and issues. Even in these times of war and terror, many young people cannot relate to the larger struggles that are tearing our world apart. The latter feels no more real than an episode of *Friends* or *Survivor*. The only real world becomes one's emotional life and the small circle of intimates that seem to shape it; everything else is reduced to the fleeting images of the electronic screen. Octavio Paz, the great South American writer, once noted that Americans spend more time studying their own selves than any people on the planet, but are more ignorant of what is happening outside of their own lives than any other people. Although this may be an exaggerated statement, there is obvious truth in the alienation and disconnection Americans feel in regard to world events—unless they directly impact our own lives. And who can deny the extraordinary ignorance that exists (and is sometimes even celebrated) in regard to knowing something about world affairs? Its results are not hard to see in our shameful misunderstanding of the sensibilities and aspirations of other people and nations in our world, and the disastrous results it sometimes produces.

THE FAILURE OF EDUCATIONAL REFORM

So we must ask, in this crisis of awareness, sensibility, and concern, what do the much publicized educational reforms contribute to the humanity and development of our young people, soon to be adult citizens of this republic? In what way has all the attention to test results, performance standards, accountability of teachers, and so on contributed to making our children more thoughtful and questioning human beings? As a result of the overhaul of school curriculum, are young people learning to become more critically reflective individuals? Does the demand for tougher grading and more rigorous classes contribute to youngsters becoming more discerning about the path to more authentically purposeful lives? Does our preoccupation with the measurability of educational "progress" have anything to do with the cultivation of sensibilities more sensitive or empathic to human needs and suffering? In our anxiety about attaining reading and math proficiency, where shall we find a similar concern for the development of imagination, or appreciation for the wonder and beauty of life in all its forms? And as the demands grow to make schooling an adjunct to the world of work, where are the voices that call for education to be a source of joy and pleasure?

Instead of the misdirected reforms that have preoccupied policymakers, we need, instead, changes that can reconnect our children's education to the imperatives and demands of our social world. We need, desperately, young people who are able to challenge the wastefulness of the earth's precious resources and our ongoing destruction of planetary life; who are able to question the extent of poverty and injustice in the world; who respond critically to the degrading and violent nature of so much human behavior; and who are encouraged to consider who or what are the primary beneficiaries, and who are the losers, in our global economic system. Our concern should be students who are encouraged to reflect on the spiritual emptiness of a culture so preoccupied with materialistic goals and superficial measures of human worth. We should want young people who can engage in the profoundly important quest for the way to live lives of purpose and meaning that are neither materialistic nor hollow. The education we offer must speak honestly to the brutal manner in which human beings have so often dealt with their differences, and the need to find ways to address conflicting relationships through nonviolent and nondominating means. Schools need to be places that can manifest relationships that do not emulate the usual hierarchical, competitive, and individualistic forms—places where young people learn of the value of caring and cooperative relationships based in mutual respect and equality. Integral to this kind of institution is the encouragement of a democratic life in which students can learn the meaning of shared responsibility in the determination of our day-to-day life together. Nor should we shrink from raising our students' awareness of the dissonance in the larger society between our democratic ideals and the actual realties of a system that places so much power in the hands of privileged elites and unaccountable interests.

Put most simply, however, our choice is whether we continue along the present intellectually deadening, soul-enervating path, or whether we can re-envisage our children's education as a vehicle that awakens minds, energizes passions, sensitizes moral capacities, and nurtures the spirit. Our choice is between an education that is mainly about having one's ticket punched—an instrumental process devoid of any real intellectual, ethical, or spiritual engagement—or a journey through which we can discover something about the meaning and significance of our connections and responsibilities toward others, as well as to the planet that is our home.

Why, we must ask, is there no real discussion concerning the proper goals of education at this time? Schools are becoming intellectually moribund places. Our kids' spirits are being killed by the dreary routines of lifeless learning. We face as a national society, and a global community, immense challenges—of social justice, of environmental sustainability, of finding common ground among differences, of bringing democratic accountability to a runaway economic system, of nurturing life-affirming values amid the preoccupations with materialism and status-seeking. For members of the younger generation, quality of life will surely depend on the answers that are found to these problems. Yet their education exists in a state of disembodied suspension—concerned, disproportionately, with drilling into students' heads abstracted information that is good fodder for testing and grading, but far removed from the life concerns and social challenges of their world that would make education truly meaningful.

We need to ask how it has come to be that education has become what it is—emotionally lifeless, separated from the challenges of the culture, and devoid of the infusion of ethical and spiritual commitment. My colleague David Purpel places some of the blame for this situation on the educational profession itself, including those who train teachers, for their willingness to acquiesce to the narrow and parochial demands of politicians and their allies in business.[2] The education profession has, with rare exceptions, been all too ready to accommodate whatever expectations are presented to them by those outside of the educational process. Public school teachers and administrators, even faculty in university schools of education, broadly accept their status as employees of the state who are expected to carry into practice whatever policies or mandates are given to them—however irrational or debilitating might be their effects. For the most part, although there may be negotiation, even contestation, over conditions of employment (pay, benefits, hours and conditions of labor), it is rare indeed for those within the profession to collectively articulate any alternative vision of the purpose and goals of education. Another colleague, Michael Apple,[3] has talked about this as the way that jobs increasingly divide "execution" from "conception": Those who do the work are not expected to have any real input into figuring out the purpose and goals of what is being done. They are simply expected to follow the rules laid down by those in authority. Its consequence, he argued, is the "teacher proof curriculum" that dictates, sometimes down to the minutest detail of time and task, what, when, and how teachers are supposed to do their work. Simply put, teaching has become another kind of "McJob." In the new, for-profit schools this process has become even more insidious and oppressive in its regimentation of pedagogy.

Sadly, even among my own colleagues within the university who have the freedom that academic life affords to think more expansively and creatively, there is a disturbing readiness to adapt their research and their teaching to the current directions of educational reform, whatever its consequences in terms of reinforcing the most banal, and limited, conceptions of education. One may speculate on the motives that maintain this slavishness to demands that make our schools increasingly dreary and educationally lifeless institutions. There is, I know, often an unwillingness among many of those who see things up close to speak out. There are also career advantages (research grants, consulting opportunities, etc.) that are consequent on playing the game, whatever the ultimate result. There is also the well-ingrained ethos of hierarchical authority that discourages employees from contesting, in any fundamental way, the direction and definition of their work. The reluctance to speak out is not just about an absence of courage or conviction—although this cannot be excluded. We must also acknowledge the very real dangers that refusing to go along with the prevailing policies and practices entails. I know from those experienced educators the price that must sometimes be paid for those who have different ideas about why and how we educate kids.

But careerism, fear, or a reluctance to articulate a different vision of education is only a part of the story. There is also what cultural critics call (after the work of the Italian thinker and political activist Antonio Gramsci) "cultural hegemony". This refers to the way that particular ideas become so widely accepted in the society that it becomes extraordinarily hard to think about something in a way that is radically different. This is surely an important part of the explanation of why it is so hard to "develop traction" for a new "bottom line" in education. So much of the way we think about education has become second nature, and hard to dislodge from our accepted notions of what and how we teach. Indeed, many of our notions have an iconic status that are beyond questioning: for example, the centrality of algebra or geometry in the curriculum, the teaching of grammar through sentence diagraming, or the place of the "big four" subjects in the curriculum. There is the peripheral role of the arts in school, and the marginal status of service learning. And there is the virtual absence of things like media literacy, peace studies, or ethics. Almost anything that involves the body is maintained as marginal to "real" learning and restricted to a specialized population. Classroom learning is dominated by "chalk and talk" methods, whereas Socratic or dialogic learning is looked on as a diversion from genuine academic activity. Work and pleasure are regarded as antithetical concepts when it comes to serious education. The value of individual competition among students for grades is assumed as a primary motivational force in learning. And primacy is given to constructing a curriculum around things that can be behaviorally demonstrated, and can be given a measurable value. The result of the latter means that much of the richness of human experience—our interior and emotional life, intuitive knowledge, religious experience—is outside of what we concern ourselves with in school. The sheer weight of habit and familiarity makes all of these aspects a part of the "common sense" of schooling—things that we think must or need to happen in school. Sometimes during periods of deep social upheavals these assumptions are disrupted (to some extent this happened in the 1960s in education, as well as in many other areas of our culture). At such times we can see that few of the things that we have accepted as part of our bedrock reality need be treated as if they are permanent and fixed. Times of change "grease" our capacity to be reflexive about our social institutions and practices. It is certainly the case that in order to transcend any kind of historically fixed reality we must have the imagination to re-envisage, in our minds, the range of human possibility. We must bring into play that uniquely human ability to creatively re-image the form and the purpose of those parts of our lives that have become so paralyzingly familiar to us. This capacity for imaginatively reconstructing our world gives us the extraordinary possibility of breaking from the treadmill of the familiar and reinventing institutions like education so that they can fit much better the demands and the challenges of our time.

Of course, the hegemony of familiar ideas is supported by more than unthinking habit. Powerful interests shape the public discourse of education. There has never been a time when the federal government has been more instrumental in setting the agenda for public schools across the United States. Against all of the traditions of local or state control of educational standards, the central government has now become the primary force in setting expectations and goals for schools. To resist these goals is to place school administrators in jeopardy, as budgets are threatened and schools are "named and shamed" through accusations of failure and lack of accountability. Such direct political pressure on schools is only the tip of a larger ideological crusade that involves economic elites and corporate interests working in tandem with politicians. This is a crusade that has its origins in the 1982 *Nation at Risk* report presented by President Reagan's Secretary of Education, Terrence Bell. That report accused schools of failing to produce a workforce with the requisite skills to ensure America's competitiveness and productivity in the emerging global economy. Since that time, whether under a Democratic or Republican President, it has become a fundamental assumption in public discussion that education is, first and foremost, a vehicle for producing suitably trained human capital. This assumption, taken up and reinforced by numerous commissions, task forces, and think-tank reports, has constantly emphasized the belief that schools' first responsibility is to ensure that new generations of workers have the skills and personal dispositions needed by employers. Of course, this has meant shaping the curriculum and practices of schools in a way that promises to meet these expectations, producing what we have seen is the stifling, regimented, top-down, system of educating kids, and an obsessive focus on narrowly defined skills and capabilities. The assimilation of educational goals and concerns to corporate economic priorities has served to narrow how we think, talk, and imagine the purposes of schools. Defined in this way, national priorities seem to have little place for the cultivation of sensitive, caring, imaginative, and critically reflective human beings. After two decades of relentless demands that schools be about generating productive and competitive "human capital," it is hard indeed for parents, teachers, or plain citizens to talk about education as a vehicle for nurturing compassionate, reflective, and joyful human beings. President Clinton's call for schools to ensure that we, as a nation, will be "number one" in the world was about our military and economic status, not about the level of our spiritual and moral maturity.

All of this can leave us in no doubt as to the difficulty of pursuing an agenda for education that is as radically different as the one we have proposed in this book. Whether because of unthinking habit, fear of making change, the erosion of imaginative possibility, or coercion to tow the line, this is a difficult time to raise the standard of deep and transformative educational change. For anyone who has followed the arguments in this book, I can offer little easy solace as to the immediate possibility of moving in the direction of a life-giving education that would nourish the ethical, spiritual and social concerns of young people. Rather than the offer of a formula for instant success (so much the American way), there is little that can be promised but the "blood, sweat, and toil" of persistent struggle. Perhaps, too, the appropriate model here for our work is that of the ancient Hebrew prophets, who knew the necessity of articulating loudly the ways in which we were falling short of our own best ideals, and did so regardless of whether they were heard by one or by many. They raised their voices in protest at the idolatry, injustice, and insensitivity they saw around them without concern as to whether this represented a pragmatic or immediately realistic course of action. To call attention to what is remiss in our world, and to the vulgarity and purposelessness of our children's education, is, quite simply, the morally right thing to do. And it is demanded of us without regard for its likelihood of success or failure. As I noted in my preface to this book, to continue to allow education to be appropriated by those who would define it in the most narrow and utilitarian of ways is to trivialize not just education but our very sense of human possibility. And here we are talking not just about being critical of what now exists, but of the need and responsibility to offer a radically different vision of human life whose foundation is that of the loving community that seeks justice, peace, and a sensitive stewardship of our natural world. The work of all of those committed to a transformative vision is, in the words of Cornel West, "to remind ourselves of what we looked like at our best."[4] And we must do this without any assurance that we can, indeed, bring about this kind of difference in who we are and in how we behave toward one another. Yet, at the same time, we work with the recognition that a deep responsibility impels us to speak out for change even in the most difficult of times when entrenched ideas, values, and interests seem the most recalcitrant. Indeed, it is in the recognition of the difficulty of such a process that we must dig deep into our own being to find those parts of ourselves that remain alive to the possibility of living our lives in other ways. It is revealing that in the research that Michael Lerner did among working people at his Institute for Mental Health and Labor[5] he found that, contrary to the conventional wisdom, material concerns were not the greatest concern among the hundreds of workers he and his colleagues interviewed. Their greatest dissatisfaction was around the lack of meaning and purpose in their work. No matter how banal, materialistic, and shallow are the values of our culture, it is hard to fully destroy that profound human quest for a moral significance to our lives, and the desire for richer and affirming human relationships.

A transformative vision is always impelled by a deep set of convictions about the meaning and purpose of human life. Many of us are hesitant to articulate these because of the fear that they will make us seem insufficiently detached or cool. There is the embarrassment that they will appear to lack the hard-nosed attitudes demanded of the "real" world. In my own setting of the university, such convictions, rooted often in people's sense of the spiritual or the religious, are chided for being "irrational" and lacking sufficient analytical justification. For my graduate students it usually comes as something of a shock when I encourage them to "name" and affirm the deep wellsprings of faith and commitment that really sustain and impel their work in the world—as teachers, administrators, nurses, social service providers, artists, or community activists. These articles of faith are almost always present, but they are rarely articulated because this is not what is typically called for in our rational, materially oriented, analytic world. They are usually expected to remain in the shadows of our identity as we go about our daily activities in the world. To talk, in the university, of the spiritual values that impel our quest for a different kind of society is to make oneself vulnerable to criticism by those who find such talk imprecise or wishy-washy. Yet if we are to speak of transforming the way we educate kids, of envisaging a radically different kind of world, of transforming our competitive, violent, and greedy society into one that is loving, just and kind, where are we to go to find the energy and faith that sustains such a vision? Although the "spiritual" is by its very nature hard to define with any precision, it offers us a shorthand way to intimate those deep human impulses, mysterious and unfathomable in all their origins, that animate our yearning for love, compassion, justice, and connection. These "angels" of our being are frequently silenced, repressed, or sometimes hideously distorted into destructive or hateful forms. Still, the yearning for a more affirming and loving human existence remains in us, awaiting their release through the power of critical reflection, the liberating possibility offered through our imagination, our courage to struggle against seemingly unmovable forces, and faith in a universe that, as Martin Luther King, asserted, "bends towards justice and love."

Each of us must find our own particular path into this power of our deepest and most hopeful convictions—certainly rooted in our life's experiences and encounters, and in the narratives of hope and faith we have each imbibed. I have earlier noted that for me these convictions have been nourished by many influences, but among them my identity as a Jew has been a central one. In the next few pages I want to sketch out aspects of this Jewish vision and sensibility that have impressed on me the importance of human freedom, social justice, the value and dignity of life, and the significance of community to human self-realization. I do this not because I have any belief about the superiority of my particular spiritual and moral path, but in my hope that it will stir you, the reader, to affirm those parts of your own identity that are the wellspring of your own sense of human goodness and possibility, and to recognize the influences—images, narratives, practices, and embodied wisdom—that influence and sustain this faith.

ELEMENTS OF A JEWISH PEDAGOGY

1. The Shofar of Awareness

The sound of the shofar or ram's horn heard in the synagogue during the days of Rosh Hashana—the Jewish New Year holiday—has a mysterious and startling quality to it. Of course for children its piercing, staccato blasts break the monotony of prayers, bringing amusement as adults try to coax the appropriate musical sounds from this obdurate instrument. It produces a sound like no other, at once a plaintive cry and a shrill demand for alert attention. The origin of the ram's horn in Jewish tradition is, we are told, in the story of Abraham's near sacrifice of his son Isaac. Although, of course, the sacrifice is thwarted at the last moment, Abraham offers up a ram in place of his son. The sound of the shofar is said to have brought down the walls of Jericho and, through the ages, it was blown at moments of great historical significance. In my own memory as a child its sound represented a kind of wild and primitive eruption in the ordered drone of the prayer service during the high holy days of the Jewish New Year. But its real purpose during that time of serious reflection on our lives was to awaken us from the tendency to "sleep walk" through our lives; its sound was intended to shake us out of the habitual routines of our existence in which our actions and behaviors lacked adequate moral and existential consideration. To be human is to be imbued with responsibility for one's life, and to have the power of choice in the ethical and social quality of the lives we lead. But such choices require awareness, a level of consciousness and conscience as to how we think, act, and respond to our world. Maxine Greene, the great educational philosopher, described as "the gas chamber of life" the great danger of living life thoughtlessly and with passivity.[5] Ordinary life, she said, is filled with distractions, comforts, escapes, and inertia that can lead us away from our human vocation to search for purpose and "the ability to make present what is absent, to summon up a condition that is not yet."[6] The sound of the shofar is the call to us to wake up and be attentive to our lives; it represents the demand that we overcome our very human tendency to resignation and passivity in the face of life. Although I do not suggest that teachers blow a ram's horn in their class room, teachers' work, I believe, is the task of what Paulo Freire called *consciencization*.[7] This is the encouragement to live life with thoughtfulness and attentiveness, and the capacity to see "reality" as humanly constructed, and always one of a number of possible ways of living. The work of teachers is always to help their students break through the sense of "this is the way it is" with its fatalistic acceptance of unkind, unjust, and degrading human behaviors. To live life with awareness means to see oneself and others possessing the power of choice—to refuse, to question, to posit alternatives to what is presented to us as, falsely, the way things are and must inevitably remain. Behind the symbolic notes of the horn are the real sounds of human beings living their lives with awareness, responsibility, and the willingness to be ethically discerning.

2. "Rabbinic" Truth

Jewish experience has taught me that to respect ideas is not the same as meekly accepting whatever one is told. One key to this readiness to contest others' assertions or beliefs seems to lie in the Jewish penchant for argument, and a deep-seated attitude of suspicion to whatever is merely given to us or presented.[8] Certainly, in whatever Jewish circles I have moved, the love of argument has seemed always to be present. From my earliest years in my parents' home I learned the pleasures of contradiction—there was parental pride in disputatious children! Somehow I learned to approach truth with a Talmudic eye. Whatever is the ultimate "Truth," the truth for each generation has to be won through the hard work of intellectual interrogation and critical reason. The text (whether in words that are spoken or written) provides no comforting certainty of established understanding—much more, it challenges human beings to elicit meaning from situation to situation, and from generation to generation. The only certainty is the knowledge that is produced in the well-known give and take of rabbinic argument. Jacob Neusner[9] described it this way:

> The Talmud taught the Jews not to be terrified by the necessity to face, and to choose among, a plurality of uncertain alternatives in an insecure world. The Talmud testified that people must choose, if tentatively and for a time, only among competing interpretations. ... So the Talmud forced choices, in a tentative and austere spirit, among the many truths available to reasonable folk. It insisted one cannot be paralyzed before contrary claims and equally persuasive reasons. (Tikkun, p. 26)

Although many of us now associate Talmudic discourse with the arcane and the esoteric, this is to miss its essence. As Neusner noted, far from a sterile intellectualism, the Talmud was, in fact, a monumental attempt to apply a practical rationality to society—an effort to figure out how a community that was dependent on the force of better argument might live. It was, he said, a document created by the intellect devoted to morality and sanctity, and one that took for granted humanity's primary capacity to think.

So here was a whole other way to view knowledge—one so different from most of our school experience. Far from evidence of disrespect or a poor attitude, to be intellectually serious means a readiness to always contest and challenge the knowledge presented to us. It means to recognize that all truth is partial at best; there are always new meanings to be mined as our situations, lives, and experiences change. This readiness to question truth is what it means to honor the extraordinary human capacity to think. But more than this, the search for what is at least partially true needs to be connected to the search for a purposeful and moral way of life. And it is always about challenging those "truths" that are dangerously deceptive or misleading to our lives and the lives of others. Put another way, the development and use of our critical reason are not about "solving" make-believe puzzles for a test or quiz, but about creating or recreating a community's cultural practices in the face of all those things that are destructive, damaging or dehumanizing. In the words of Judith Plaskow[10] we are always "Standing at Sinai." Far from being revealed all at once, our knowledge is always in process, and meanings are not fixed but fluid. Although our understanding is shaped by the social context in which it arises, each generation can and must find new layers of significance and insight into the purpose and quality of our lives. All of this will require that we can be, at once, accepting of the uncertainty of our always unfinished understanding, while restlessly committed to putting what we know to work so as to make a better world.

3. The Calendar of Survival

Although my parents were born and grew up in London, the children of recently arrived immigrants from Eastern Europe, for them English people were always the *goyim*—strangers quite different from themselves. They consciously marked themselves as living at the cultural periphery of a society. Notwithstanding the considerable common ground they shared with other working-class Londoners in language, attitudes, and values, the latter seemed to exist on the other side of a powerful, if invisible, social and cultural divide. There was a sense of cultural difference that, to an extent, was passed on to their children. It was fomented by things seemingly trivial, such as our taste in food and attitudes toward drink, as well as much more substantial differences around religious practices and identity. Of major importance was the celebration of events in the Jewish calendar. At their most mundane these holidays were a break from school, a time to eat tasty foods and be with friends or family. At another level they represented a serious separation from the overwhelming cultural hegemony of Christian culture. Here was not just a distinction of significant dates in the yearly round and a reminder of our differences from the non-Jewish majority, but the seeds, as I now see it, of a quite different view of history and celebration.

From my earliest years, the Jewish calendar reminded me again and again that (to paraphrase Walter Benjamin) a relentless barbarism has been the underside of history. History, at least for some, I learned, was a constant struggle against oppression and persecution. My history was nothing, I saw, if not a document of savage human brutality and a people's resistance to physical and spiritual annihilation. This is the repeated saga played out in the traditional observances of Passover, Purim, Tisha B'Av, and Chanukah, as well as in other holidays and events (including the recently added Yom Hashoa or Holocaust commemoration day). In all of them, injustice and brutal oppression are the repeated refrains that echo through the cyclical telling of our Jewish history. And survival and redemption are ultimately the achievements not of individuals, but of a people. Judaism deals with the fate of a community, not of a person alone. How different this is (as I am reminded so often in my classes) from the Protestant view with its highly individualistic form of redemption. In Jewish history, I learned, justice is always social justice.

It is not surprising that I count myself among those many Jews whose tradition has inspired in them a deep sense of solidarity with all those who struggle against the unjust power of ruling elites and the privileged. I have always identified with those movements of resistance against those who would deny human beings the ability to give shape and meaning to their world. I have always been profoundly moved by those human struggles that seek to increase democracy, human rights, and equality. The meaningful life, I have come to believe, is inseparable from the quest for a more socially just world. In this sense, for me, the purpose of education is always linked to the critical spirit that seeks a full and liberated existence for all human beings. Education must constantly help us root out and challenge all those ways that privilege some human lives over others—to help resist the imposition of demeaning and exploitative relationships. An education imbued with this spirit has been called "prophetic," after the role of the ancient Hebrew prophets. No one has described their quest with greater power than the late Abraham Joshua Heschel[11]:

> The prophet is an iconoclast, challenging the apparently holy, revered, and awesome. Beliefs cherished as certainties, institutions endowed with supreme sanctity, he exposes as scandalous pretensions. ... The prophet faces a coalition of callousness and established authority, and undertakes to stop a mighty stream with mere words. Had the purpose been to express great ideas, prophecy would have led to be acclaimed as a triumph. Yet the pursuit of prophecy is to conquer callousness, to change the inner man as well as to revolutionize history.

4. A World of Possibility

Of all my childhood experiences it is the Passover celebration that is most memorable. At the center of this holiday stood the Seder, the ritual meal celebrating the ancient Israelites' liberation from Egyptian bondage. It was an annual event lit up with the festive pleasures of family conviviality, song, food, wine, stories, and humor. But beyond the immediacy of the celebration were, as I have come to see, messages of extraordinary power and significance. Here was conveyed not simply history but memory. The contemporary commentator Lawrence Kushner,[12] delineated this distinction well:

We take a memory of four hundred years of slavery and set it into a larger context of liberation and redemption. We then celebrate that slavery with a ban-
quet. We further find in those four hundred years of servitude a continuing
admonition to be ever mindful of the affliction of others. We find purpose and
mission in our slavery. If slaveries can become freedoms and miseries can become meaningful, then the game is never over. ... Through the dynamic
search for meaning the past remains eternally fluid before our eyes.

The Seder becomes much more than a retelling of long-ago historical events. Its
purpose is clearly to interrogate our present world to find in it current forms of
enslavement and suffering, but to do that from the vantage point of hope and possibility
about a world in which exile and injustice have ended. The injunction to remember in
this Jewish sense is a clearly ethical and transformative one: "You shall not wrong a
stranger or oppress him, for you were strangers in the land of Egypt" (Exodus 22:20).
The extraordinary pedagogy of the Seder (one aimed especially at children) manages to
fuse a celebration of survival, the demand to see the oppressions of our present world,
and the imaginary re-envisioning of a world of wholeness and justice. In all of this there
is our own personal and collective responsibility for social change. And, most of all,
there is the emphasis on possibility and hope. Remembering the past is the way to
infuse our present with energy, passion, and imagination as to the continuing
opportunity to transform the future world. This is a lesson that is the very opposite of
the cynicism and despair that afflicts so many young people. It is the antithesis to the
mentality of "why bother?"; the ennui expressed in "whatever"; or the jadedness of
"been there, done that." There is, instead, the fierce assertion that the realities of a world
that seem so solid and unmovable can indeed crumble; things can change, and we can
be agents of transformation.

There is joy and excitement in this recognition of human possibility and our
capacity to affect how things are. We do not have to see ourselves as stuck in a
groove and having to be nothing more than "bricks in the wall" of reality. In
thinking about Passover, or those other holidays of remembrance, it is often
laughter that comes to mind in spite of the weightiness of their concerns. And this is
true also of my best classes, where students have grasped the power of human
possibility. I believe that this laughter is not an escape from the seriousness of the
issues considered or commemorated, but an important way we find to resist the
spiritual, emotional, and political suffocation of oppressive situations. Laughter at
sad times not only relieves tension, it also promotes healing. It reminds us of
another dimension of our psyche. (There is much in Jewish humor, as well as in the
humor of other minority groups, that works in that way to turn the oppressive world
upside-down; the victim becomes a winner, the fool the smart one, the most
pathetic the one with truth on his or her side). In all of this, laughter provides an
emotional transcendence of the world; what appeared fixed and immutable
suddenly seems arbitrary and changeable. Such humor deconstructs a world that
moments before appeared so unalterable. We do not simply see the world in a new

and fluid light, but perhaps more importantly, we feel it in our bellies. Humor dissolves the overwhelming "facticity" of a threatening world. It helps us to fully grasp that with understanding, commitment, and creativity, human beings are not destined to merely reproduce the old ways of doing things. We have the capacity—as well as the moral obligation—of recreating our world!

5. The Language of the Body

Education, Paulo Freire famously asserted, suffers from "narration sickness." This condition leads not just to too much talk by teachers, and too little participation by students, in the classroom; it also means that pedagogy suffers from an overemphasis on the cerebral at the expense of human feeling. Knowing, in our schools, focuses overwhelmingly on analysis, problem solving, and memorization of information. In many ways, success in education is defined by one's capacity to be successful at learning tasks that may be said to be disembodied. To a very great extent, we have learned to define being "smart" in this very limited way as thinking that is separated from what Terry Eagleton[13] once described as the "the territory that is nothing less than the whole of our sensate life." Post-Cartesian philosophy has led us, he argued, to distinguish between "things and thoughts, sensations and ideas, that which is bound up with our creaturely life as opposed to that which conducts some shadowy existence in the recesses of the mind." How apparent this is in our schooling, which seeks (at best) intellectual capability that is divorced from passionate concern, sensitivity or awareness of our interiority.

I don't know how much my aversion to such a limited version of pedagogy is rooted in my Jewish experience, but there are certainly dimensions of this that may have given me the seeds of a different, more embodied educational vision. There is, in this experience, a strong emphasis on the connection between one's internal life and how one acts in the public world. The modern concept of praxis, the unity of thought and action, has always seemed to me to be foreshadowed in the prophetic demand that the spiritual life is not something purely personal but is lived out in our pursuit of a more just and compassionate world. Understanding that is divorced from what we do is a form of idolatry. There is, too, a fierce protection of the human body, which makes it incumbent on Jews to break any and all religious restrictions in pursuit of saving a life (it is asserted that "in saving a single life it is as if one has saved an entire world"). There is the tradition of *brachot* or blessings in Jewish life, which provides an appropriate moment of reflection and appreciation on the most mundane aspects of a human being's daily existence, including those bodily processes that permit life to continue. These draw our attention to the extraordinary, if taken for granted, dimensions of what it means for us to be embodied creatures. And there is the celebratory view of human sexuality, in which the pleasure of sexual experience is a positive expectation in the life of both men and women. (Of course I don't ignore the fact that orthodox Judaism, like most other religious traditions also defines women's sexuality in highly patriarchal and often demeaning ways.)

My view of education is rooted in the belief that knowledge and understanding should not be separated from the embodied life. Education could, and should, be a process that is joyful and playful. Something that is a celebration of human inquiry and curiosity. How different this is from the public discourse of education today in which notions of joy and pleasure in the context of learning are rarely articulated, as we emphasize only the importance of acquiring competencies, skills, and measurable gains. Even among young children, play and recess are increasingly viewed as expendable frills. Against all of our understanding of children's psychological development, experiential and sensory learning are viewed as taking time away from serious academic instruction. Sex education, too, is often taught today in such clinical, abstract, and threatening terms that it seems disconnected from any affirmation of the wonderful, and wondrous, nature of human desire and pleasure. In our pursuit of more efficient and cost-effective means of "delivering" schooling, distance learning is increasingly embraced. This depersonalization of education ignores the importance of shared human presence: the warmth and immediacy of being present in the same physical space with others that is an irreplaceable dimension of the dialogue and communication that might lead to greater human empathy and understanding. Indeed, our embrace of computer-assisted learning takes place without any serious consideration of the physical isolation implied in such learning. Nor is their much concern that the logical and linear forms of cognition associated with computers, as well as the increasing rapidity of electronic processing, are antithetical to the slow and messy business of self-reflection and the discernment of our inner lives.

Given our distorted sense of what constitutes significant learning, it is hardly surprising that all that is concerned with the aesthetic—the exploration of feeling, subjectivity, and the senses—should play so little role in education. Our emphasis on the knowledge that is "out there" and needs to be acquired leaves little room for understanding our subjective life—who we are, or what we desire, fear, or hope for. Of course, those whose business it is to shape our wants and needs have no such reluctance to focus on our interior being. Advertising is a relentless "education" of the body and human desires. The goal of self-understanding and awareness in our consumer culture would mean an education that enables young people to critically grasp the way their emotional lives are influenced, and their bodies "inscribed," with the desire for commodified solutions to human concerns. Sherry Shapiro,[14] a dance educator, pointed to the way understanding our embodied lives can enable us to grasp the social forces that influence and shape the most visceral dimensions of our identities. She noted:

> A language that emerges from our bodily living speaks of a kind of rationality distinct from one that is intellectually rooted. It demands that we listen to our bodies, feel our emotions, release our passions, and reunite our critical powers of thinking with our feelings, in hopes of a fuller humanity.

Shapiro went on to argue that recognizing our own embodied knowledge is a crucial vehicle for being better able to grasp the nature of our identity—who we are and how we have been shaped by culture, the meanings we give to gender, and the effects of media and popular representations on our experience.

Our education needs a new sense of balance. Intellectual development must be accompanied by emotional development. We might ask how would it be if schools recognized not just the smartest kids (or at least those who are best at playing the academic game), but students who are compassionate, have a profound sense of justice, and have a concern for the well-being of others. My interest here is not a new form of competitive ranking. It is the recognition that our technological advances as a nation are not matched by the extent of our sensitivity and concern for others. Our obsessive focus on "getting ahead," and our instrumental view of knowledge have depleted the attention we need to give to understanding ourselves better and figuring out what it might mean to live our lives with authenticity and meaning. Of course, as we make education a place of feeling—inspiration, outrage, compassion, and human concern—the expectation that action follows from what we know will surely grow. Community service and social action will become something more than a necessary way to enhance one's college application. They will be, instead, a way of living out an education that unites both body and mind, thought and action, passion and understanding.

6. The Sabbath of Being

Little in my childhood life is more vivid than the rituals attached to the making of the Sabbath in my home. In the way of the orthodox Jewish celebration of this day (that actually begins on the Friday evening and concludes Saturday at dusk), the Sabbath began with the lighting of candles followed by recitation of the *Kiddush*, the sanctification and drinking of a cup of wine. Our modest living room, with lit candles and white tablecloth, seemed to glow with special warmth as we enjoyed the traditional chicken soup and boiled chicken dinner. Still, as a child, much about the Sabbath rankled because of the restrictions imposed by orthodox observance of the day: limitations on travel, the use of money, even writing; restrictions on watching TV; and the need to attend synagogue prayers whose recitation always felt endlessly repetitive. Much later in my life, however, I came to appreciate the wisdom of this day in ways I did not as a child. In particular, reading Abraham Heschel's extraordinary little book *The Sabbath*[15] enabled me to gain insight into the idea of the Sabbath as a day devoted to purposes that set it apart from our work- and consumer-oriented culture. From this book I began to see the importance of time devoted to the beauty and preciousness of life and the celebration of the simple fact of being. Such a time would allow us respite from the constant imperative to do, to work, and to produce, in order to appreciate the extraordinary and wondrous nature of creation. Drawing on Heschel, Letty Cottin Pogrebin,[16] a contemporary Jewish writer, expressed this notion of the Sabbath in these words:

The Sabbath is pure time: "The hours of the seventh-day are significant in themselves; their significance and beauty do not depend on any work, profit or progress we may achieve." On that one day, we are supposed to enter time's realm and treasure time for its own sake. We are not only expected to desist from manual labor ("labor is a craft, but perfect rest is an art") but to contemplate creation, the product of God's labor. ... Rather than communicate through productivity, we are to communicate through inaction. Not writing, driving, all this proclaims that humanity is connected to a source of productivity greater than its own.

The Sabbath represented a temporal space—for stillness, reflection, appreciation of relationships, and most of all time to appreciate the deep mystery of creation. It offered us a short period that provided a contrast to our production-driven culture's notion of time with its demand for a frantic way of life in which "doing" is everything and "being" is regarded has having little useful value. The "doing" culture was one in which our instrumental view of the world meant that we lived always in anticipation of our future achievements, rather than allowing ourselves to be fully present to the moment of our existence. Sometimes in class I amuse students with a Buddhist inspired quip that says "don't just do something, sit there." It is probably not surprising that capitalism's spiraling obsession with work, and the increasing compulsion to spend and consume, has made many individuals more receptive to the Sabbath concept—the need for time to "just be."

But the need for contemplative time is about more than "reenergizing our batteries" so that we can return to the task of doing and making more effectively. We need alternative ways to be in the world to allow us to see life, and all of creation, in its extraordinary beauty and magnificence—the opportunity to be filled with awe and wonder at our universe, and the extraordinary fecundity, diversity, and interconnectedness of life. We live at a time of unparalleled destructiveness toward the earth: the elimination of whole living species; potentially cataclysmic alterations in our climate; deadly erosion of the protective layers of our atmosphere; abuse of our air, seas, and rivers; a dangerous diminishing of the rainforests with their vital regenerative role; and the proliferation of pollutants and radioactive waste that threatens organic life. We are in desperate need of a change in consciousness that will allow us to see nature as something other than a limitless set of inert resources that can endlessly "feed" our system of production and profit making. Environmental report after report tells us that we are driving ourselves to destruction, even extinction. At the very least, our dominant culture of doing and using must be balanced by one of appreciation for being that will lead us to care for the precious and sacred beauty of creation. We need not add that school, to a very great extent, is the very embodiment of the culture of production; doing, performing, showing is the very axis of school life. We so much need there opportunities that can cultivate the Sabbath consciousness of stillness, reflection, and appreciation for what is. Others have written movingly of an education that can encourage our students' recognition of the wonder and beauty of existence and respect for life in all its rich diversity, amid the environmental destruction that our present way of living is producing.[17] I have not tried to duplicate that work here. But its appalling prognosis for the future of our natural habitat is far more clear than anything I can say here concerning the full dimensions of the destructive path the human species is now on. A recent study by 1,360 researchers in 95 nations—the largest study of the earth's life-support systems ever undertaken, showed that in the last 50 years the rising human population had polluted or overexploited two-thirds of the ecological systems on which life depends, including clean air and fresh water. This report noted that the strain on the natural functions of the earth was so great that the ability to sustain future generations cannot now be taken for granted.

An education concerned with sensitivity toward our ecological plight means taking seriously the interior lives of young people and their sense of spiritual awareness, the value of intuitive knowledge and meanings, and the capacity for empathy and connection. Central to this is the recognition of the damage we produce when we see ourselves as independent, self-sufficient, and self-contained beings, instead of indissolubly connected to, and dependent on, others. To quietly contemplate the human condition is to see ourselves embedded in the chain of existence that links us back and forward through the infinity of time. It is to appreciate the extraordinary webs of life that nourish and support our existence. And it is to see how each seemingly distinct individual has his or her origins in the same star dust from which we are all materialized. To engage in the quiet contemplation of the wondrous nature of life and existence is also to see ourselves through new eyes that refuse the steady despiritualization and disenchantment of our world. Commodification and objectification insinuate themselves into every area of life on this planet, turning human beings into measurable and quantifiable human resources, treating animals with a callous and cruel disregard for their sentient natures, and appropriating the genetic codes that govern life itself as the saleable items of corporate possession and trading. The Shabbat consciousness of contemplation and heightened awareness does indeed offer a window into a culture that affirms life (not, we need add, to be confused with the cynically manipulated "culture of life" that some politicians refer to). Making a space in our education for developing such a consciousness might at least provide a window into the possibility of another way of being in this world that is apart from the instrumental, coldly calculating, and cash-dominated character of our workaday institutions. This window, at least for a limited time, might allow us to reflect on a world that recognized the extraordinary nature of creation, the irreplaceable preciousness of life, and our responsibility toward all that sustains it.

BETWEEN FUNDAMENTALISMS

As I conclude this book, the nation is mourning the death of President Ronald Reagan. Of course it is natural that at his passing, commentary on his tenure as

President should focus on his positive achievements and legacy. It was, however, too little noted by these commentators that it was Reagan who inaugurated the modern era of free-market "fundamentalism." More than anything else, I believe, it is this ideology that has shaped the world over the past quarter of a century, and now dominates the way that life is lived in most of the world. The fundamentalism of the marketplace means a belief that all aspects of our collective needs as human beings can be best met through the unregulated competitive quest for profit among those who sell goods and services. In such a world, economic considerations alone hold sway in determining the benefits and costs of what is produced, and the consequences of production. Anything that attempts to intervene and detract from this process—that questions the social value of what is produced, the way workers are treated or paid by employers, the environmental consequences of what is being manufactured or consumed—is considered dysfunctional to the economic "good." Naturally, the free-market fundamentalists are hostile to anything that gets in the way of the pure pursuit of profits, whether this be trade union activity by workers to enhance their rights, environmental regulation, demands for corporate accountability to the society as a whole, or the need for investment in areas that may be unprofitable but are socially needed, such as health care, housing, and transportation for those unable to afford the costs of these items. With a religious zeal, advocates for such an ideology hold the right to untrammeled economic freedom as the virtually sole measure of positive political action. It is hardly surprising that with such zeal comes a blindness to many of the consequences of such unconstrained freedom: the spreading tide of poverty in the world, the erosion of workers' basic economic security, environmental destruction, wasteful depletion of the earth's resources, unmet health needs, under-addressed scourges such as HIV/AIDS and TB. For free-market zealots the good world is one in which every aspect of our lives submits to the test of marketability. Something's social value inheres, first and foremost, in its ability to sell. Although, paradoxically, the advocates of this view will often speak about the need for moral or religious rejuvenation, in reality they have little sympathy with anything that gets in way of the pursuit of cold cash. Their politics is often articulated in moralistic tones, but we can be in no doubt that the policies that get their support are the ones that make it possible to amass the largest profits with the least hindrance. Indeed, little remains in our world that is not now the product of the crassest materialistic thinking. The untrammeled freedom of the market is in fact the unhindered ability to transform every part of our human culture into a vulgar opportunity to make a sale. More and more, the measure of the products and meanings that constitute the human culture is the simple quest to amass more money. However much right-wing politicians wring their hands over the moral state of the nation, they see no contradiction between this and the pursuit of a world that is actually about little more than "making a deal"—a world whose moral axis is constituted by greed, self-interest, and economic advantage over others. Nor does there seem to be much anguish at the increasing insecurity of so many people's lives as jobs become more uncertain, unemployment insurance more meager, pensions in one's old age less reliable, and health insurance unavailable or unaffordable. As the shrillness of the Right's moral arguments increase, its sphere of concerns seem to contract away from those things that shape the everyday lives of most people.

The ideology of the free-market is the reigning viewpoint of our time. Yet its control has not entirely thwarted growing moral repugnance to the kind of world it is spawning, with all of its grotesque social inequities, environmental irresponsibility, shallow manufactured meanings, and callous indifference to others lives. Far from being at an "end to history," it is hard to doubt that we are on the edge of major new resistance to the distorted priorities and fixations of the global market place. Increasingly, questions are raised regarding the erosion of democratic accountability in the "new world order" in which corporations wield so much power. And challenges now abound as to the unfairness of the system of world trade, indebtedness of the poor to the rich, the destruction of traditional ways of life as the homogenizing culture of mass merchandizing spreads across continents, and the increasing dangers to our climatic system from the unrestrained buildup of greenhouse gases.

The world is also confronted by another kind of blind zealotry. This is one whose roots go far back in history but that is surely nourished by the social conditions we have already described. Religious authoritarianism, in whatever form it takes, offers an answer to the moral disintegration and cultural emptiness of a world ruled by money and self-interest. In place of postmodern uncertainties about truth and meaning, believers can find existential comfort in the precise and incontrovertible absolutes of the faith. In place of the flux and insecurity of a world buffeted by the tumultuous consequences of capitalism's disruption of traditional ways of life, religious fundamentalism offers the assurance of a spiritual order purified of the tawdriness, vulgarity, and permissiveness unleashed by the consumer culture. Of course, the most virulent form of contemporary religious absolutism is that found within the extreme sects of Islam. These, as we know to our great human cost, have produced a fanatical, intolerant, and bloodthirsty strain of political expression. It stands in furious opposition to those values of the Enlightenment that are at the core of liberal democracy. Fanatical Islam confronts the world with a belief system that is deeply repressive toward women, eschews tolerance or respect toward others' religious or political beliefs, disparages individual freedom and personal choice, and encourages indiscriminate violence against nonbelievers.

Such extremist beliefs threaten lives here and elsewhere, with their call for acts of terror and bloody vengeance. That is a dangerous enough reality with which we must now all deal. But they have also produced, in their train, a series of other threats to our individual and collective well-being. They have renewed the strain of fearful insecurity, and the siege mentality, that was so much a part of the Cold War era but that had begun to abate in the short interregnum between the collapse of the Soviet Union and September 11, 2001. Such insecurity is now fueled by the constant sense of being on alert for new attacks, and the heightened sense of alarm about our safety.

The suspicion and distrust of this new era of global terrorism fuel the justification for a more intrusive curtailment of our civil liberties. Core dimensions of a democratic society, such as the right to face charges in a court of law, are now endangered, as the state claims the right to detain individuals without trial for indefinite periods. Our leaders justify the need to torture "detainees." It has become more dangerous to express dissent or disagreement with government policy, and the government is much more freely able to invade and limit citizens' ability to express or organize in dissenting ways. Dissent is frequently identified as expressing a lack of patriotism. Perhaps it is not surprising, in this context, that a Knight Foundation survey found that only half of America's high school students think newspapers should be free to publish without government approval. It has fueled, too, a remilitarization of our national culture. All talk of a "peace dividend" following the end of the Cold War has disappeared. In its place is a near political consensus on the need for open-ended military budgets. Beyond this is the notion that our new more dangerous world, demands a much greater readiness to engage in military intervention wherever threats to our national security emerge, or even might be expected to emerge at some later time. This strategy of "preemptive" action licenses our government to military action even where there is no immediate threat or danger. Such action, which can be taken without significant support or agreement with other nations, abrogates processes of international deliberation and consensus that are the foundation for a more ordered and secure world. This is, I believe, likely to encourage the resort of other countries to military "solutions" to conflicts rather than reductions of the likelihood of wars. The overreliance on a military response is also a product of a simplistic view of the nature of the current conflict, obscuring underlying issues and causes. The simple pitting of good versus evil makes it possible to avoid consideration of our own nation's responsibility or culpability in the emergence of terrorism. There is our support for repressive and privileged governing elites in other countries such as Saudi Arabia, Pakistan, Egypt, Kuwait, and Iraq. There is our lack of consistency in supporting Palestinian rights and the need to finally end the Israeli occupation. We should not forget our cynically motivated support for Islamic fundamentalists, such as the Taliban, when it suited our own national interests. And there is the willful pursuit of an energy policy that demands unlimited cheap oil from the Middle East to fuel our own wasteful preference for gas-guzzling cars and SUVs. The rhetoric of good versus evil in this conflict also draws our attention away from attending to the conditions that produce so much rage and frustration in the world—the terrible social and economic inequities both within and between countries, an existence for so many blighted by lack of education, decent jobs, and the hope for a worthwhile, dignified life.

From all of this, the world our children must expect, as they grow up in this 21st century, will be one of immense difficulties and challenges. It is one in which we may expect human beings to be positioned between forces that, in very different ways, make the quest for a humane, free, and secure existence much harder to come by. The world we and our children face confronts us with growing economic disparities, threats to our physical safety and well-being, an erosion of democratic influence over the institutions that shape our lives, an increasing recourse to violent solutions to our differences, insecurity that breeds suspicion and hostility toward strangers, and a culture that is ever more focused on wealth and self-interest. Yet for all of these dangers, this is also a time of extraordinary possibility. Medical advances offer the possibilities of cures for a whole range of diseases; technological innovations can reduce some of the most onerous kinds of human labor as well as the amount of time that must be expended at paid work; and extraordinary developments in communications electronics open up whole new vistas for personal connection, broad access to information, and opportunities for democratic participation. The growing recognition of our interconnectedness as a species, and of all our dependence on nature, has brought with it the flourishing of a global civic community concerned with the need for sustainable economic systems, a just distribution of the earth's resources, and the intellectual or political indefensibility of racism and ethnic chauvinism. The great revolution in women's rights that began in the 1970s continues, globally, to batter structures of patriarchal power and to open new possibilities and opportunities for half the human race. Modernity continues to encourage extraordinary creativity and innovative thinking in every area of culture. In every field of human knowledge and understanding, from science to aesthetics, from spiritual awareness to our understanding of the body, from our insights into time, matter, and space, to the ecology of life on this planet, this is a time of unbelievably imaginative and generative thinking.

It is in this context—of great danger and of great possibility—that we must examine what it means to educate our children for the 21st century. We need to remind ourselves again of the distinction between schooling and education. The former can be made fairer and less subject to the advantages and disadvantages of race, social class, gender, immigrant status, and so on. We can distribute resources more fairly, be less culturally biased in our teaching and testing, and certainly open up more opportunity for those who have been disadvantaged to find new possibilities in their lives. Make no mistake, all of this would be a good thing for both individuals and for our society as a whole. But none of this, in itself, would bring us much closer to what it might mean to educate for the challenges of our new century. For this, we need something far more transformative in our thinking. This will require us to think of education in ways that are far more holistic than we typically do, as something that is not just about the learning of skills, or the capacity to solve problems, or the ingesting of information. We need to think of the education we give our children as a process that addresses mind, heart, and spirit—in other words, as a process that forms us as mature individuals, and as people who live in relationship with others. Can we really doubt that what we need today are human beings, not who know how to play the grading and testing games that schools now encourage, but who have the capacity to meet the extraordinary challenges and demands that are before us as a civilization? We know something about the education that this will entail. We know that it must engage students in terms of the totality of their beings, not in the shrunken and limited way that our schools now demand. As I have tried to make clear in this book, to educate our children in the ways that allow them to meet the human challenges of our time means to teach them a number of things. It means to take seriously the quest for citizens who can discern truth (or at least what is truer) from the distortions and deceit that surrounds us in our culture—students, in other words, who can think critically and can problematize the knowledge and meanings they are presented with in their everyday world. It means to take very seriously the goal of an education that is concerned with the ethical quality of our lives and our society, central to which is the quest for a global culture that ensures the dignity and well-being of each and every person. Finally, it means an education that can affirm the spiritual dimension of our existence—one that awakens in each person the sense of beauty, wonder, and preciousness of all life on our planet, and the interdependence that makes continuation of this life possible. Of course, the task before us and our children, to transform the world of so much unnecessary suffering, hurt, indignity, and injustice, is too great for any one person to contemplate addressing. It is clearly a task that must employ the minds and bodies of many of us if change is to come. We must teach the value of our participation in the task of *Tikkun Olam*—the repair and healing of our world—without either the sense of futility that may come from minimizing what we can do, or exaggerating the contributions that one individual may make. The first leads to cynicism and the latter to hubris. More realistically, in our work with young people, we may emphasize the teaching of Rabbi Tarfon, who asserted that "it is not your duty to complete the work, but neither are you excused from participating in it." We must teach the young that while it may be important to have a realistic appreciation of the limits of what may be possible, the only justifiable purpose of education in our time is that of bettering the world we have all been given. All the rest is mere commentary.

NOTES

1. Christopher Lasch. (1991). *The culture of narcissism.* New York: W. W. Norton.
2. David E. Purpel. (2004). *Reflections on the moral and spiritual crisis of education.* New York: Peter Lang.
3. Michael Apple. (1995). *Education and power.* New York: Routledge.
4. Cornel West. (2004, April). *Speech to the Tikkun Convention*, Washington, DC.
5. Michael Lerner. (1997). *The politics of meaning.* New York: Perseus.
6. Maxine Greene. (1988). *The dialectic of freedom.* New York: Teachers College Press.
7. Paulo Friere. (2000). *Pedagogy of the oppressed.* New York: Continuum.
8. I have drawn here from my essay in H. Svi Shapiro (ed.). (1999). *Strangers in the land.* New York: Peter Lang.

9. Jacob Neusner. (1973). *Invitation to the Talmud* (pp. 291–292). San Francisco: Harper and Row.

10. Judith Plaskow. (1991). *Standing again at Sinai*. New York: Harper Collins.

11. Abraham Heschel. (1962). *The prophet* (p. 10). New York: Jewish Publication Society of America.

12. Lawrence Kushner. (1993). *The book of words* (p. 88). Vermont: Jewish Lights Publishing.

13. Terry Eagleton. (1990). *The ideology of the aesthetic* (p. 13). Cambridge: Basil Blackwell.

14. Sherry Shapiro. (1999). *Pedagogy and the politics of the body* (p. 27). New York: Garland.

15. Abraham Heschel. (1951). *The Sabbath*. New York: Farrar, Straus and Giroux.

16. Letty Cottin Pogrebin. (1996). Time is all there is. In *Meaning Matters* (p. 5). The Foundation for Ethics and Meaning, NY.

17. See for example, James Moffet. (1998). *The universal schoolhouse*. San Francisco: Jossey-Bass. David W. Orr. (1994). *Ecological literacy*. New York: SUNY Press. Michael Lerner. (2000). *Spirit matters*. New York: Hampton Roads. And Jane Roland Martin. (1995). *Schoolhome*. Cambridge, MA: Harvard University Press.

Author Index

Subject Index

B'tselem Elohim, 60, 128, 172–176
Buber, Martin, 2, 37
Bullying, 154, 161
Burkett, Elinor, 11–12
Bush, George W., 10, 128
Bush, Jeb, 24

C

Calvin Klein, 32
Capitalism, xvii, 11, 28, 71, 144–147, 198, 201
"Chalk and talk" methods, 113, 186
Channel One, 39
Chanukah, 68, 72, 193
Character
 amoral
 apocalyptic, 159
 cash-dominated, 199
 developing, ix
 education, 20, 98
 moral, xi, 75
 results-driven, 9
 violent, 179
Charity, 60
Cheating, 9–12, 17, 26, 34–35, 57, 60
Cheating Culture, The, 10
Childhood, 47
Children
 of adult violence, 155
 African-American, 82
 Black, 122, 138
 Brown, 138
 challenging, 4
 dignity of, 164
 educating, xvi, 4, 51–52, 88, 139, 157, 169, 184–185, 188, 203–204
 exploitation of, 37
 homicide amongst, 154
 of immigrants, 158, 192
 judging, 141
 Latino, 138
 as a market, 31–34
 mining for commercial advantage, 38
 minority, 138
 normalizing, 49
 in poverty, 141, 163
 slavery of, 96

 spiritual developmental needs of, 74–75
 upper-class, 130
 valuing, 54
 White, 165
Children's
 values, 38
Children's Defense Fund, 165
Christian
 communities, 84–85
 culture, 192
 milieu, 68
 oriented agenda, xi
Christianity, 49, 73, 82
Citizenship, xii, xvi, 24, 71, 90, 95, 99–100, 103, 110, 112, 146, 163
Civil rights, 81, 102, 146
Classroom
 achievement, 60
 ambience of, 109
 disruptions, 86
 evaluation, 55
 instruction, 10
 learning, 186
 moral code of, 60
 peer learning in, 64
 tasks, 96
 typical American, 40, 59, 177
Classrooms, 7–8, 21–22, 39–40, 43, 93, 96–97, 99, 106, 109, 120–124, 128–134, 141, 161–162
 college, 13
 competition in, 57
 lack of change in, 15
Clerks of the empire, 63
Closed communities of meaning, 84–87
Coca-cola, 39
Cold War, 201
Columbine, 23, 25, 58, 155, 165–168
Commitment, 18, 39, 42, 51–52, 84–86, 107, 141, 146, 156, 174, 178, 182, 189, 195
 to community, xi
 ethical, 16, 185
 moral, 75
 political, 126
 spiritual, 68, 185
Communities of resistance, 81

of consumption, 109
crisis of, 115–116
educating for, 98–101
of expression, 108–112
liberal, 201
as a lived experience, 112–113
promise of, 15
threat to, 97
versus capitalism, 144–147
Democracy Matters, 103, 164
Democratic
accountability, 105, 185, 201
community, 71–72, 112
creed, 60
culture, 75, 98–99, 105
education, 99, 109
ethos, ix, xi
ideas, 85
influence, 203
rights, 146, 171
society, 67, 100, 105, 202
values, 95, 99, 128, 148
Depersonalization of education, 196
Depression, 28, 73, 79, 97, 167
Detachment, 73, 80, 98, 154
Dewey, John, 52
Dialogue, 8, 109, 139, 156, 162, 188, 196
Diploma, 21, 39, 42
Discipline (*see also* Self-discipline), 23, 85
desire for, 73
fiscal, 29
Distance learning, 42, 196
Divide and rule, 133

E

Earth
destructiveness toward, 198
Earth's
life support systems, 199
resources, 30, 184, 200, 203
Economy
globalization of, 115, 197
market, 41
moral, 56–64, 134
post-Fordist, 157
structure of, 26
Education (*see also* Banking education
     and Crisis of education *and*

Nonschool Education *and* Peace
     Education)
Afrocentric, 82
bilingual, 82
as a commodity, 41–42
conceptualizing, 59
conservative approach to, 85–86
cynical message of, 9
degeneration of, 5
de-meaning, 10–14
democratic, 99, 116
fundamental purpose of, 77
of the heart, 81
Jewish, 67–69
leaders, 3
multi-cultural, 139
performance-driven, 61
public, 5, 10, 14, 67, 71, 86, 97, 106,
     147–148, 172, 182
as a race or as a community, 128–132
relevance of, 46
result-centered, 21
rethinking, 16
for scarcity or abundance, 132–135
as socialization, 51–53
Educational
challenge, 155–157
communities, 75
concerns, 78
goals, 98, 100, 121, 126, 187
health of children, 5
leadership, 87–90
reform, 5, 13–16, 138
     failure of, 184–190
     rethinking, 14–16
standards, 6, 14, 133, 187
vision, 75, 77, 195
Educational Testing Service, 131
Eichmann, Adolph, 94–95, 99
Elementary
education, 122, 125
level, 162
rights, 159
school children, 38
schools, 4, 7, 53, 67
Elimidate, 32
Emulation process, 26
End of Homework, The, 7
Environment, 115